STERLING
Test Prep

AP
Physics 2

Practice Questions

5th edition

www.Sterling–Prep.com

Copyright © 2021 Sterling Test Prep

Our books are of the highest quality and error-free.

Be the first to report a content error and receive a $10 reward
or a typo or grammatical mistake for a $5 reward.

info@sterling–prep.com

*We reply to all emails – **check your spam folder***

5   4   3   2   1

ISBN-13: 978-1-9475563-2-4

Sterling Test Prep products are available at special quantity discounts for sales, promotions, academic counseling offices and other educational purposes.

Contact our sales department at: info@sterling–prep.com

Sterling Test Prep
6 Liberty Square #11
Boston, MA 02109

© 2021 Sterling Test Prep

Published by Sterling Test Prep

 Printed in the U.S.A.

Congratulations on joining thousands of students using our study aids to achieve high test scores!

Scoring well on the AP exams is essential to earn placement credits and admission into a competitive college, which will position you for a successful future. This book prepares you to achieve a high score on the AP Physics 2 exam by developing the ability to apply your knowledge and quickly choose the correct answer. Solving targeted practice questions builds your understanding of fundamental physics concepts and is a more effective strategy than merely memorizing terms.

This book has more than 765 high-yield practice questions covering all AP Physics 2 topics. Physics instructors with years of teaching experience prepared this material by analyzing the exam content and developing practice material that builds your knowledge and skills crucial for success on the test. Our editorial team reviewed and systematized the content to ensure adherence to the current College Board AP Physics 2 curriculum. Our editors are experts on preparing students for standardized tests and have coached thousands of undergraduate and graduate school applicants on test preparation and admission strategies.

Our detailed explanations describe why an answer is correct and – more important for your learning – why another attractive choice is wrong. They provide step-by-step solutions for quantitative questions and teach the scientific foundations and details of essential physics topics needed to answer conceptual exam questions. Read all the explanations carefully to understand how they apply to the question and learn important physics concepts and the relationships between them. With the practice material contained in this book, you will significantly improve your AP score.

We wish you great success in your academics and look forward to being an important part of your successful test preparation!

Visit www.sterling-prep.com for more test prep resources.

201117gdx

Higher score money back guarantee!

What some students say about this book

★★★★★ ***Did great on the exam***

... It was great to use the diagnostic tests before studying the chapters. The chapters had many questions that let me learn the material. The step by step and detailed explanations are what makes this book so great. ... Really targeted my studying. I was able to gain confidence from all my practice, learn the concepts and be very efficient in my study time. ... Thanks to Sterling the tests are behind me and I have the scores I hoped for.

Bonnie Eldrige (Amazon verified purchase)

★★★★★ ***Did well on the exam and thanks to this book***

The diagnostic tests are great because they were representative of my understanding of the material. Different than other books my friends owned, they are a great tool in the book. I learned from the detailed explanations to the questions. The large number of questions allowed me to focus my studying. I did great on the test and was much better prepared by using this book for the AP physics 2 test.

Tiffany Fields (Amazon verified purchase)

★★★★★ ***Parents ask me for suggestions on prep books***

... I reviewed several prep books and I recommend this book to my students and their parents. There is a large selection of varied problems with different ranges of difficulty. I like that the book offers both conceptual and calculation-based questions. My experience shows that both skills needed to be mastered by students to do well both in class and on the AP. Initial feedback from several students in my AP 2 class shows that they have derived benefits from using the book.

Mr. Sam V (Amazon verified purchase)

★★★★★ ***practice problems have answers that are clear***

Great to practice the AP physics 2 topics. Chapters allow me to focus on discrete topics. The best thing is that the questions are solved in a clear fashion. Really helps me.

Ted (Amazon verified purchase)

★★★★★ ***Solutions helped me learn the concepts***

Great practice problems. Diagnostic tests really helped. I then used the chapters to focus on topics covered in class. Solutions were complete and very clear that really helped me learn. I feel that I am getting prepared to ace my class and have a solid foundation to crush the AP exam.

M Childs (Amazon verified purchase)

★★★★★ ***Best among all the physics books I previewed***

The questions and detailed explanations were great. I like that the solutions are detailed so I could learn from reading the solutions and comparing them to my work. ... It was difficult to find a book that had challenging questions and detailed explanations. This book has both of these important features. Great learning from using this book...

Bethany Sanchez (Amazon verified purchase)

AP online practice tests at www.Sterling-Prep.com

Our advanced online testing platform allows you to take AP practice questions on your computer to generate a Diagnostic Report for each test.

By using our online AP tests and Diagnostic Reports, you will:

- Assess your knowledge of topics tested on the AP exam

- Identify your areas of strength and weakness

- Learn important scientific topics and concepts

- Improve your test-taking skills

Book owners

Check the last page for special pricing access
to our online resources

**For best results, supplement this book with
"AP Physics 2 Complete Content Review"**

AP Physics 2 Complete Content Review provides a detailed and thorough review of topics tested on the AP Physics 2 exam. The content covers foundational principles and concepts necessary to answer related questions on the test.

· Thermodynamics

· Fluid statics & dynamics

· Geometric & physical optics

· Atomic & nuclear physics

· Particle physics

· Electrostatics & magnetism

· DC & RC circuits

· Quantum mechanics

AP prep books by Sterling Test Prep

- AP Chemistry Practice Questions
- AP Chemistry Review
- AP Biology Practice Questions
- AP Biology Review
- AP Physics 1 Practice Questions
- AP Physics 1 Review
- AP Environmental Science

- AP Psychology
- AP U.S. History
- AP World History
- AP European History
- AP U.S. Government and Politics
- AP Comparative Government and Politics
- AP Human Geography

Table of Contents

We want to hear from you

Your feedback is important to us because we strive to provide the highest quality prep materials. Email us any comments or suggestions.

info@sterling–prep.com

Customer Satisfaction Guarantee

Contact us to resolve any issues to your satisfaction.

*We reply to all emails – **check your spam folder***

Thank you for choosing our products to achieve your educational goals!

AP Physics 2 Test-Taking Strategies

The best way to do well on AP Physics 2 is to be good at physics. There is no way around that. Prepare for the test as much as you can, so you can answer with confidence as many questions as possible. With that being said, there are strategies you should employ when you approach a question on the exam.

The task of pacing yourself will become easier if you are aware of the number of questions you need to answer to reach the score you want to get. Always strive for the highest score, but also be realistic about your level of preparation. It may be helpful if you research what counts as a good score for the colleges you are applying to. You can talk to admissions offices at colleges, research college guidebooks or specific college websites, or talk to your guidance counselor. You should find out which score would earn you a college placement credit and which score would be beneficial to your application without earning credit.

Below are some test-taking strategies to help you maximize your score. Many of these strategies you already know and they may seem like common sense. However, when you are feeling the pressure of a timed test, these common-sense strategies might be forgotten.

Mental Attitude

If you psych yourself out, chances are you will do poorly on the test. To do well on the test, particularly physics, which calls for cool, systemic thinking, you must remain calm. If you start to panic, your mind won't be able to find correct solutions to the questions. Many steps can be taken before the test to increase your confidence level. Buying this book is a great start because you can begin to practice, learn the information you should know to master the topics and get used to answering physics questions. However, there are other things you should keep in mind:

Study in advance. The information will be more manageable, and you will feel more confident if you've studied at regular intervals during the weeks leading up to the test. Cramming the night before is not a successful tactic.

Be well rested. If you are up late the night before the test, chances are you will have a difficult time concentrating and focusing on the day of the test, as you will not feel fresh and alert.

Come up for air. The best way to take this three-hour-long test is not to keep your head down, concentrating intensely for the entire time. Even though you only have 1 minute and 48 seconds per question (on the multiple-choice section) and there is no time to waste, it is recommended to take a few seconds between the questions to take a deep breath and relax your muscles.

Time Management

Aside from good preparation, time management is the most important strategy that you should know how to use on any test. You have an average time of 1 minute 48 seconds for each question on the multiple choice section. Even though, you will breeze through some in less than a minute, with others you may be stuck on for three minutes.

Don't dwell on any one question for too long. You should aim to look at every question on the test. It would be unfortunate to not earn the points for a question you could have easily answered just because you did not get a chance to look at it. If you are still in the first half of the test and find yourself spending more than a minute on one question and don't see yourself getting closer to solving it, it is better to move on. It will be more productive if you come back to this question with a fresh mind at the end of the test. You do not want to lose points because you were stuck on one or few questions and did not get a chance to work with other questions that are easy for you.

Nail the easy questions quickly. Everyone has their strong and weak topics, and you might be a master on a certain type of questions that are normally considered difficult. Skip the questions you are struggling with and nail the easy ones.

Skip the unfamiliar. If you come across a question that is totally unfamiliar to you, skip it. Do not try to figure out what is going on or what they are trying to ask. At the end of the test, you can go back to these questions if you have time. If you are encountering a question that you have no clue about, most likely you won't be able to answer it through analysis. The better strategy is to leave such questions to the end and use the guessing strategy on them at the end of the test.

Understanding the Question

It is important that you know what the question is asking before you select your answer choice. This seems obvious, but it is surprising how many students don't read a question carefully because they rush through the test and select a wrong answer choice.

A successful student will not just read the question but will take a moment to understand the question before even looking at the answer choices. This will allow you to separate the important information from distracters and you will not get confused on the questions that are asking to identify a false statement (which is the correct answer).

Once you've identified what you're dealing with and what is being asked, you should be able to spend less time picking the right answer. If the question is asking for a general concept, try to answer the question before looking at the answer choices, then look at the choices. If you see a choice that matches the answer you thought of, most likely it is the correct choice.

Correct Way to Guess

Random guessing won't help you on the test, but educated guessing is the strategy you should use in certain situations if you can eliminate at least one (or even two) of the four possible choices.

If you just randomly entered responses for the first 20 questions, there is a 25% chance of guessing correctly on any given question. Therefore, the odds are you would guess right on 5 questions and wrong on 15 questions. However, if for each of the 20 questions you can eliminate one answer choice because you know it to be wrong (e.g., wrong order of magnitude, wrong units), you will have a 33% chance of being correct and your odds would move to 7 questions right and 13 questions wrong. Correspondingly, if you can eliminate 2 wrong answers, you can increase your odds to 50%.

Guessing is not cheating and should not be viewed that way. Rather it is a form of "partial credit" because while you might not be sure of the correct answer, you do have relevant knowledge to identify one or two choices that are wrong.

AP Physics 2 Tips

Tip 1: Know the formulas

Since 70–80% of the test requires that you know how to use the formulas, it is imperative that you memorize and understand when to use each one. It is not permitted to bring any papers with notes to the test, but you will be given a sheet with formulas allowed by the College Board.

As you work with this book, you will learn the application of all the important physical formulas and will use them in many different question types.

Tip 2: Know how to manipulate the formulas

You must know how to apply the formulas in addition to just memorizing them. Questions will be worded in ways unfamiliar to you to test whether you can manipulate equations to calculate the correct answer. Knowing that $P = I \Delta V$ is not helpful without understanding that $\Delta V = P / I$ because it is very unlikely that a question will ask to calculate the power with a given current and voltage. Rather you are likely to be asked to calculate the acceleration of an object of a given mass with force acting on it.

Tip 3: Estimating

This tip is only helpful for quantitative questions. For example, estimating can help you choose the correct answer if you have a general sense of the order of magnitude. This is especially applicable to questions where all answer choices have different orders of magnitude, and you can save time that you would have to spend on actual calculations.

Tip 4: Draw the question

Don't hesitate to write, draw or graph your thought process once you have read and understood the question. This can help you determine what kind of information you are dealing with. Draw the force and velocity vectors, ray/wave paths, or anything else that may be helpful. Even if a question does not require a graphic answer, drawing a graph (for example, a sketch of a particle's velocity) can allow a solution to become obvious.

Tip 5: Eliminating wrong answers

This tip utilizes the strategy of educated guessing. You can usually eliminate one or two answer choices right away in many questions. Also, there are certain types of questions for which you can use a particular elimination method.

By using logical estimations for qualitative questions, you can eliminate the answer choices that are unreasonably high or unreasonably low.

Last helpful tip: fill in your answers carefully

This seems like a simple thing, but it is extremely important. Many test takers make mistakes when filling in answers whether it is a paper test or computer-based test. Make sure you pay attention and check off the answer choice you actually chose as correct.

Common Physics Formulas & Conversions

Constants and Conversion Factors

1 unified atomic mass unit	$1 \text{ u} = 1.66 \times 10^{-27} \text{ kg}$
	$1 \text{ u} = 931 \text{ MeV}/c^2$
Proton mass	$m_p = 1.67 \times 10^{-27} \text{ kg}$
Neutron mass	$m_n = 1.67 \times 10^{-27} \text{ kg}$
Electron mass	$m_e = 9.11 \times 10^{-31} \text{ kg}$
Electron charge magnitude	$e = 1.60 \times 10^{-19} \text{ C}$
Avogadro's number	$N_0 = 6.02 \times 10^{23} \text{ mol}^{-1}$
Universal gas constant	$R = 8.31 \text{ J/(mol·K)}$
Boltzmann's constant	$k_B = 1.38 \times 10^{-23} \text{ J/K}$
Speed of light	$c = 3.00 \times 10^8 \text{ m/s}$
Planck's constant	$h = 6.63 \times 10^{-34} \text{ J·s}$
	$h = 4.14 \times 10^{-15} \text{ eV·s}$
	$hc = 1.99 \times 10^{-25} \text{ J·m}$
	$hc = 1.24 \times 10^3 \text{ eV·nm}$
Vacuum permittivity	$\varepsilon_0 = 8.85 \times 10^{-12} \text{ C}^2/\text{N·m}^2$
Coulomb's law constant	$k = 1/4\pi\varepsilon_0 = 9.0 \times 10^9 \text{ N·m}^2/\text{C}^2$
Vacuum permeability	$\mu_0 = 4\pi \times 10^{-7} \text{ (T·m)/A}$
Magnetic constant	$k' = \mu_0/4\pi = 10^{-7} \text{ (T·m)/A}$
Universal gravitational constant	$G = 6.67 \times 10^{-11} \text{ m}^3/\text{kg·s}^2$
Acceleration due to gravity at Earth's surface	$g = 9.8 \text{ m/s}^2$
1 atmosphere pressure	$1 \text{ atm} = 1.0 \times 10^5 \text{ N/m}^2$
	$1 \text{ atm} = 1.0 \times 10^5 \text{ Pa}$
1 electron volt	$1 \text{ eV} = 1.60 \times 10^{-19} \text{ J}$
Balmer constant	$B = 3.645 \times 10^{-7} \text{ m}$
Rydberg constant	$R = 1.097 \times 10^7 \text{ m}^{-1}$
Stefan constant	$\sigma = 5.67 \times 10^{-8} \text{ W/m}^2\text{K}^4$

Units			Prefixes	
Name	**Symbol**	**Factor**	**Prefix**	**Symbol**
meter	m	10^{12}	tera	T
kilogram	kg	10^{9}	giga	G
second	s	10^{6}	mega	M
ampere	A	10^{3}	kilo	k
kelvin	K	10^{-2}	centi	c
mole	mol	10^{-3}	mili	m
hertz	Hz	10^{-6}	micro	μ
newton	N	10^{-9}	nano	n
pascal	Pa	10^{-12}	pico	p
joule	J			
watt	W			
coulomb	C			
volt	V			
ohm	Ω			
henry	H			
farad	F			
tesla	T			
degree Celsius	°C			
electronvolt	eV			

Values of Trigonometric Functions for Common Angles

θ	$\sin\theta$	$\cos\theta$	$\tan\theta$
0°	0	1	0
30°	1/2	$\sqrt{3}/2$	$\sqrt{3}/3$
37°	3/5	4/5	3/4
45°	$\sqrt{2}/2$	$\sqrt{2}/2$	1
53°	4/5	3/5	4/3
60°	$\sqrt{3}/2$	1/2	$\sqrt{3}$
90°	1	0	∞

Electricity and Magnetism

		A = area
Electric Field	$\vec{E} = \dfrac{\vec{F}_E}{q}$	B = magnetic field
		C = capacitance
Electric Field Strength	$\left|\vec{E}\right| = \dfrac{1}{4\pi\varepsilon_0}\dfrac{\left|q\right|}{r^2}$	d = distance
		E = electric field
Electric Field Strength	$\left|\vec{E}\right| = \dfrac{\left|\Delta V\right|}{\left|\Delta r\right|}$	ϵ = emf
		F = force
Electrostatic Force Between Charged Particles	$\left|\vec{F}_E\right| = \dfrac{1}{4\pi\varepsilon_0}\dfrac{\left|q_1 q_2\right|}{r^2}$	I = current
		l = length
Electric Potential Energy	$\Delta U_E = q\Delta V$	P = power
		Q = charge
Electrostatic Potential due to a Charge	$V = \dfrac{1}{4\pi\varepsilon_0}\dfrac{q}{r}$	q = point charge
		R = resistance
Capacitor Voltage	$V = \dfrac{Q}{C}$	r = separation
		t = time
Capacitance of a Parallel Plate Capacitor	$C = \kappa\varepsilon_0\dfrac{A}{d}$	U = potential energy
		V = electric potential
Electric Field Inside a Parallel Plate Capacitor	$E = \dfrac{Q}{\varepsilon_0 A}$	v = speed
		κ = dielectric constant
Capacitor Potential Energy	$U_C = \frac{1}{2}Q\Delta V = \frac{1}{2}C(\Delta V)^2$	ρ = resistivity
		θ = angle
Current	$I = \dfrac{\Delta Q}{\Delta t}$	Φ = flux
Resistance	$R = \dfrac{\rho l}{A}$	
Power	$P = I\Delta V$	

Current	$I = \dfrac{\Delta V}{R}$
Resistors in Series	$R_s = \sum_i R_i$
Resistors in Parallel	$\dfrac{1}{R_p} = \sum_i \dfrac{1}{R_i}$
Capacitors in Parallel	$C_p = \sum_i C_i$
Capacitors in Series	$\dfrac{1}{C_s} = \sum_i \dfrac{1}{C_i}$
Magnetic Field Strength (from a long straight current-carrying wire)	$B = \dfrac{\mu_0 I}{2\pi r}$
Magnetic Force	$\vec{F}_M = q\vec{v} \times \vec{B}$ $\vec{F}_M = |q\vec{v}||\sin\theta||\vec{B}|$ $\vec{F}_M = I\vec{l} \times \vec{B}$ $\vec{F}_M = |I\vec{l}||\sin\theta||\vec{B}|$
Magnetic Flux	$\Phi_B = \vec{B} \cdot \vec{A}$ $\Phi_B = |\vec{B}|\cos\theta\,|\vec{A}|$
Electromagnetic Induction	$\epsilon = \dfrac{-\Delta\Phi_B}{\Delta t}$ $\epsilon = Blv$

Fluid Mechanics and Thermal Physics

Density	$\rho = \dfrac{m}{V}$	A = area
		c = specific heat
Pressure	$P = \dfrac{F}{A}$	d = thickness
		e = emissivity
Absolute Pressure	$P = P_0 + \rho g h$	F = force
Buoyant Force	$F_b = \rho V g$	h = depth
Fluid Continuity Equation	$A_1 v_1 = A_2 v_2$	k = thermal conductivity
		K = kinetic energy
Bernoulli's Equation	$P_1 + \rho g y_1 + \dfrac{1}{2}\rho v_1^2 = P_2 + \rho g y_2 + \dfrac{1}{2}\rho v_2^2$	l = length
		L = latent heat
Heat Conduction	$\dfrac{Q}{\Delta t} = \dfrac{kA\Delta T}{d}$	m = mass
		n = number of moles
		n_c = efficiency
Thermal Radiation	$P = e\sigma A(T^4 - T_C^4)$	N = number of molecules
Ideal Gas Law	$PV = nRT = Nk_B T$	P = pressure or power
		Q = energy transferred to
Average Energy	$K = \dfrac{3}{2}k_B T$	a system by heating
		T = temperature
Work	$W = -P\Delta V$	t = time
Conservation of Energy	$\Delta E = Q + W$	E = internal energy
Linear Expansion	$\Delta l = \alpha l_o \Delta T$	V = volume
		v = speed
Heat Engine Efficiency	$n_c = |W/Q_H|$	W = work done on a
		system
Carnot Heat Engine Efficiency	$n_c = \dfrac{T_H - T_C}{T_H}$	y = height
		σ = Stefan constant
Energy of Temperature Change	$Q = mc\Delta T$	α = coefficient of linear expansion
Energy of Phase Change	$Q = mL$	ρ = density

Optics

Wavelength to Frequency	$\lambda = \dfrac{v}{f}$	$d = separation$
		$f = frequency\ or\ focal\ length$
Index of Refraction	$n = \dfrac{c}{v}$	$h = height$
		$L = distance$
Snell's Law	$n_1 \sin \theta_1 = n_2 \sin \theta_2$	$M = magnification$
		$m = an\ integer$
Thin Lens Equation	$\dfrac{1}{s_i} + \dfrac{1}{s_0} = \dfrac{1}{f}$	$n = index\ of\ refraction$
		$R = radius\ of\ curvature$
Magnification Equation	$\lvert M \rvert = \left\lvert \dfrac{h_i}{h_o} \right\rvert = \left\lvert \dfrac{s_i}{s_o} \right\rvert$	$s = distance$
		$v = speed$
Double Slit Diffraction	$d \sin \theta = m\lambda$	$x = position$
	$\Delta L = m\lambda$	$\lambda = wavelength$
		$\theta = angle$
Critical Angle	$\sin \theta_c = \dfrac{n_2}{n_1}$	
Focal Length of Spherical Mirror	$f = \dfrac{R}{2}$	

Modern Physics

		B = Balmer constant
Photon Energy	$E = hf$	c = speed of light
Photoelectric Electron Energy	$K_{max} = hf - \phi$	E = energy
		f = frequency
Electron Wavelength	$\lambda = \dfrac{h}{p}$	K = kinetic energy
		m = mass
Energy Mass Relationship	$E = mc^2$	p = momentum
Rydberg Formula	$\dfrac{1}{\lambda} = R\left(\dfrac{1}{n_f^2} - \dfrac{1}{n_i^2}\right)$	R = Rydberg constant
		v = velocity
Balmer Formula	$\lambda = B\left(\dfrac{n^2}{n^2 - 2^2}\right)$	λ = wavelength
		ϕ = work function
Lorentz Factor	$\gamma = \dfrac{1}{\sqrt{1 - \dfrac{v^2}{c^2}}}$	γ = Lorentz factor

Geometry and Trigonometry

Rectangle	$A = bh$	A = area
		C = circumference
Triangle	$A = \dfrac{1}{2}bh$	V = volume
		S = surface area
Circle	$A = \pi r^2$	b = base
	$C = 2\pi r$	h = height
		l = length
Rectangular Solid	$V = lwh$	
		w = width
Cylinder	$V = \pi r^2 l$	r = radius
	$S = 2\pi rl + 2\pi r^2$	θ = angle
Sphere	$V = \dfrac{4}{3}\pi r^3$	
	$S = 4\pi r^2$	
Right Triangle	$a^2 + b^2 = c^2$	
	$\sin\theta = \dfrac{a}{c}$	
	$\cos\theta = \dfrac{b}{c}$	
	$\tan\theta = \dfrac{a}{b}$	

AP Physics 2

Diagnostic Tests

Diagnostic Test #1

Answer Sheet

#	Answer:				Mark for review	#	Answer:				Mark for review
1:	A	B	C	D	____	26:	A	B	C	D	____
2:	A	B	C	D	____	27:	A	B	C	D	____
3:	A	B	C	D	____	28:	A	B	C	D	____
4:	A	B	C	D	____	29:	A	B	C	D	____
5:	A	B	C	D	____	30:	A	B	C	D	____
6:	A	B	C	D	____	31:	A	B	C	D	____
7:	A	B	C	D	____	32:	A	B	C	D	____
8:	A	B	C	D	____	33:	A	B	C	D	____
9:	A	B	C	D	____	34:	A	B	C	D	____
10:	A	B	C	D	____	35:	A	B	C	D	____
11:	A	B	C	D	____	36:	A	B	C	D	____
12:	A	B	C	D	____	37:	A	B	C	D	____
13:	A	B	C	D	____	38:	A	B	C	D	____
14:	A	B	C	D	____	39:	A	B	C	D	____
15:	A	B	C	D	____	40:	A	B	C	D	____
16:	A	B	C	D	____	41:	A	B	C	D	____
17:	A	B	C	D	____	42:	A	B	C	D	____
18:	A	B	C	D	____	43:	A	B	C	D	____
19:	A	B	C	D	____	44:	A	B	C	D	____
20:	A	B	C	D	____	45:	A	B	C	D	____
21:	A	B	C	D	____	46:	A	B	C	D	____
22:	A	B	C	D	____	47:	A	B	C	D	____
23:	A	B	C	D	____	48:	A	B	C	D	____
24:	A	B	C	D	____	49:	A	B	C	D	____
25:	A	B	C	D	____	50:	A	B	C	D	____

This Diagnostic Test is designed for you to assess your proficiency on each topic and NOT to mimic the actual test. Use your test results and identify areas of your strength and weakness to adjust your study plan and enhance your fundamental knowledge.

The length of the Diagnostic Tests is proven to be optimal for a single study session.

1. A thermally-isolated system is made up of a hot piece of aluminum and a cold piece of copper, with the aluminum and copper in thermal contact. The specific heat capacity of aluminum is more than double that of copper. Which object experiences the greater magnitude of gain or loss of heat during the time the system takes to reach thermal equilibrium?

    A. Aluminum

    B. Copper

    C. Neither, because both undergo the same magnitude of gain or loss of heat

    D. Requires knowing the masses

2. As a lead weight drops into the water of uniform density and continues to sink deeper, what happens to the buoyant force on the lead weight from its origin above the surface of the water?

    A. First increases, then remains constant   **C.** Increases steadily

    B. First decreases, then remains constant   **D.** First decreases, then increases steadily

3. What is the focal length of a lens if a candle is placed at a distance of 4 m from the lens and the image is 2 m from the other side of the lens?

    A. –2 m   **B.** –4/3 m   **C.** 3/4 m   **D.** 4/3 m

4. When a nucleus captures a β^- particle, the atomic number of the nucleus:

    A. increases by two   **C.** increases by one

    B. decreases by one   **D.** remains the same

5. A charged particle that is moving in a uniform static magnetic field:

    A. may experience a magnetic force, but its speed does not change

    B. may experience a magnetic force, but its direction of motion does not change

    C. always experiences a magnetic force, and its direction of motion does change

    D. always experiences a magnetic force, and its speed does not change

6. Which statement is true for two conductors that are joined by a long copper wire?

    A. One conductor must have a lower potential than the other conductor

    B. Shortening the wire increases the potential of both conductors

    C. Each conductor must have the same potential

    D. The potential on the wire is the sum of the potentials of each conductor

7. As a solid goes through a phase change to a liquid, heat is absorbed and the temperature:

    A. fluctuates   **B.** remains the same   **C.** decreases   **D.** increases

8. Stress is:

A. strain per unit length

B. applied force per cross-sectional area

C. the ratio of the change in force

D. equivalent to force

9. A light ray in glass arrives at the glass-water interface at an angle of $\theta = 48°$ with respect to the normal. The refracted ray in the water makes an angle of $\phi = 61°$ with respect to the normal. If the angle of incidence changes to $\theta = 25°$, what is the new angle of refraction ϕ in the water? (Use the index of refraction of water = 1.33)

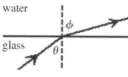

A. 16°   B. 54°   C. 30°   D. 24°

10. What is the name of the type of radiation that has the atomic notation $_0^0\gamma$?

A. Gamma   B. Neutron   C. Alpha   D. Beta

11. Which characteristic is required for a mass spectrometer?

A. Perpendicular electric and gravitational fields

B. Perpendicular gravitational and magnetic fields

C. Perpendicular magnetic and electric fields

D. Collinear magnetic and electric fields

12. What is the capacitance of a capacitor having an impedance of 4 kΩ when operating at 0.6 kHz?

A. 96 μF   B. 2.4 μF   C. 0.15 μF   D. 0.066 μF

13. What is the average kinetic energy of a molecule in an ideal gas at 740 K? (Use Boltzmann's constant $k = 1.38 \times 10^{-23}$ J/K)

A. 3.9×10^{-19} J   B. 2.4×10^{-17} J   C. 5.8×10^{-21} J   D. 1.5×10^{-20} J

14. The density of the material at the center of a neutron star is about 1×10^{18} kg/m³. Calculate the approximate mass of a cube of this material that is 1.76 microns on each side. 1 micron = 1×10^{-6} m.

A. 5.5 kg   B. 4.8 kg   C. 7.8 kg   D. 6.4 kg

15. What happens to an atom when it absorbs energy?

    A. The atom re-emits the energy as light

    B. The atom stores the energy as potential energy

    C. The average distance between the electron and nucleus is reduced

    D. The atom stores the energy as kinetic energy

16. A Sievert is the SI unit for:

    A. measuring the amount of low radiation absorbed per kilogram of tissue

    B. measuring the energy of different types of radiation

    C. measuring the amount of radiation absorbed per gram of tissue

    D. the amount of radiation that produces one-unit charge in 1 cm^3 of water

17. A conductor differs from an insulator in that a conductor has:

    A. slower moving molecules   **C.** more protons than electrons

    B. tightly-bound outer electrons   **D.** none of the above

18. Two objects, I and II, have equal charge and mass. Because of equal gravitational and electrostatic forces between them, neither body is in motion. If the mass of object I is halved, equilibrium is maintained if which change occurs for object II:

    A. mass is quadrupled   **C.** charge is doubled

    B. mass is halved   **D.** charge is halved

19. Aluminum has a positive coefficient of thermal expansion. Consider a round hole that has been drilled in a large sheet of aluminum. As the temperature increases and the surrounding metal expands, the diameter of the hole:

    A. either increases or decreases, depending on how much metal surrounds the hole

    B. remains constant

    C. decreases

    D. increases

20. When an 8.8 kg mass is suspended from a 4.4 m long wire with 1.6 mm diameter, the wire stretches by 3.3 mm. What is Young's modulus for the wire? (Use the acceleration due to gravity $g = 9.8 \text{ m/s}^2$)

    A. $2.4 \times 10^{10} \text{ N/m}^2$ **B.** $3.6 \times 10^{11} \text{ N/m}^2$ **C.** $5.7 \times 10^{10} \text{ N/m}^2$ **D.** $7.1 \times 10^{12} \text{ N/m}^2$

21. The rear-view mirror on the passenger side of many cars has a warning: *objects in mirror are closer than they appear*. This implies that the mirror must be:

    A. convex   **B.** transparent   **C.** concave   **D.** plane

22. The nuclear particle described by the symbol $_2^4$He is a(n):

A. positron   **B.** neutron   **C.** electron   **D.** alpha particle

23. Which of the following is a TRUE statement?

A. It is impossible to convert work entirely into heat
B. It is impossible to transfer heat from a cooler to a hotter body
C. The second law of thermodynamics is a consequence of the first law of thermodynamics
D. All of these statements are false

24. A pipe with a 3 cm radius carries water at a velocity of 4 m/s. What is the volume flow rate?

A. 1.1×10^{-2} m^3/s   **C.** 7.5×10^{-3} m^3/s
B. 48 m^3/s   **D.** 2.7×10^2 m^3/s

25. If two converging lenses with focal lengths of 10 cm and 20 cm are placed in contact, what is the power of the combination?

A. 10 D   **B.** 15 D   **C.** 20 D   **D.** 30 D

26. What type of radioactive decay produces a daughter nuclide that is the same element as the parent nuclide?

     I. Alpha   II. Gamma   III. Beta

A. I only   **B.** II only   **C.** III only   **D.** I and II only

27. Two parallel metal plates, separated by a 0.05 m distance, are charged to produce a uniform electric field between them that points down. What is the magnitude of the force experienced by a proton between the two plates? (Use acceleration due to gravity $g = 10$ m/s^2, charge of a proton $= 1.6 \times 10^{-19}$ C and uniform electric field $= 4 \times 10^4$ N/C)

A. 6.4×10^{-10} N   **C.** 3.2×10^{-15} N
B. 3.2×10^{-10} N   **D.** 6.4×10^{-15} N

28. Initially, for the circuit shown, the switch S is open, and the capacitor voltage is 295 V. The switch S is closed at time $t = 0$. What is the charge on the capacitor when the current in the circuit is 33 μA?

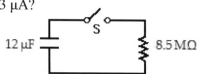

A. 3,400 μC   **B.** 2,600 μC   **C.** 3,000 μC   **D.** 1,800 μC

29. Objects 1 and 2 are heated from the same initial temperature (T_i) to the same final temperature (T_f). Object 1 has three times the specific heat capacity of Object 2 and four times the mass. If Object 1 absorbs heat Q during this process, what is the amount of heat absorbed by Object 2?

   A. $(4/3)Q$ **B.** $(3/4)Q$ **C.** $6Q$ **D.** $(1/12)Q$

30. What force needs to be applied to a 6 cm diameter piston to lift a 12,000 N container with a hydraulic piston that has a diameter of 25 cm?

   A. 26 N   **B.** 691 N   **C.** 1,040 N   **D.** 2,080 N

31. A girl of height h stands in front of a plane mirror. What must the minimum length of the mirror be so that she can view her entire body?

   A. ¼h **B.** $2h$ **C.** ½h **D.** h

32. The fission of an atom that has a larger atomic number (e.g., uranium) can be induced by bombarding the atom with:

   A. electrons   **B.** positrons   **C.** neutrons   **D.** protons

33. Which is an important feature of the Carnot cycle?

   A. Efficiency is determined only by the properties of the working substance used
   B. It is the most efficient engine operating between two temperatures
   C. Efficiency can be 100%
   D. Efficiency depends only on the absolute temperature of the hot reservoir used

34. The two strongest forces that act between protons in a nucleus are the:

   A. electrostatic and gravitational forces
   B. strong nuclear and electrostatic forces
   C. weak nuclear and electrostatic forces
   D. strong nuclear and gravitational forces

35. The transfer of energy from molecule to molecule is:

   A. conduction   **B.** equilibrium   **C.** convection   **D.** condensation

36. A marble cube is lowered at a steady rate into the ocean by a crane, while its top and bottom surfaces remain parallel with the water's surface. Which graph describes the buoyant force (*B*) on this cube as a function of time (*t*), if the cube enters the water at time *t* = 0 s and is lowered until its top surface is well below the water?

A.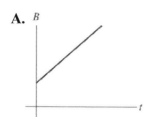

C.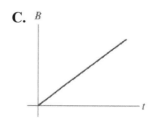

B.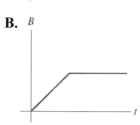

D.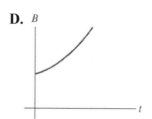

37. Two antennas 130 m apart on a North-South line radiate in phase at a frequency of 3.6 MHz and all radio measurements are recorded far away from the antennas. What is the smallest angle, East of North from the antennas, for constructive interference of the two radio waves? (Use the speed of light $c = 3 \times 10^8$ m/s)

A. 45°   **B.** 60°   **C.** 50°   **D.** 30°

38. According to the quantum mechanical model of the He atom, if the orbital angular momentum quantum number is ℓ, how many magnetic quantum numbers are possible?

A. $2\ell + 1$ **B.** $2\ell - 1$ **C.** 2ℓ **D.** $\ell/2$

39. Which statement regarding the electric charge is NOT correct if the electric charge is conserved?

A. Will not interact with neighboring electric charges
B. Can neither be created nor destroyed
C. Is a whole-number multiple of the charge of one electron
D. May occur in an infinite variety of quantities

40. When connected to a household voltage of 120 V, a light bulb draws 2 A of current. How many watts is the light bulb?

A. 30 W   **B.** 120 W   **C.** 180 W   **D.** 240 W

41. A few 10 cm long aluminum rods and 8 cm long steel rods are at 5 °C temperature and are joined together to form a 60 cm long rod. What is the increase in the length of the joined rod when the temperature is raised to 80 °C? (Use a coefficient of linear expansion for aluminum = $2.4 \times 10^{-5} \text{ K}^{-1}$ and coefficient of linear expansion for steel = $1.2 \times 10^{-5} \text{ K}^{-1}$)

    A. 0.3 mm   **B.** 0.5 mm   **C.** 1.8 mm   **D.** 0.72 mm

42. A water tank open to the atmosphere is elevated above the ground by 25 m and is filled to a depth of 12 m. What is the approximate water pressure in a hose with a 2 cm diameter at ground level? (Use acceleration due to gravity $g = 9.8 \text{ m/s}^2$, density of water $\rho = 1{,}000 \text{ kg/m}^3$ and atmospheric pressure P = 1 atm or 101,325 N/m^2)

    A. 8.4 N/m^2 **B.** 3.2×10^5 N/m^2 **C.** 4.6×10^5 N/m^2 **D.** 5.6 N/m^2

43. Optical density is proportional to:

    A. index of refraction   **C.** mass density

    B. index of reflection   **D.** light speed

44. Which radiation type penetrates about 1 cm of human tissue and requires a minimum protective shielding made of wood or aluminum?

    A. Gamma   **B.** Beta   **C.** Alpha   **D.** Nuclide

45. The process whereby heat flows by the mass movement of molecules from one place to another is known as:

    A. inversion   **B.** radiation   **C.** convection   **D.** conduction

46. When fully charged, a particular battery provides 1 mW of power at 9 V. What is the current that it delivers?

    A. 0.13 kA   **B.** 9 kA   **C.** 0.11 mA   **D.** 18 mA

47. Relative to the mirror, where is the resulting image when a light source is placed 12 m in front of a diverging mirror that has a focal length of 6 m?

    A. 2 m in front   **B.** 2 m behind   **C.** 4 m in front   **D.** 4 m behind

48. Monochromatic light is incident on a metal surface and electrons are ejected. How do the ejection rate and the maximum energy of the electrons change if the intensity of the light is increased?

    A. Same rate; same maximum energy   **C.** Same rate; lower maximum energy

    B. Greater rate; greater maximum energy   **D.** Greater rate; same maximum energy

49. Which of the following diagrams is correct for a circuit with a battery connected to four resistors, R_1, R_2, R_3, and R_4? Resistors R_1 and R_2 are connected in parallel, resistors R_3 and R_4 are connected in parallel, and both parallel sets of resistors are connected in series across the battery.

A.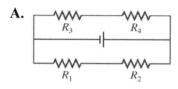

C.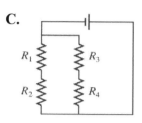

B.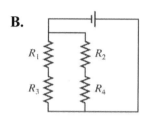

D.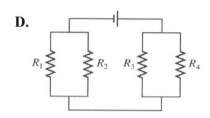

50. Light refracts when traveling from air into glass because light:

   A. travels slower in glass than in air

   B. travels slower in the air than in glass

   C. has a frequency that is greater in glass than in air

   D. travels at the same speed in glass and air

Check your answers using the answer key. Then, go to the explanations section and review the explanations in detail, paying particular attention to questions you didn't answer correctly or marked for review. Note the topic that those questions belong to.

We recommend that you do this BEFORE taking the next Diagnostic Test.

Diagnostic test #1 – Answer Key

1	C	Thermodynamics	**26**	B	Atomic, nuclear & quantum physics
2	A	Fluid statics & dynamics	**27**	D	Electrostatics & magnetism
3	D	Geometric & physical optics	**28**	A	DC and RC circuits
4	B	Atomic, nuclear & quantum physics	**29**	D	Thermodynamics
5	A	Electrostatics & magnetism	**30**	B	Fluid statics & dynamics
6	C	DC and RC circuits	**31**	C	Geometric & physical optics
7	B	Thermodynamics	**32**	C	Atomic, nuclear & quantum physics
8	B	Fluid statics & dynamics	**33**	B	Thermodynamics
9	C	Geometric & physical optics	**34**	B	Atomic & nuclear physics
10	A	Atomic, nuclear & quantum physics	**35**	A	Thermodynamics
11	C	Electrostatics & magnetism	**36**	B	Fluid statics & dynamics
12	D	DC and RC circuits	**37**	C	Geometric & physical optics
13	D	Thermodynamics	**38**	A	Atomic, nuclear & quantum physics
14	A	Fluid statics & dynamics	**39**	A	Electrostatics & magnetism
15	A	Geometric & physical optics	**40**	D	DC and RC circuits
16	A	Atomic, nuclear & quantum physics	**41**	D	Thermodynamics
17	D	Electrostatics & magnetism	**42**	C	Fluid statics & dynamics
18	D	Electrostatics & magnetism	**43**	A	Geometric & physical optics
19	D	Thermodynamics	**44**	B	Atomic, nuclear & quantum physics
20	C	Fluid statics & dynamics	**45**	C	Thermodynamics
21	A	Geometric & physical optics	**46**	C	DC and RC circuits
22	D	Atomic, nuclear & quantum physics	**47**	D	Geometric & physical optics
23	D	Thermodynamics	**48**	D	Atomic, nuclear & quantum physics
24	A	Fluid statics & dynamics	**49**	D	DC and RC circuits
25	B	Geometric & physical optics	**50**	A	Geometric & physical optics

Diagnostic Test #2

Answer Sheet

#	Answer:				Mark for review	#	Answer:				Mark for review
1:	A	B	C	D	____	26:	A	B	C	D	____
2:	A	B	C	D	____	27:	A	B	C	D	____
3:	A	B	C	D	____	28:	A	B	C	D	____
4:	A	B	C	D	____	29:	A	B	C	D	____
5:	A	B	C	D	____	30:	A	B	C	D	____
6:	A	B	C	D	____	31:	A	B	C	D	____
7:	A	B	C	D	____	32:	A	B	C	D	____
8:	A	B	C	D	____	33:	A	B	C	D	____
9:	A	B	C	D	____	34:	A	B	C	D	____
10:	A	B	C	D	____	35:	A	B	C	D	____
11:	A	B	C	D	____	36:	A	B	C	D	____
12:	A	B	C	D	____	37:	A	B	C	D	____
13:	A	B	C	D	____	38:	A	B	C	D	____
14:	A	B	C	D	____	39:	A	B	C	D	____
15:	A	B	C	D	____	40:	A	B	C	D	____
16:	A	B	C	D	____	41:	A	B	C	D	____
17:	A	B	C	D	____	42:	A	B	C	D	____
18:	A	B	C	D	____	43:	A	B	C	D	____
19:	A	B	C	D	____	44:	A	B	C	D	____
20:	A	B	C	D	____	45:	A	B	C	D	____
21:	A	B	C	D	____	46:	A	B	C	D	____
22:	A	B	C	D	____	47:	A	B	C	D	____
23:	A	B	C	D	____	48:	A	B	C	D	____
24:	A	B	C	D	____	49:	A	B	C	D	____
25:	A	B	C	D	____	50:	A	B	C	D	____

This Diagnostic Test is designed for you to assess your proficiency on each topic and NOT to mimic the actual test. Use your test results and identify areas of your strength and weakness to adjust your study plan and enhance your fundamental knowledge.

The length of the Diagnostic Tests is proven to be optimal for a single study session.

1. Once a steady-state heat flow is established, the thickness of a wall built from solid uniform material is doubled. Relative to the original value, what is the result for the rate of heat loss for a given temperature difference across the wall?

   A. $1/\sqrt{2}$ **B.** ¼   **C.** 2 times   **D.** ½

2. A tank of water has a hose, filled with water, projecting from the top. The system acts as a siphon as the other end of the hose is below the tank. The end of the hose outside the tank is at height $h = 0$ m. The bottom of the tank is at height h_1, the end of the hose inside the tank is at height h_2, and the top of the water is at height h_3. Assuming that the flow is without viscosity, which is the best expression for the pressure at the bottom of the tank?

   A. $P_{atm} + \rho g(h_3 + h_1)$ **C.** $P_{atm} + \rho g(h_3 - h_1)$

   B. $P_{atm} - \rho g(h_3 + h_1)$ **D.** $P_{atm} - \rho g(h_3 - h_1)$

3. Which of the following types of electromagnetic radiation has the highest energy per photon?

     I. Microwave   II. Infrared   III. Ultraviolet

   A. I only   **B.** II only   **C.** III only   **D.** I and II only

4. This is an example of what type of nuclear reaction: $^{126}_{50}Sn \rightarrow {}^{126}_{51}Sb$?

   A. Beta emission   **B.** Gamma particle   **C.** Fusion   **D.** Fission

5. A likely cause for the existence of Earth's magnetic field is:

     I. moving charges in the liquid part of Earth's core
     II. convection currents in the liquid part of Earth's core
     III. great numbers of very slow moving charges in the Earth

   A. I only   **B.** II only   **C.** III only   **D.** I, II and III

6. Which statement(s) is/are correct?

     I. Current results in voltage
     II. Current flows through a circuit
     III. Voltage flows through a circuit

   A. I only   **B.** II only   **C.** III only   **D.** I and II only

7. If 60 g of material at 100 °C is mixed with 200 g of water at 0 °C, the final temperature is 40 °C. What is the specific heat of the material?

   A. 2.2 kcal/kg·°C   **C.** 0.4 kcal/kg·°C

   B. 6.3 kcal/kg·°C   **D.** 4.6 kcal/kg·°C

8. The tires support the weight of a stationary car. If one tire has a slow leak, the air pressure within the tire [   ], the surface area between the tire and the road [   ] and the net force the tire exerts on the road [   ]. (Assume the car is nearly level and remains nearly level, and that initially, each tire supports the same force)

A. decreases … increases … remains constant

B. increases … increases … increases

C. decreases … increases … increases

D. decreases … increases … decreases

9. A blue object appears black when illuminated with which color of light?

A. Green   **B.** Yellow   **C.** Cyan   **D.** Blue

10. What type of radiation is released when $^{220}_{86}Rn \rightarrow {}^{216}_{84}Po$?

     I. Gamma   II. Beta   III. Alpha

A. I only   **B.** II only   **C.** III only   **D.** I and II only

11. Consider two current-carrying circular loops. Both are made from one strand of wire each, and both carry the same amount of current, but one has double the radius. Compared to the magnetic moment of the smaller loop, the magnetic moment of the larger loop is:

A. $\sqrt{2}$ times stronger   **B.** 4 times stronger   **C.** $\sqrt{2}$ times weaker   **D.** 2 times stronger

12. How often does the polarity of the voltage reverse in a 60 Hz circuit?

A. 60 times/s   **B.** 120 times/s   **C.** 90 times/s   **D.** 1/60 times/s

13. According to the laws of thermodynamics:

A. heat energy cannot be completely converted into mechanical energy

B. heat flows naturally from a region of lower to a region of higher temperature

C. mechanical energy cannot be completely converted into heat

D. at a constant temperature, entropy increases as heat is extracted from a system

14. In Egypt, the Aswan Dam on the Nile River is 110 m high. Assuming the density of water is 1,000 kg/m^3, what is the gauge pressure of the water at the foot of the dam? (Use the acceleration due to gravity $g = 10$ m/s^2)

A. 2.1×10^5 Pa   **B.** 2.9×10^3 Pa   **C.** 1.8×10^7 Pa   **D.** 1.1×10^6 Pa

15. A simple compound microscope normally uses a:

    A. short focal length objective and a long focal length eyepiece

    B. long focal length objective and a short focal length eyepiece

    C. focal length objective and focal length eyepiece of the same length

    D. short focal length objective and a shorter focal length eyepiece

16. What happens to the de Broglie wavelength for a particle as it increases its velocity?

    A. Increases   **C.** Remains constant

    B. Decreases   **D** Increases by $\sqrt{\Delta v}$

17. Two solenoids are close to each other with the switch S open. In which direction does the induced current flow through the galvanometer in the left-hand solenoid when the switch is closed?

    A. From left to right

    B. From right to left

    C. There will be no induced current through the galvanometer

    D. It depends on the amount of the induced current

18. The water fountain pump recirculates water from a pool and pumps it up to a trough, where it flows along the trough and passes through a hole in the bottom of it. As the water falls back into the pool, it turns a water wheel. What aspect of this water fountain is analogous to an electric current within an electric circuit?

    A. Volume flow rate   **C.** Density of water

    B. Height of water   **D.** Flow velocity

19. When 110 J of heat is added to a system that performs 40 J of work, the total thermal energy change of the system is:

    A. 2.8 J   **B.** 40 J   **C.** 70 J   **D.** 0 J

20. A pump uses a piston with a 20 cm diameter that moves at 3 cm/s to push a liquid through a pipe. Assuming that the liquid is ideal and incompressible, what is the speed of the liquid when it enters a portion of the pipe that is 4 mm in diameter?

    A. 5 m/s   **B.** 60 cm/s   **C.** 22 m/s   **D.** 75 m/s

21. The image of a real object from a plane mirror has the following characteristics:

   A. real, erect, with magnification = 1   **C.** real, erect, with magnification > 1

   B. real, inverted, with magnification = 1   **D.** virtual, erect, with magnification = 1

22. In β⁻ decay, the number of protons in the nucleus:

   A. increases by 2   **C.** decreases by 2

   B. increases by 1   **D.** decreases by 1

23. In the equation $PV = NkT$, k is known as:

   A. the spring (compressibility) constant   **C.** Planck's constant

   B. Boltzmann's constant   **D.** Avogadro's number

24. What would be the apparent mass of a 2 in × 4 in × 6 in lead brick, if it was placed in oil? (Use the acceleration due to gravity $g = 9.8$ m/s², density of oil $\rho = 0.92$ g/cm³, density of lead $\rho = 11.4$ g/cm³ and 1 in³ = 16.4 cm³)

   A. 8.2 kg   **C.** 0.3 kg

   B. 6 kg   **D.** 1.8 kg

25. Light in a vacuum has a speed of 3×10^8 m/s as it enters a liquid with a refractive index of 2. What is the speed of light in this liquid?

   A. 7.5×10^8 m/s   **C.** 6×10^8 m/s

   B. 1.5×10^8 m/s   **D.** 3×10^8 m/s

26. In a transition from one vibrational state to another, a molecule emits a photon of wavelength 6.5 μm. What is the energy difference between these two states? (Use the speed of light $c = 3 \times 10^8$ m/s and Planck's constant $h = 4.136 \times 10^{-15}$ eV·s)

   A. 11.1 eV   **C.** 0.28 MeV

   B. 11.1 MeV   **D.** 0.19 eV

27. Which statement is accurate?

   A. The magnetic force on a moving charge does not change its energy

   B. The magnetic force on a current-carrying wire is minimal when the wire is perpendicular to the magnetic field

   C. All magnetic fields originate from the North and South poles

   D. By definition, a magnetic field line is a tangent to the direction of the magnetic force on a moving charge at a given point in space

28. If the length and the cross-sectional diameter of wire are both doubled, the resistance is:

    A. halved

    B. increased fourfold

    C. doubled

    D. decreased by one fourth

29. An engineer is studying the rate of heat loss, $\Delta Q / \Delta t$ through a sheet of insulating material as a function of the thickness of the sheet. Assuming fixed temperatures on the two faces of the sheet and steady-state heat flow, which of the graphs best represents the rate of heat transfer as a function of the thickness of the insulating sheet?

A.
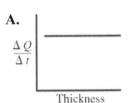

C.
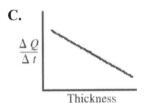

B.
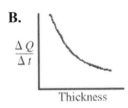

D.
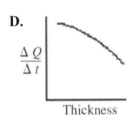

30. Jack is breathing through a snorkel as he swims in the Caribbean Sea. He experiences difficulty breathing when his chest is submerged about 1 meter under water. Which expression gives the force that his muscles must exert to expand his chest?

    A. (atmospheric pressure) × (area of his chest)

    B. (atmospheric pressure) × (area of snorkel hole + area of his chest)

    C. (gauge pressure of the water) × (area of his chest)

    D. (gauge pressure of the water) × (area of snorkel hole)

31. Which expression describes the critical angle for the interface of water with air? (Use index of refraction for water n = 1.33 and index of refraction for air n = 1)

    A. $\sin^{-1}(1/3)$ **B.** $\sin^{-1}(3/4)$ **C.** $\sin^{-1}(2/3)$ **D.** $\sin^{-1}(4/3)$

32. What is the amount of energy required to ionize a hydrogen atom from the ground state? (Use Rydberg formula where $E_0 = -13.6$ eV)

    A. 4.1 eV   **B.** 9.8 eV   **C.** 13.6 eV   **D.** 22.3 eV

33. Which two temperature scales have the same interval size?

A. Kelvin and Celsius

B. Fahrenheit and Centigrade

C. Celsius and Fahrenheit

D. Fahrenheit and Kelvin

34. What is the mass of a cylindrical rod with a length of 14 cm and a diameter of 2 cm that just barely floats in water? (Use density of water $\rho = 1,000$ kg/m^3)

A. 44 g   **B.** 70 g   **C.** 140 g   **D.** 28 g

35. Using a mirror with a focal length of 10 m, an object is viewed at various distances. What is its magnification and orientation when the object is 5 m in front of the mirror?

A. Twice as large and upright

B. Twice as large and inverted

C. Half as large and upright

D. Same size and inverted

36. Which energy source provides most of a person's annual exposure to radiation?

A. Cell phones and hand-held electronic devices

B. Televisions (i.e., cathode ray tubes)

C. Background radiation

D. Sunlight and UV rays

37. A magnet is always surrounded by a(n):

I. electric field   II. magnetic field   III. declination field

A. I only   **B.** II only   **C.** III only   **D.** I and II only

38. Which quantity is expressed in units of $\Omega \cdot$m?

A. Flow   **B.** Capacitance   **C.** Resistivity   **D.** Potential

39. Compared to a giant iceberg, a hot cup of coffee has:

A. a higher temperature, but more thermal energy

B. a greater specific heat and more thermal energy

C. a higher temperature, but less thermal energy

D. more thermal energy and lower temperature

40. A pipe with a circular cross-section has water flowing from the point I to point II. The radius of the pipe is 6 cm at the point I, while the radius at point II is 3 cm. At the end of the point I, the flow rate is 0.04 m^3/s. What is the velocity of the water at the point I?

A. 3.5 m/s   **B.** 22 m/s   **C.** 18.5 m/s   **D.** 6 m/s

41. A candle is viewed through a converging lens. What is the magnification of the image when the candle is 6 m from the lens, and the image is 3 m from the lens on the other side?

  A. Twice as large and upright

  B. Same size and inverted

  C. Half as large and upright

  D. Half as large and inverted

42. Uranium has an atomic number of 92, but often contains 146 or more neutrons and undergoes radioactive decay. Which statement describes why this occurs?

    I. The electromagnetic repulsion overcomes the strong nuclear force

    II. Excess neutrons increase the electromagnetic repulsion

    III. The strong nuclear force has a limited range

  A. I only   **B.** II only   **C.** III only   **D.** I and III only

43. By what magnitude does a magnetic field produced by a wire decrease when the distance from a long current-carrying wire is doubled?

  A. $1/\sqrt{2}$ **B.** ½   **C.** ¼   **D.** 1/6

44. Which diagram represents a circuit with two batteries that connects a negative pole to a positive pole, a resistor between them, and a capacitor in parallel with the resistor?

A. 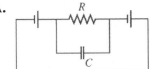   **C.**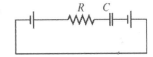

B. 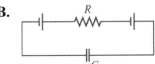   **D.**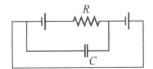

45. An 830 g meteor impacts the Earth at a speed of 1,250 m/s. If its kinetic energy is entirely converted to heat of the meteorite, by what temperature does it increase? (Use the specific heat for the meteor = 108 cal/kg·°C and 1 cal = 4.186 Joules)

  A. 1,728 °C   **B.** 1,346 °C   **C.** 2,628 °C   **D.** 7,142 °C

46. A small aircraft is traveling at a constant speed in a circular path with a radius of 200 m parallel to the ground. The center of the circular path is 400 m above an air traffic control tower. Its engine is the source of audible sound waves of a fixed frequency. To a stationary observer in the tower, how would the detected frequency (f_d) of the engine differ from that of the source (f_s) while the aircraft circled above?

A. Remains constant and equal to f_s

B. Higher than f_s during one orbit, and lower during each subsequent orbit

C. Higher than f_s during half the orbit, and lower during each subsequent half-orbit

D. Remains constant, but is lower than f_s

47. What is the focal length of the mirror if, when an object is 24 cm in front of a concave spherical mirror, the image is formed 3 cm in front of the mirror?

A. 1.5 cm   **B.** 2.7 cm   **C.** 5 cm   **D.** 6.3 cm

48. The isotope $^{238}_{92}\text{U}$ is most likely to emit:

A. a γ ray

B. a β particle

C. an α particle

D. both an α and β particle

49. A proton, moving in a uniform magnetic field, moves in a circle perpendicular to the field. If the proton's speed is tripled, what happens to the time needed to complete a circular path?

A. Increases   **B.** Remains constant   **C.** Decreases   **D.** Doubles

50. Which of the following is an accurate statement?

A. The magnetic force on a current-carrying wire is the smallest when the wire is perpendicular to the magnetic field

B. The magnetic force on a moving charge does not change its energy

C. A magnetic field line is, by definition, tangent to the direction of the magnetic force on a moving charge at a given point in space

D. All magnetic fields have North and South poles as their sources

Check your answers using the answer key. Then, go to the explanations section and review the explanations in detail, paying particular attention to questions you didn't answer correctly or marked for review. Note the topic that those questions belong to.

We recommend that you do this BEFORE taking the next Diagnostic Test.

Diagnostic test #2 – Answer Key

1	D	Thermodynamics	**26**	D	Atomic, nuclear & quantum physics
2	C	Fluid statics & dynamics	**27**	A	Electrostatics & magnetism
3	C	Geometric & physical optics	**28**	A	DC and RC circuits
4	A	Atomic, nuclear & quantum physics	**29**	B	Thermodynamics
5	D	Electrostatics & magnetism	**30**	C	Fluid statics & dynamics
6	B	DC and RC circuits	**31**	B	Geometric & physical optics
7	A	Thermodynamics	**32**	C	Atomic, nuclear & quantum physics
8	A	Fluid statics & dynamics	**33**	A	Thermodynamics
9	B	Geometric & physical optics	**34**	A	Fluid statics & dynamics
10	C	Atomic, nuclear & quantum physics	**35**	A	Geometric & physical optics
11	B	Electrostatics & magnetism	**36**	C	Atomic, nuclear & quantum physics
12	B	DC and RC circuits	**37**	B	Electrostatics & magnetism
13	A	Thermodynamics	**38**	C	DC and RC circuits
14	D	Fluid statics & dynamics	**39**	C	Thermodynamics
15	A	Geometric & physical optics	**40**	A	Fluid statics & dynamics
16	B	Atomic, nuclear & quantum physics	**41**	D	Geometric & physical optics
17	B	Electrostatics & magnetism	**42**	D	Atomic, nuclear & quantum physics
18	A	DC and RC circuits	**43**	B	Electrostatics & magnetism
19	C	Thermodynamics	**44**	A	DC and RC circuits
20	D	Fluid statics & dynamics	**45**	A	Thermodynamics
21	D	Geometric & physical optics	**46**	A	Fluid statics & dynamics
22	B	Atomic, nuclear & quantum physics	**47**	B	Geometric & physical optics
23	B	Thermodynamics	**48**	C	Atomic, nuclear & quantum physics
24	A	Fluid statics & dynamics	**49**	B	Electrostatics & magnetism
25	B	Geometric & physical optics	**50**	B	DC and RC circuits

Diagnostic Test #3

Answer Sheet

#	Answer:				Mark for review	#	Answer:				Mark for review
1:	A	B	C	D	____	26:	A	B	C	D	____
2:	A	B	C	D	____	27:	A	B	C	D	____
3:	A	B	C	D	____	28:	A	B	C	D	____
4:	A	B	C	D	____	29:	A	B	C	D	____
5:	A	B	C	D	____	30:	A	B	C	D	____
6:	A	B	C	D	____	31:	A	B	C	D	____
7:	A	B	C	D	____	32:	A	B	C	D	____
8:	A	B	C	D	____	33:	A	B	C	D	____
9:	A	B	C	D	____	34:	A	B	C	D	____
10:	A	B	C	D	____	35:	A	B	C	D	____
11:	A	B	C	D	____	36:	A	B	C	D	____
12:	A	B	C	D	____	37:	A	B	C	D	____
13:	A	B	C	D	____	38:	A	B	C	D	____
14:	A	B	C	D	____	39:	A	B	C	D	____
15:	A	B	C	D	____	40:	A	B	C	D	____
16:	A	B	C	D	____	41:	A	B	C	D	____
17:	A	B	C	D	____	42:	A	B	C	D	____
18:	A	B	C	D	____	43:	A	B	C	D	____
19:	A	B	C	D	____	44:	A	B	C	D	____
20:	A	B	C	D	____	45:	A	B	C	D	____
21:	A	B	C	D	____	46:	A	B	C	D	____
22:	A	B	C	D	____	47:	A	B	C	D	____
23:	A	B	C	D	____	48:	A	B	C	D	____
24:	A	B	C	D	____	49:	A	B	C	D	____
25:	A	B	C	D	____	50:	A	B	C	D	____

This Diagnostic Test is designed for you to assess your proficiency on each topic and NOT to mimic the actual test. Use your test results and identify areas of your strength and weakness to adjust your study plan and enhance your fundamental knowledge.

The length of the Diagnostic Tests is proven to be optimal for a single study session.

1. A solid cylindrical bar conducts heat at a rate of 30 W from a hot to a cold reservoir under steady-state conditions. What is the rate at which it conducts heat between these reservoirs if both the diameter and length of the bar are doubled? Assume heat transfer is lengthwise and sides of the bar are perfectly insulated.

    A. 30 W   **B.** 60 W   **C.** 15 W   **D.** 120 W

2. A 600 N weight sits on the small piston of a hydraulic machine. The small piston has an area of 5 cm². If the large piston has an area of 50 cm², how much force can the large piston support?

    A. 200 N   **B.** 300 N   **C.** 3,000 N   **D.** 6,000 N

3. What color light allows the investigator to see with the greatest resolution in a light microscope?

    A. Red light because it is refracted less than other colors by the objective lens
    B. Blue light because it has a shorter wavelength
    C. Violet light because it has a longer wavelength
    D. Blue light because it is brighter

4. A blue laser beam is incident on a metallic surface, causing electrons to be ejected from the metal. What is the effect on the rate of ejected electrons if the frequency of the laser beam is increased, while the intensity of the beam is held fixed?

    A. Remains the same, but the maximum kinetic energy decreases
    B. Decreases and the maximum kinetic energy decreases
    C. Decreases, but the maximum kinetic energy remains the same
    D. Decreases, but the maximum kinetic energy increases

5. A cube with 0.1 m sides is constructed of six insulated metal plates. Plates I and IV are opposite to each other and are maintained at 500 V. Plates II and V are opposite to each other and are maintained at 0 V. Plates III and VI are opposite to each other and are maintained at −500 V. What is the change in potential energy, if an electron is transferred from plate I to plate III? (Use the charge of e = 1.6 × 10⁻¹⁹ C)

    A. -3.2×10^{-14} J   **B.** -1.6×10^{-15} J   **C.** 3.2×10^{-12} J   **D.** 1.6×10^{-16} J

6. A series circuit has a 50 Hz AC source, a 0.4 H inductor, a 50 μF capacitor and a 30 Ω resistor. If the rms current in the circuit is 1.8 A, what is the voltage of the source?

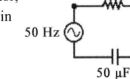

    A. 142 V   **C.** 75.5 V
    B. 124 V   **D.** 96.7 V

7. With all other factors equal, the most likely situation in which a person burns her mouth is with food that has:

A. specific heat is not applicable

B. requires more information

C. higher specific heat

D. lower specific heat

8. How many grams of ethanol should be added to 5 grams of chloroform for the resulting mixture to have a specific gravity of 1.2? (Use the specific gravity of ethanol = 0.8, specific gravity of chloroform = 1.5 and conversion factor of 1 mL = 1 g)

A. 1.5 g   B. 2.6 g   C. 2.0 g   D. 1.0 g

9. What is the distance between a lens and a screen so that when the screen and the converging lens of focal length f are arranged, an image of the Moon falls on the screen? Assume that the Moon is infinity ∞ away from the lens.

A. $f/2$ B. $2f$ C. f D. infinity

10. What is the nuclear particle which is described by the symbol $_1^1H$?

A. positron   B. β particle   C. γ particle   D. proton

11. A charged particle is traveling in a circular path of radius r in a uniform magnetic field. The plane of the circular path is perpendicular to the magnetic field. What is the radius of the circular path if the particle travels twice as fast?

A. $\sqrt{2}r$ B. $r/2$ C. $4r$ D. $2r$

12. For a graph of potential vs. power, what does the slope represent for a DC circuit?

A. 1 / resistance

B. current

C. 1 / current

D. resistance

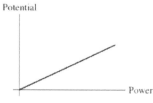

13. Two identical blocks of steel, one at 20 °C and the other at 30 °C, are placed into contact. Suppose the cooler block cools to 15 °C and the warmer block warms to 35 °C. This violates the:

    I. First law of thermodynamics

    II. Second law of thermodynamics

    III. Third law of thermodynamics

A. I only   B. II only   C. III only   D. I and II only

14. A silver necklace that has a mass of 60 grams and a volume of 5.7 cm³ is lowered into a container of water and is tied to a string connected to a force meter. What is the reading on the force meter? (Use the density of water = 1 g/cm³ and acceleration due to gravity $g = 9.8$ m/s²)

    A. 0.53 N   **B.** 0.22 N   **C.** 0.62 N   **D.** 0.38 N

15. Which statement is true for the angle of incidence?

    A. It may be greater than or less than, but never equal to, the angle of reflection
    B. It is always greater than the angle of reflection
    C. It must equal the angle of reflection
    D. It is always less than the angle of reflection

16. ¹⁴C is generated in the atmosphere by the nuclear reaction: $^{14}_{7}N + ^{1}_{0}n \rightarrow ^{14}_{6}C + \_\_$?

What species is not shown?

    A. neutron   **B.** positron   **C.** α particle   **D.** proton

17. In which direction is the magnetic field if a positive charge is moving to the right and experiences a vertical (upward) magnetic force?

    A. Out of the page   **C.** To the left
    B. Into the page   **D.** To the right

18. How much current flows through a 57 m length of copper wire with a radius of 5.7 mm if it is connected to a source supplying 70 V? (Use resistivity of copper = 1.68×10^{-8} Ω·m)

    A. 180 nA   **B.** 3,600 A   **C.** 7,447 A   **D.** 3.7×10^8 A

19. A 1,140 g empty iron kettle is on a hot stove. How much heat must it absorb to raise its temperature from 18 °C to 90 °C? (Use the specific heat for iron = 113 cal/kg·°C and 1 cal = 4.186 J)

    A. 8,230 J   **B.** 20,340 J   **C.** 38,825 J   **D.** 41,650 J

20. A water tank is filled to a depth of 6 m, and the bottom of the tank is 22 m above ground. A water-filled hose that is 2 cm in diameter extends from the bottom of the tank to the ground, but no water is flowing in the hose. What is the gauge water pressure at ground level in the hose? (Use the density of water $\rho = 1,000$ kg/m³ and acceleration due to gravity $g = 9.8$ m/s²)

    A. 2.7×10^5 N/m²   **C.** 8.7 N/m²
    B. 5.3×10^4 N/m²   **D.** Requires the cross-sectional area of the tank

21. What is the orientation and magnification of the image of a light bulb if the light bulb is placed 2 m in front of a mirror and the image is 6 m behind the mirror?

A. Upright and × 3

B. Inverted and × 3

C. Upright and × 0.5

D. Inverted and × 1.5

22. What is the amount of energy required to ionize a hydrogen atom from the ground state? (Use Rydberg formula where $E_0 = -13.6$ eV)

A. 4.1 eV   **B.** 9.8 eV   **C.** 13.6 eV   **D.** 22.3 eV

23. How much heat is needed to melt a 70 kg sample of ice that is at 0 °C? (Use latent heat of fusion for water $L_f = 334{,}000$ J/kg and heat of vaporization for water $L_v = 2.3 \times 10^6$ J/kg)

A. 1.3×10^5 kJ

B. 5.7×10^4 kJ

C. 4.0×10^6 kJ

D. 2.3×10^4 kJ

24. When a dam began to leak, Mike placed his finger in the hole to stop the flow. The dam is 20 m high and 100 km long and sits on top of a lake which is another 980 m deep, 100 km wide, and 100 km long. The hole that Mike blocked is a square 0.01 m by 0.01 m located 1 m below the surface of the water. Assuming that the viscosity of the water is negligible, what force does Mike have to exert to prevent water from leaking? (Use atmospheric pressure $P_{atm} = 10^5$ Pa, the density of water $\rho = 10^3$ kg/m^3 and the acceleration due to gravity $g = 10$ m/s^2)

A. 10 N   **B.** 1 N   **C.** 1,000 N   **D.** 0.1 N

25. The index of refraction of the core of a piece of fiber optic cable is 1.6. If the index of the surrounding cladding is 1.3, what is the critical angle for total internal reflection of a light ray in the core, incident on the core-cladding interface?

A. 82°   **B.** 40°   **C.** 34°   **D.** 54°

26. The image shows three beams of radiation passing between two electrically-charged plates. Which of the beams is due to a high-energy electron?

     I. a

     II. b

     III. c

A. I only   **B.** II only   **C.** III only   **D.** I and II only

27. Two parallel metal plates separated by a distance of 0.03 m are charged to create a uniform electric field (4×10^4 N/C) between them, which points down. How does the force exerted on an α particle between the plates compare with the force exerted on a proton between the plates? (Use acceleration due to gravity $g = 10$ m/s^2 and the charge on a proton = 1.6×10^{-19} C)

    A. Twice as large and in the same direction
    B. Four times as large and in the same direction
    C. The same magnitude, but in the opposite direction
    D. The same magnitude and in the same direction

28. Which graph is representative for a semiconductor material? R = resistivity, T = temperature.

A.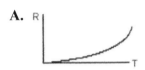

C.

B.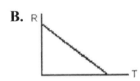

D.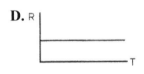

29. What is the primary heat transfer mechanism by which the sun warms the Earth?

    I. Convection   II. Radiation   III. Conduction

    A. I only   **B.** II only   **C.** III only   **D.** I and II only

30. What is the density of an object if it weighs 7.86 N when it is in air and 6.92 N when it is immersed in water? (Use the acceleration due to gravity $g = 9.8$ m/s^2 and the density of water $\rho = 1,000$ kg/m^3)

    A. 6,042 kg/m^3 **B.** 7,286 kg/m^3 **C.** 8,333 kg/m^3 **D.** 9,240 kg/m^3

31. A light ray in water passes into the air where the angle of incidence in the water is 42°. What is the angle of refraction in the air? (Use the index of refraction of air n = 1 and the index of refraction of water = 1.33)

    A. 63°   **B.** 18°   **C.** 46°   **D.** 74°

32. ^{3}Hydrogen can be used as a chemical tracer. What is the half-life of the radionuclide if 3,200 μg decays to 800 μg after 24.6 years?

    A. 6.1 years   **B.** 12.3 years   **C.** 24.6 years   **D.** 49.2 years

33. A 500 g empty iron pot is put on a stove. How much heat must it absorb to raise its temperature from 20 °C to 70 °C? (Use the specific heat c of iron = 92 cal/kg·°C and 1 cal = 4.186 J)

   A. 8,110 J   **B.** 9,628 J   **C.** 20,100 J   **D.** 12,500 J

34. Which statement is accurate?

   A. Tensile stress is measured in N·m
   B. Stress has a meaning similar to work

   C. Strain has a meaning similar to force
   D. The elastic modulus is the stress/strain ratio

35. The image of an object placed outside the focal point of a concave mirror is:

   A. virtual and inverted
   B. virtual and upright

   C. real and inverted
   D. real and upright

36. What is the term for the amount of radiation that produces 2.1×10^9 units of charge in 1 cm^3 of air?

   A. gray   **B.** rad   **C.** curie   **D.** roentgen

37. The H nucleus, which has a charge of e^+, is situated to the left of a C nucleus, which has a charge of $6\ e^+$. Which is true regarding the direction and magnitude of the electrical force experienced by the H nucleus?

   A. To the right and equal to the force exerted on the C nucleus
   B. To the left and less than the force exerted on the C nucleus
   C. To the right and greater than the force exerted on the C nucleus
   D. To the left and equal to the force exerted on the C nucleus

38. Consider two copper wires of equal length. How do the resistances of these two wires compare if one wire has twice the cross-sectional area?

   A. The thicker wire has one-half the resistance of the thinner wire
   B. The thicker wire has four times the resistance of the thinner wire
   C. The thicker wire has twice the resistance of the thinner wire
   D. The thicker wire has eight times the resistance of the thinner wire

39. Two metal rods are made of the same material and have the same cross-sectional area. The two rods differ only in their lengths of L and $3L$. The two rods are heated from the same initial temperature to the same final temperature. The short rod expands its length by an amount of ΔL. What is the amount by which the length of the long rod increases?

   A. $\sqrt{3}\Delta L$ **B.** $3\Delta L$ **C.** ΔL **D.** $3/2\Delta L$

40. As a cubical block of marble is lowered at a steady rate into the ocean by a crane, the top and bottom faces are kept horizontal. Which graph depicts the total pressure (P) on the bottom of the block as a function of time (*t*) as the block just enters the water at *t* = 0 s?

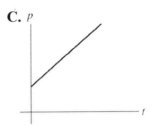

A. *p*

C. *p*

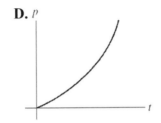

B. *p*

D. *P*

41. Which statement about images is correct?

    A. A real image is always upright
    B. A virtual image cannot be photographed
    C. A virtual image cannot be seen by the unaided eye
    D. A virtual image cannot be formed on a screen

42. When a β^+ particle is emitted from an unstable nucleus, the atomic number of the nucleus:

    A. decreases by 2   **C.** decreases by 1
    B. increases by 2   **D.** increases by 1

43. If a sheet of copper is quickly passed through a strong permanent magnet with the plane of the sheet perpendicular to the magnetic field, which statement is true?

    A. There is no movement because there is no magnetic force
    B. The force experienced by the sheet of copper is due mainly to lead impurities in the copper, since copper is not magnetic
    C. There is a magnetic force opposing the motion of the sheet
    D. There is a magnetic force assisting the motion of the sheet

44. A water fountain pump recirculates water from a pool and pumps it up to a trough, where it flows along the trough and passes through a hole in the bottom of it. As the water falls back into the pool, it turns a water wheel. What aspect of this water fountain is analogous to an electric potential within an electric circuit?

A. Height of water

B. Volume flow rate

C. Flow velocity

D. Mass of water

45. When grinding a culinary knife, the 70 g of metal becomes heated to 450 °C. What is the minimum amount of 25 °C water is needed if the water is to remain liquid and not rise above 100 °C when the hot knife is cooled in it? (Use the specific heat of the knife = 0.11 cal/g·°C and the specific heat of water = 1 cal/g·°C)

A. 36 g   **B.** 28 g   **C.** 47 g   **D.** 18 g

46. A spherical inflated balloon is submerged in a swimming pool. How is the buoyant force affected if the balloon is inflated to double its radius?

A. 8 times larger

B. 2 times larger

C. 4 times larger

D. 2 times smaller

47. If n_1 is the index of refraction for the incident medium, and n_2 is the index of the refracting medium, what conditions are necessary for the critical angle to exist?

A. $n_1 = n_2$ **B.** $n_1 < n_2$ **C.** $n_1 < 2n_2$ **D.** $n_1 > n_2$

48. For a given value of the principal quantum number n, what are the allowable orbital angular momentum quantum numbers?

A. $\ell = 1, 2, 3, \ldots, n$

B. $\ell = 0, 1, 2, \ldots, (n-1)$

C. $\ell = 0, 1, 2, \ldots, n$

D. $\ell = 1, 2, 3, \ldots, (n-1)$

49. A volt is a unit of electrical:

A. resistance   **B.** current   **C.** potential difference   **D.** charge

50. It is necessary to determine the specific heat of a 185 g object. It is determined experimentally that it takes 14 J to raise the temperature 10° C. What is the specific heat of the object?

A. 343 J/kg·K   **B.** 1.6 J/kg·K   **C.** 25.9 J/kg·K   **D.** 7.6 J/kg·K

Diagnostic test #3 – Answer Key

1	B	Thermodynamics	26	A	Atomic, nuclear & quantum physics
2	D	Fluid statics & dynamics	27	A	Electrostatics & magnetism
3	B	Geometric & physical optics	28	B	DC and RC circuits
4	D	Atomic, nuclear & quantum physics	29	B	Thermodynamics
5	D	Electrostatics & magnetism	30	C	Fluid statics & dynamics
6	B	DC and RC circuits	31	A	Geometric & physical optics
7	C	Thermodynamics	32	B	Atomic, nuclear & quantum physics
8	C	Fluid statics & dynamics	33	B	Thermodynamics
9	C	Geometric & physical optics	34	D	Fluid statics & dynamics
10	D	Atomic, nuclear & quantum physics	35	C	Geometric & physical optics
11	D	Electrostatics & magnetism	36	D	Atomic, nuclear & quantum physics
12	C	DC and RC circuits	37	D	Electrostatics & magnetism
13	B	Thermodynamics	38	A	DC and RC circuits
14	A	Fluid statics & dynamics	39	B	Thermodynamics
15	C	Geometric & physical optics	40	C	Fluid statics & dynamics
16	D	Atomic, nuclear & quantum physics	41	D	Geometric & physical optics
17	B	Electrostatics & magnetism	42	C	Atomic, nuclear & quantum physics
18	C	DC and RC circuits	43	C	Electrostatics & magnetism
19	C	Thermodynamics	44	A	DC and RC circuits
20	A	Fluid statics & dynamics	45	A	Thermodynamics
21	A	Geometric & physical optics	46	A	Fluid statics & dynamics
22	C	Atomic, nuclear & quantum physics	47	D	Geometric & physical optics
23	D	Thermodynamics	48	B	Atomic, nuclear & quantum physics
24	B	Fluid statics & dynamics	49	C	Electrostatics & magnetism
25	D	Geometric & physical optics	50	D	Thermodynamics

Diagnostic Test #4

Answer Sheet

#	Answer:				Mark for review	#	Answer:				Mark for review
1:	A	B	C	D	____	26:	A	B	C	D	____
2:	A	B	C	D	____	27:	A	B	C	D	____
3:	A	B	C	D	____	28:	A	B	C	D	____
4:	A	B	C	D	____	29:	A	B	C	D	____
5:	A	B	C	D	____	30:	A	B	C	D	____
6:	A	B	C	D	____	31:	A	B	C	D	____
7:	A	B	C	D	____	32:	A	B	C	D	____
8:	A	B	C	D	____	33:	A	B	C	D	____
9:	A	B	C	D	____	34:	A	B	C	D	____
10:	A	B	C	D	____	35:	A	B	C	D	____
11:	A	B	C	D	____	36:	A	B	C	D	____
12:	A	B	C	D	____	37:	A	B	C	D	____
13:	A	B	C	D	____	38:	A	B	C	D	____
14:	A	B	C	D	____	39:	A	B	C	D	____
15:	A	B	C	D	____	40:	A	B	C	D	____
16:	A	B	C	D	____	41:	A	B	C	D	____
17:	A	B	C	D	____	42:	A	B	C	D	____
18:	A	B	C	D	____	43:	A	B	C	D	____
19:	A	B	C	D	____	44:	A	B	C	D	____
20:	A	B	C	D	____	45:	A	B	C	D	____
21:	A	B	C	D	____	46:	A	B	C	D	____
22:	A	B	C	D	____	47:	A	B	C	D	____
23:	A	B	C	D	____	48:	A	B	C	D	____
24:	A	B	C	D	____	49:	A	B	C	D	____
25:	A	B	C	D	____	50:	A	B	C	D	____

This Diagnostic Test is designed for you to assess your proficiency on each topic and NOT to mimic the actual test. Use your test results and identify areas of your strength and weakness to adjust your study plan and enhance your fundamental knowledge.

The length of the Diagnostic Tests is proven to be optimal for a single study session.

1. A fluid in an insulated, flexible bottle is heated by a high-resistance wire and expands. If 9 kJ of heat is applied to the system and the system does 5 kJ of work, how much does the internal energy change?

    A. –4 kJ   **B.** 32 kJ   **C.** 4 kJ   **D.** 12 kJ

2. A 4.2 m steel wire has a diameter of 1.8 mm. The wire stretches 1.8 mm when it bears a load. What is the mass of the load? (Use Young's modulus for steel $= 2 \times 10^{11}$ N/m^2 and the acceleration due to gravity $g = 9.8$ m/s^2)

    A. 22 kg   **B.** 26 kg   **C.** 30 kg   **D.** 16 kg

3. Which statement about thin, single lenses is correct?

    A. A diverging lens can only sometimes produce a virtual, erect image
    B. A diverging lens always produces a virtual, erect image
    C. A converging lens always produces a real, inverted image
    D. A diverging lens always produces a real, inverted image

4. During β^+ decay:

    A. a proton is transformed into a neutron
    B. an electron is released from its orbit
    C. a neutron is transformed into a positron
    D. a neutron is transformed into a proton

5. A circular loop of wire is positioned in a region of changing magnetic field; the direction of the field remains constant, but the magnitude is fluctuating. What must the orientation of the loop's area vector be in relation to the magnetic field direction to create the maximum induced emf?

    A. An angle of 45° to the magnetic field
    B. An angle of –45° to the magnetic field
    C. An angle of 90° to the magnetic field
    D. Parallel to the magnetic field

6. An alternating voltage, oscillating at 60 Hz, has a maximum value of 200 V during each cycle. What would be the reading if an rms (root mean square) voltmeter is connected to the circuit?

    A. 142 V   **B.** 100 V   **C.** 35 V   **D.** 284 V

7. A person running in place on an exercise machine for 10 min expends 19 kcal. Another person exercises by repeatedly lifting two 3 kg weights a distance of 50 cm. How many repetitions of this exercise are equivalent to 10 minutes of running in place? Assume that the person uses negligible energy in letting down the weights after each lift. (Use the acceleration due to gravity $g = 9.8$ m/s^2 and 1 kcal = 1,000 cal and 1 cal = 4.186 J)

    A. 2,705 repetitions   **C.** 1,360 repetitions
    B. 1,800 repetitions   **D.** 3,940 repetitions

8. A plastic container in the shape of a cube with 0.2 m sides is suspended in a vacuum. The container is filled to 3 atm with 10 g of N$_2$ gas. What is the force that the N$_2$ gas exerts on one face of the cube? (Use the ideal gas constant $R = 0.0821$ L atm/K mol and 1 atm = 1.01×10^5 Pa)

    A. 2.1×10^3 N   **C.** 1.2×10^4 N
    B. 5.6×10^4 N   **D.** 4.2×10^4 N

9. Where is the resulting image if a candle 21 cm tall is placed 4 m away from a diverging lens with a focal length of 3 m?

    A. 12/7 m from the lens on the opposite side from the object
    B. 12 m from the lens on the opposite side from the object
    C. 12/7 m from the lens on the same side as the object
    D. 12 m from the lens on the same side as the object

10. An energy level diagram of a certain atom is shown below whereby the energy difference between levels 1 and 2 is twice the energy difference between levels 2 and 3. A wavelength λ is emitted when an electron makes a transition from level 3 to 2. What possible radiation λ might be produced by other transitions between the three energy levels?

    A. 2λ only   **B.** both 2λ and 3λ   **C.** ½λ only   **D.** both ½λ and λ/3

11. A charged, parallel-plate capacitor has an electric field E_0 between its plates. The bare nuclei of ^{1}H and ^{3}H, both at rest, are placed between the plates. Ignoring the force of gravity, how does the force, F_1, of the light ^{1}H nucleus compare with the force, F_3, of the heavy ^{3}H nucleus?

    A. $F_3 = 3F_1$ **B.** $F_3 = \sqrt{2}F_1$ **C.** $F_3 = F_1$ **D.** $F_3 = (1/3)F_1$

12. In Experiment 1, a magnet was moved toward the end of a solenoid, and a voltage was induced between the two ends of the solenoid wire. In Experiment 2, a higher voltage was observed. What might have changed between the two experiments?

     I. A stronger magnet replaced the bar magnet
     II. The solenoid was replaced by one with more loops but the same length
     III. The speed of the magnet increased

  A. I only   **B.** II only   **C.** III only   **D.** I, II and III

13. An object having an emissivity 0.867 radiates heat at a rate of 15 W when it is at a temperature T. If its temperature is doubled, what is the rate at which it radiates heat?

  A. 30 W   **B.** 60 W   **C.** 80 W   **D.** 240 W

14. If the amount of fluid flowing through a tube remains constant, by what factor does the speed of the fluid change when the radius of the tube decreases from 16 cm to 4 cm?

  A. Increases by $\sqrt{2}$ **B.** Increases by 16   **C.** Decreases by 16   **D.** Decreases by 4

15. Which statement is true if the magnification of a mirror or lens is negative?

  A. Object is closer to the mirror or lens than to the image
  B. Image is inverted
  C. Image is erect and smaller than the object
  D. Image is smaller than the object

16. The masses of all isotopes are based on a comparison to the mass of which isotope?

  A. ^{232}Uranium   **B.** ^{13}Carbon   **C.** ^{12}Carbon   **D.** ^{1}Hydrogen

17. What is the maximum magnetic field for a wave if an electromagnetic wave is traveling in a vacuum that has a maximum electric field of 1,200 V/m? (Use the speed of light c in a vacuum = 3×10^8 m/s)

  A. 4×10^{-6} T   **B.** 2×10^{-5} T   **C.** 3.3×10^{-4} T   **D.** 8×10^{-6} T

18. Magnetic field lines about a current-carrying wire:

I. extend radially from the wire
II. circle the wire in closed loops
III. circle the wire in a spiral

A. I only **B.** II only **C.** III only **D.** I and II only

19. A gas is confined to a rigid container that cannot expand as heat energy is added to it. This process is referred to as:

A. isokinetic **B.** isentropic **C.** isothermal **D.** isometric

20. In the equation PV = NkT, the k is known as:

A. Planck's constant **C.** Avogadro's number
B. Boltzmann's constant **D.** The spring (compressibility) constant

21. A lens of focal length 50 mm is used as a magnifier to view a 6.4 mm object that is positioned at the focal point of the lens. The user of the magnifier has a near point at 25 cm. What is the angular magnification of the magnifier?

A. 5 **B.** 6.9 **C.** 5.8 **D.** 8.1

22. Which forces hold the protons in a nucleus together?

A. dipole–dipole **C.** nuclear
B. gravitational **D.** electrostatic attraction

23. How much heat is required to raise the temperature of a 300 g lead ball from 20 °C to 30 °C? The specific heat of lead is 128 J/kg·K.

A. 224 J **B.** 168 J **C.** 576 J **D.** 384 J

24. A viscous oil flows through a narrow pipe at a constant velocity. By what factor does the flow rate increase if the diameter of the pipe is doubled?

A. 4 **B.** $\sqrt{2}$ **C.** 6 **D.** 8

25. Which form of electromagnetic radiation has the lowest frequency?

A. X-rays **B.** γ rays **C.** Radio waves **D.** Microwaves

26. Why do heavy nuclei contain more neutrons than protons?

   A. Neutrons are heavier than protons

   B. Neutrons and heavy nuclei are not radioactive

   C. Neutrons reduce the electric repulsion of the protons

   D. Neutrons are lighter than protons

27. Three particles travel through a region of space where the magnetic field is pointing out of the page. What are the signs of the charges of these three particles?

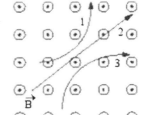

   A. 1 is negative, 2 is positive, and 3 is neutral

   B. 1 is negative, 2 is neutral, and 3 is positive

   C. 1 is positive, 2 is neutral, and 3 is negative

   D. 1 is neutral, 2 is positive, and 3 is negative

28. Which statement applies to the 120 V circuit shown?

   A. 120 J of energy are given to each Coulomb of charge making up the current in the circuit

   B. 120 J of energy is equally shared among all Coulombs in the circuit at any instant

   C. 120 C of charge flow through the lamp every second

   D. 120 C of energy is converted to heat and light in the circuit every second

29. An aluminum rod 10 cm long and a steel rod 80 cm long are joined end-to-end. Both rods are at a temperature of 15 °C and have the same diameter. What is the increase in the length of the joined rod when the temperature is raised to 90 °C? (Use the coefficient of linear expansion α for aluminum = $2.4 \times 10^{-5}\ K^{-1}$ and α for steel = $1.2 \times 10^{-5}\ K^{-1}$)

   A. 0.7 mm   **B.** 1.1 mm   **C.** 0.9 mm   **D.** 0.8 mm

30. A wire circle and solid circle of the same diameter are resting on the surface of the water. Which one can have the larger maximum mass without sinking?

   A. The solid circle, by a factor of 2   **C.** The wire circle, by a factor of 2

   B. The solid circle, by a factor of 4   **D.** They have the same maximum mass

31. How does an image appear if an object is placed in front of a convex mirror at a distance larger than twice the magnitude of the focal length of the mirror?

   A. upright and smaller   **C.** inverted and smaller

   B. inverted and larger   **D.** inverted and the same size

32. According to the de Broglie hypothesis, the idea of matter waves describes the wave-like behavior of:

      I. Positively-charged stationary particles
      II. Negatively-charged stationary particles
      III. Particles that are moving

  A. I only   **B.** II only   **C.** III only   **D.** I and II

33. At constant pressure and temperature, Graham's Law states that the diffusion rate for a gas molecule is:

  A. inversely proportional to √mass
  B. inversely proportional to mass
  C. proportional to the log of the mass
  D. proportional to mass

34. Determine the speed at which water exits a tank through a very small hole in the bottom of the tank that is 20 cm in diameter and filled with water to a height of 50 cm. (Use the acceleration due to gravity $g = 9.8$ m/s^2)

  A. 3.1 m/s   **B.** 17.8 m/s   **C.** 31.2 m/s   **D.** 21.6 m/s

35. A 1.8×10^{14} Hz electromagnetic wave propagates in CCl$_4$ with a speed of 2.43×10^8 m/s. The wave then leaves the CCl$_4$ and enters a vacuum. What is the wavelength of the wave in the vacuum? (Use the speed of light in a vacuum $c = 3 \times 10^8$ m/s)

  A. 2,260 nm   **B.** 1,280 nm   **C.** 1,040 nm   **D.** 1,667 nm

36. How much energy does a photon of wavelength 580 nm have? (Use Planck's constant $h = 6.626 \times 10^{-34}$ J·s and speed of light $c = 3 \times 10^8$ m/s)

  A. 6.4×10^{-32} J   **B.** 8.8 eV   **C.** 3.4×10^{-19} J   **D.** 1.3×10^{-19} eV

37. What is the path for an electron moving on the page toward the right when subjected to a magnetic field pointing out of the page?

  A. Curves upward (path X)
  B. Continues straight ahead (path Y)
  C. Curves downward (path Z)
  D. Decelerates

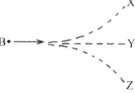

38. How many electrons pass a given point in a minute for a wire that has a current of 6 mA? (Use the charge of an electron $= 1.602 \times 10^{-19}$ C)

  A. 5.3×10^{14} electrons
  B. 5.4×10^{-15} electrons
  C. 2.3×10^{18} electrons
  D. 3.7×10^{12} electrons

39. A 0.4 kg ice cube at 0 °C has sufficient heat added to it to cause total melting, and the resulting water is heated to 60 °C. How much heat is added? (Use the latent heat of fusion for water $L_f = 334,000$ J/kg, the latent heat of vaporization for water $L_v = 2.256 \times 10^6$ J/kg and the specific heat $c = 4.186 \times 10^3$ J/kg·°C)

    A. 56 kJ   **B.** 84 kJ   **C.** 470 kJ   **D.** 234 kJ

40. A pipe with a circular cross-section has water flowing within it from point I to point II. The radius of the pipe at point I is 12 cm, while the radius at point II is 6 cm. If at the end of point I the flow rate is 0.09 m³/s, what is the flow rate at the end of point II?

    A. 0.6 m³/s   **B.** 0.09 m³/s   **C.** 0.15 m³/s   **D.** 1.2 m³/s

41. If parallel light rays were incident on a lens of power 4 D, which statement is true for the rays on the other side of the lens?

    A. The rays diverge as if from a point 4 m behind the lens
    B. The rays diverge as if from a point ¼ m in front of the lens
    C. The rays converge with a focal length of ¼ m
    D. The rays converge with a focal length of 4 m

42. The α particle has twice the electric charge of the β particle but deflects less than the β in a magnetic field because it:

    A. is smaller   **B.** has less inertia   **C.** moves slower   **D.** has more inertia

43. A positively-charged particle is traveling on a path parallel to a straight wire that contains a current. Which change increases the magnetic field at a point along the particle's path?

    A. Increasing the speed of the particle
    B. Increasing the distance of the particle from the wire
    C. Decreasing the distance of the particle from the wire
    D. Decreasing the current in the wire

44. How do the resistances of two copper wires compare where one has twice the length and twice the cross-sectional area?

    A. The longer wire has one fourth the resistance of the shorter wire
    B. The shorter wire has √2 times the resistance of the longer wire
    C. The shorter wire has twice the resistance of the longer wire
    D. Both wires have the same resistance

45. A sphere of surface area 1.25 m² and emissivity 1 is at a temperature of 100 °C. What is the rate at which it radiates heat into space? (Use the Stefan-Boltzmann constant $\sigma = 5.67 \times 10^{-8}$ W/m²K⁴)

    A. 1.4 kW   **B.** 7.6 kW   **C.** 27.3 kW   **D.** 0.63 kW

46. Which answer best describes what happens to a spherical lead ball with a density of 11.3 g/cm³ when it is placed in a tub of mercury with a density of 13.6 g/cm³?

    A. It sinks slowly to the bottom of the mercury
    B. It floats with about 17% of its volume above the surface of the mercury
    C. It floats with its top exactly even with the surface of the mercury
    D. It floats with about 83% of its volume above the surface of the mercury

47. A concave spherical mirror has a focal length of 20 cm. Where, relative to the mirror, is the image located if an object is placed 10 cm in front of the mirror?

    A. 7.5 cm in front   **C.** 20 cm in front
    B. 7.5 cm behind   **D.** 20 cm behind

48. Which type of emission from the reactant nucleus causes the transformation: $^{15}_{8}\text{O} \rightarrow {}^{15}_{7}\text{N}$?

    A. Neutron emission   **C.** Positron emission
    B. Alpha particle   **D.** Proton emission

49. Two identical metal balls, each with a radius of 0.15 m, are located 4 m apart, are neutral and have an electrical potential of zero. Electrons are transferred as an isolated system from ball I to II. After the transfer, ball I has acquired a potential of 8,000 V and ball II a potential of –8,000 V. How much work is required to transfer 10^{-10} C from ball I to ball II?

    A. -1.6×10^{-6} J   **B.** -4.7×10^{-7} J   **C.** 7.1×10^{-5} J   **D.** 3.3×10^{-6} J

50. Which is an example of a reversible process?

    A. Hooke's cycle   **C.** Swinn cycle
    B. Carnot cycle   **D.** Boltzmann's cycle

Diagnostic test #4 – Answer Key

1	C	Thermodynamics	26	C	Atomic, nuclear & quantum physics
2	A	Fluid statics & dynamics	27	B	Electrostatics & magnetism
3	B	Geometric & physical optics	28	A	DC and RC circuits
4	A	Atomic, nuclear & quantum physics	29	C	Thermodynamics
5	D	Electrostatics & magnetism	30	C	Fluid statics & dynamics
6	A	DC and RC circuits	31	A	Geometric & physical optics
7	A	Thermodynamics	32	C	Atomic, nuclear & quantum physics
8	C	Fluid statics & dynamics	33	A	Thermodynamics
9	C	Geometric & physical optics	34	A	Fluid statics & dynamics
10	D	Atomic, nuclear & quantum physics	35	D	Geometric & physical optics
11	C	Electrostatics & magnetism	36	C	Atomic, nuclear & quantum physics
12	D	DC and RC circuits	37	A	Electrostatics & magnetism
13	D	Thermodynamics	38	C	DC and RC circuits
14	B	Fluid statics & dynamics	39	D	Thermodynamics
15	B	Geometric & physical optics	40	B	Fluid statics & dynamics
16	C	Atomic, nuclear & quantum physics	41	C	Geometric & physical optics
17	A	Electrostatics & magnetism	42	D	Atomic, nuclear & quantum physics
18	B	DC and RC circuits	43	C	Electrostatics & magnetism
19	D	Thermodynamics	44	D	DC and RC circuits
20	B	Fluid statics & dynamics	45	A	Thermodynamics
21	A	Geometric & physical optics	46	B	Fluid statics & dynamics
22	C	Atomic, nuclear & quantum physics	47	D	Geometric & physical optics
23	D	Thermodynamics	48	C	Atomic, nuclear & quantum physics
24	A	Fluid statics & dynamics	49	A	Electrostatics & magnetism
25	C	Geometric & physical optics	50	B	Thermodynamics

AP Physics 2

Topical
Practice Questions

Thermodynamics

1. Compared to the initial value, what is the resulting pressure for an ideal gas that is compressed isothermally to one-third of its initial volume?

   A. Equal   **C.** Larger, but less than three times larger

   B. Three times larger   **D.** More than three times larger

2. A uniform hole in a brass plate has a diameter of 1.2 cm at 25 °C. What is the diameter of the hole when the plate is heated to 225 °C? (Use the coefficient of linear thermal expansion for brass = $19 \times 10^{-6} \text{ K}^{-1}$)

   A. 2.2 cm   **B.** 2.8 cm   **C.** 1.2 cm   **D.** 1.6 cm

3. A student heats 90 g of water using 50 W of power, with 100% efficiency. How long does it take to raise the temperature of the water from 10 °C to 30 °C? (Use the specific heat of water $c = 4.186$ J/g·°C)

   A. 232 s   **B.** 81 s   **C.** 59 s   **D.** 151 s

4. A runner generates 1,260 W of thermal energy. If her heat is to be dissipated only by evaporation, how much water does she shed in 15 minutes of running? (Use the latent heat of vaporization of water $L_v = 22.6 \times 10^5$ J/kg)

   A. 500 g   **B.** 35 g   **C.** 350 g   **D.** 50 g

5. Phase changes occur as temperature:

     I. decreases   II. increases   III. remains the same

   A. I only   **B.** II only   **C.** III only   **D.** I and II only

6. How much heat is needed to melt a 55 kg sample of ice that is at 0 °C? (Use latent heat of fusion for water $L_f = 334$ kJ/kg and latent heat of vaporization $L_v = 2,257$ kJ/kg)

   A. 0 kJ   **C.** 3×10^5 kJ

   B. 1.8×10^4 kJ   **D.** 4.6×10^6 kJ

7. Metals are both good heat conductors and good electrical conductors because of the:

   A. relatively high densities of metals

   B. high elasticity of metals

   C. ductility of metals

   D. looseness of outer electrons in metal atoms

8. Solar houses are designed to retain the heat absorbed during the day so that the stored heat can be released during the night. A botanist produces steam at 100 °C during the day, and then allows the steam to cool to 0 °C and freeze during the night. How many kilograms of water are needed to store 200 kJ of energy for this process? (Use the latent heat of vaporization of water $L_v = 22.6 \times 10^5$ J/kg, the latent heat of fusion of water $L_f = 33.5 \times 10^4$ J/kg, and the specific heat capacity of water $c = 4{,}186$ J/kg·K)

   A. 0.066 kg   **B.** 0.103 kg   **C.** 0.482 kg   **D.** 1.18 kg

9. The heat required to change a substance from the solid to the liquid state is referred to as the heat of:

   A. condensation   **B.** freezing   **C.** fusion   **D.** vaporization

10. A rigid container holds 0.2 kg of hydrogen gas. How much heat is needed to change the temperature of the gas from 250 K to 280 K? (Use specific heat of hydrogen gas = 14.3 J/g·K)

   A. 46 kJ   **B.** 72 kJ   **C.** 56 kJ   **D.** 86 kJ

11. An aluminum electric tea kettle with a mass of 500 g is heated with a 500 W heating coil. How many minutes are required to heat 1 kg of water from 18 °C to 98 °C in the tea kettle? (Use the specific heat of aluminum = 900 J/kg·K and specific heat of water = 4,186 J/kg·K)

   A. 16 min   **B.** 12 min   **C.** 8 min   **D.** 4 min

12. Heat is added at a constant rate to a pure substance in a closed container. The temperature of the substance as a function of time is shown in the graph. If L_f = latent heat of fusion and L_v = latent heat of vaporization, what is the value of the ratio L_v / L_f for this substance?

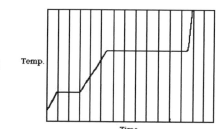

   A. 3.5   **B.** 7.2   **C.** 4.5   **D.** 5.0

13. The moderate temperatures of islands throughout the world have much to do with water's:

   A. high evaporation rate   **C.** vast supply of thermal energy
   B. high specific heat capacity   **D.** poor conductivity

14. A 4.5 g lead BB moving at 46 m/s penetrates a wood block and comes to rest inside the block. If the BB absorbs half of the kinetic energy, what is the change in the temperature of the BB? (Use the specific heat of lead = 128 J/kg·K)

   A. 2.8 K   **B.** 3.6 K   **C.** 1.6 K   **D.** 4.1 K

15. The heat required to change a substance from the liquid to the vapor state is referred to as the heat of:

   A. melting   **B.** condensation   **C.** vaporization   **D.** fusion

16. A Carnot engine operating between a reservoir of liquid mercury at its melting point and a colder reservoir extracts 18 J of heat from the mercury and does 5 J of work during each cycle. What is the temperature of the colder reservoir? (Use the melting temperature of mercury = 233 K)

    A. 168 K   **B.** 66 K   **C.** 57 K   **D.** 82 K

17. A 920 g empty iron pan is put on a stove. How much heat in joules must the iron pan absorb to raise its temperature from 18 °C to 96 °C? (Use the specific heat for iron = 113 cal/kg·°C and 1 cal = 4.186 J)

    A. 50,180 J   **B.** 81,010 J   **C.** 63,420 J   **D.** 33,940 J

18. When a solid melts, what change occurs in the substance?

    A. Heat energy dissipates   **C.** Temperature increases
    B. Heat energy enters   **D.** Temperature decreases

19. Which of the following is an accurate statement about the work done for a cyclic process carried out in a gas? (Use P for pressure and V for volume on the graph)

    A. It is equal to the area under *ab* minus the area under *dc*
    B. It is equal to the area under the curve *adc*
    C. It is equal to the area enclosed by the cyclic process
    D. It equals zero

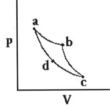

20. Substance A has a higher specific heat than substance B. With all other factors equal, which substance requires more energy to be heated to the same temperature?

    A. Substance A   **C.** Both require the same amount of heat
    B. Substance B   **D.** Depends on the density of each substance

21. A 6.5 g meteor hits the Earth at a speed of 300 m/s. If the meteor's kinetic energy is entirely converted to heat, by how much does its temperature rise? (Use the specific heat of the meteor = 120 cal/kg·°C and the conversion of 1 cal = 4.186 J)

    A. 134 °C   **B.** 68 °C   **C.** 120 °C   **D.** 90 °C

22. When a liquid freezes, what change occurs in the substance?

    A. Heat energy dissipates   **C.** Temperature increases
    B. Heat energy enters   **D.** Temperature decreases

23. A monatomic ideal gas ($C_v = 3/2$ R) undergoes an isothermal expansion at 300 K, as the volume increases from 0.05 m^3 to 0.2 m^3. The final pressure is 130 kPa. What is the heat transfer of the gas? (Use the ideal gas constant R = 8.314 J/mol·K)

    A. −14 kJ   **B.** 36 kJ   **C.** 14 kJ   **D.** −21 kJ

24. What is the maximum temperature rise expected for 1 kg of water falling from a waterfall with a vertical drop of 30 m? (Use the acceleration due to gravity $g = 9.8$ m/s^2 and the specific heat of water = 4,186 J/kg·K)

A. 0.1 °C   **B.** 0.06 °C   **C.** 0.15 °C   **D.** 0.07 °C

25. When 0.75 kg of water at 0 °C freezes, what is the change in entropy of the water? (Use the latent heat of fusion of water $L_f = 33,400$ J/kg)

A. –92 J/K   **B.** –18 J/K   **C.** 44 J/K   **D.** 80 J/K

26. When a bimetallic bar made of a copper and iron strip is heated, the copper part of the bar bends toward the iron strip. The reason for this is:

A. copper expands more than iron   **C.** iron gets hotter before copper
B. iron expands more than copper   **D.** copper gets hotter before iron

27. In a flask, 110 g of water is heated using 60 W of power, with perfect efficiency. How long does it take to raise the temperature of the water from 20 °C to 30 °C? (Use the specific heat of water $c = 4,186$ J/kg·K)

A. 132 s   **B.** 57 s   **C.** 9.6 s   **D.** 77 s

28. When a liquid evaporates, what change occurs in the substance?

A. Heat energy dissipates   **C.** Temperature increases
B. Heat energy enters   **D.** Temperature decreases

29. A flask of liquid nitrogen is at a temperature of –243 °C. If the nitrogen is heated until the average energy of the particles is doubled, what is the new temperature?

A. 356 °C   **B.** –356 °C   **C.** –213 °C   **D.** 134 °C

30. If a researcher is attempting to determine how much the temperature of a particular piece of material would rise when a known amount of heat is added to it, knowing which of the following quantities would be most helpful?

A. Density   **C.** Initial temperature
B. Coefficient of linear expansion   **D.** Specific heat

31. A substance has a density of 1,800 kg/m^3 in the liquid state. At atmospheric pressure, the substance has a boiling point of 170 °C. The vapor has a density of 6 kg/m^3 at the boiling point at atmospheric pressure. What is the change in the internal energy of 1 kg of the substance, as it vaporizes at atmospheric pressure? (Use the heat of vaporization $L_v = 1.7 \times 10^5$ J/kg)

A. 180 kJ   **B.** 170 kJ   **C.** 6 kJ   **D.** 12 kJ

32. If an aluminum rod that is at 5 °C is heated until it has twice the thermal energy, its temperature is:

    A. 10 °C   **B.** 56 °C   **C.** 278 °C   **D.** 283 °C

33. A thermally isolated system is made up of a hot piece of aluminum and a cold piece of copper, with the aluminum and the copper in thermal contact. The specific heat capacity of aluminum is more than double that of copper. Which object experiences the greater temperature change during the time the system takes to reach thermal equilibrium?

    A. Both experience the same magnitude of temperature change   **C.** The copper
    B. The mass of each is required   **D.** The aluminum

34. In liquid water of a given temperature, the water molecules are moving randomly at different speeds. Electrostatic forces of cohesion tend to hold them together. However, occasionally one molecule gains enough energy through multiple collisions to pull away from the others and escape from the liquid. Which of the following is an illustration of this phenomenon?

    A. When a large steel suspension bridge is built, gaps are left between the girders
    B. When a body gets too warm, it produces sweat to cool itself down
    C. Increasing the atmospheric pressure over a liquid causes the boiling temperature to decrease
    D. If snow begins to fall when Mary is skiing, she feels colder than before it started to snow

35. A 2,200 kg sample of water at 0 °C is cooled to −30 °C, and freezes in the process. Approximately how much heat is liberated during this process? (Use heat of fusion for water $L_f = 334$ kJ/kg, heat of vaporization $L_v = 2,257$ kJ/kg and specific heat for ice = 2,050 J/kg·K)

    A. 328,600 kJ   **B.** 190,040 kJ   **C.** 637,200 kJ   **D.** 870,100 kJ

36. Object 1 has three times the specific heat capacity and four times the mass of Object 2. The same amount of heat is transferred to the two objects. If the temperature of Object 1 changes by an amount of ΔT, what is the change in temperature of Object 2?

    A. $12\Delta T$ **B.** $3\Delta T$ **C.** ΔT **D.** $(3/4)\Delta T$

37. The process whereby heat flows through molecular collisions is known as:

    A. radiation   **B.** inversion   **C.** conduction   **D.** convection

38. The graph shows a PV diagram for 5.1 g of oxygen gas in a sealed container. The temperature of T_1 is 20 °C. What are the values for temperatures of T_3 and T_4, respectively? (Use the gas constant R= 8.314 J/mol·K)

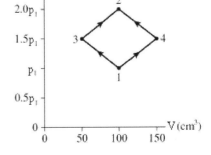

    A. −53 °C and 387 °C   **C.** 210 °C and 640 °C
    B. −14 °C and 34 °C   **D.** 12 °C and 58 °C

39. On a cold day, a piece of steel feels much colder to the touch than a piece of plastic. This is due to the difference in which one of the following physical properties of these materials?

A. Emissivity   **B.** Thermal conductivity   **C.** Density   **D.** Specific heat

40. What is the term for a process when a gas is allowed to expand as heat is added to it at constant pressure?

A. Isochoric   **B.** Isobaric   **C.** Adiabatic   **D.** Isothermal

41. A Carnot engine is used as an air conditioner to cool a house in the summer. The air conditioner removes 20 kJ of heat per second from the house, and maintains the inside temperature at 293 K, while the outside temperature is 307 K. What is the power required for the air conditioner?

A. 2.3 kW   **B.** 3.22 kW   **C.** 1.6 kW   **D.** 0.96 kW

42. Heat energy is measured in units of:

    I. Joules   II. calories   III. work

A. I only   **B.** II only   **C.** I and II only   **D.** III only

43. The process in which heat flows by the mass movement of molecules from one place to another is known as:

    I. conduction   II. convection   III. radiation

A. I only   **B.** II only   **C.** III only   **D.** I and II only

44. The process whereby heat flows in the absence of any medium is known as:

A. radiation   **C.** conduction
B. inversion   **D.** convection

45. The figure shows 0.008 mol of gas that undergoes the process $1 \rightarrow 2 \rightarrow 3$. What is the volume of V_3?

(Use ideal gas constant R = 8.314 J/mol·K and 1 atm = 101,325 Pa)

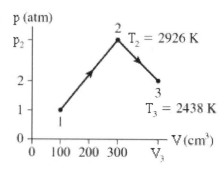

A. 435 cm³   **C.** 656 cm³
B. 568 cm³   **D.** 800 cm³

46. When a gas expands adiabatically:

A. it does no work   **C.** the internal (thermal) energy of the gas decreases
B. work is done on the gas   **D.** the internal (thermal) energy of the gas increases

47. Why is it that when a swimmer gets out of a swimming pool and stands in a breeze dripping wet, he feels much colder compared to when he dries off?

  A. This is a physiological effect resulting from the skin's sensory nerves
  B. To evaporate a gram of water from his skin requires heat and most of
        this heat flows out of his body
  C. The moisture on his skin has good thermal conductivity
  D. Water has a relatively small specific heat

48. Which method of heat flow requires the movement of energy through solid matter to a new location?

        I. Conduction   II. Convection   III. Radiation

  A. I only   **B.** II only   **C.** III only   **D.** I and II only

49. An ideal gas is compressed via an isobaric process to one-third of its initial volume. Compared to the initial pressure, the resulting pressure is:

  A. more than three times greater   **C.** three times greater
  B. nine times greater   **D.** the same

50. Which of the following would be the best radiator of thermal energy?

  A. A metallic surface   **B.** A black surface   **C.** A white surface   **D.** A shiny surface

51. A brass rod is 59.1 cm long, and an aluminum rod is 39.3 cm long when both rods are at an initial temperature of 0 °C. The rods are placed with a distance of 1.1 cm between them. The distance between the far ends of the rods is maintained at 99.5 cm. The temperature is raised until the two rods are barely in contact.

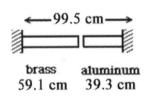

In the figure, what is the temperature at which contact of the rods barely occurs? (Use the coefficient of linear expansion of brass $= 2 \times 10^{-5}$ K^{-1} and the coefficient of linear expansion of aluminum $= 2.4 \times 10^{-5}$ K^{-1})

  A. 424 °C   **B.** 588 °C   **C.** 518 °C   **D.** 363 °C

52. At room temperature, a person loses energy to the surroundings at the rate of 60 W. If an equivalent food intake compensates this energy loss, how many kilocalories does he need to consume every 24 hours? (Use the conversion of 1 cal = 4.186 J)

  A. 1,240 kcal   **B.** 1,660 kcal   **C.** 600 kcal   **D.** 880 kcal

53. By what primary heat transfer mechanism does one end of an iron bar become hot when the other end is placed in a flame?

  A. Convection   **B.** Forced convection   **C.** Radiation   **D.** Conduction

> Questions **54-55** are based on the following:

Two experiments are performed to determine the calorimetric properties of an alcohol which has a melting point of –10 °C. In the first trial, a 220 g cube of frozen alcohol, at the melting point, is added to 350 g of water at 26 °C in a Styrofoam container. When thermal equilibrium is reached, the alcohol-water solution is at a temperature of 5 °C. In the second trial, an identical cube of alcohol is added to 400 g of water at 30 °C, and the temperature at thermal equilibrium is 10 °C. (Use the specific heat of water = 4,190 J/kg·K and assume no heat exchange between the Styrofoam container and the surroundings).

54. What is the specific heat capacity of the alcohol?

　A. 2,150 J/kg·K　　**B.** 2,475 J/kg·K　　**C.** 1,175 J/kg·K　　**D.** 1,820 J/kg·K

55. What is the heat of fusion of the alcohol?

　A. 7.2×10^3 J/kg　　**B.** 1.9×10^5 J/kg　　**C.** 5.2×10^4 J/kg　　**D.** 10.3×10^4 J/kg

56. The silver coating on the glass surface of a Thermos bottle reduces the energy that is transferred by:

　　I. conduction　　　　II. convection　　　　III. radiation

　A. I only　　**B.** II only　　**C.** III only　　**D.** I and II only

57. A person consumes a snack containing 16 kcal. What is the power this food produces if it is to be expended during exercise in 5 hours? (Use the conversion 1 cal = 4.186 J)

　A. 0.6 W　　**B.** 3.7 W　　**C.** 9.7 W　　**D.** 96.3 W

58. If 50 kcal of heat is added to 5 kg of water, what is the resulting temperature change? (Use the specific heat of water = 1 kcal/kg·°C)

　A. 10 °C　　**B.** 20 °C　　**C.** 5 °C　　**D.** 40 °C

59. How much heat is needed to melt a 30 kg sample of ice that is at 0 °C? (Use t latent heat of fusion for water L_f = 334 kJ/kg and latent heat of vaporization for water L_v = 2,257 kJ/kg)

　A. 0 kJ　　**B.** 5.6×10^4 kJ　　**C.** 1×10^4 kJ　　**D.** 2.4×10^6 kJ

60. A 6 kg aluminum rod is originally at 12 °C. If 160 kJ of heat is added to the rod, what is its final temperature? (Use the specific heat capacity of aluminum = 910 J/kg·K)

　A. 32 °C　　**B.** 41 °C　　**C.** 54 °C　　**D.** 23 °C

61. A solid sample of a pure compound is contained in a closed, well-insulated container. Heat is added at a constant rate, and the sample temperature is recorded. The resulting data is shown in the graph. Which of the following statements is true?

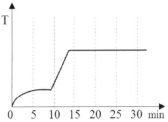

A. After 5 minutes, the sample was a mixture of solid and liquid
B. The heat capacity of the solid phase is greater than that of the liquid phase
C. The sample never boiled
D. The heat of fusion is greater than the heat of vaporization

62. Warm air rises because it tends to move to regions of less:

I. density   II. pressure   III. friction

A. I only   B. II only   C. III only   D. I and II only

63. A machine part consists of 0.15 kg of iron and 0.20 kg of copper. How much heat must be added to the material to raise its temperature from 23 °C to 58 °C? (Use the specific heat for iron = 470 J/kg·K and the specific heat for copper = 390 J/kg·K)

A. 2,800 J   B. 5,198 J   C. 910 J   D. 5,200 J

64. How much heat is required to raise the temperature of 300 g of lead by 20 °C? (Use the specific heat c of lead = 0.11 kcal/kg·°C)

A. 6 kcal   B. 0.33 cal   C. 660 cal   D. 66 cal

65. A large and a small container are filled with water of the same temperature. In comparison, they have:

A. the same amounts of internal energy less external energy
B. different amounts of internal energy
C. the same amounts of internal energy and external energy
D. the same amounts of internal energy

66. A 200 L electric water heater uses 4 kW. Assuming no heat loss, how many hours would it take to heat the water in this tank from 28 °C to 80 °C? (Use the specific heat of water = 4,186 J/kg·K, density of water = 1,000 kg/m³ and the conversion of 1 L = 0.001 m³)

A. 12 h   B. 9 h   C. 1.5 h   D. 3 h

67. The First Law of Thermodynamics is equivalent to:

A. the law of conservation of energy
B. Newton's First Law of motion
C. the law of conservation of momentum
D. Newton's Third Law of motion

68. A glass window pane is 3.1 m high, 1.8 m wide and 9 mm thick. The temperature at the inner surface of the glass is 22 °C and at the outer surface 7 °C. Given the properties of glass listed below, how much heat is lost through the window every hour?

Density	2,150 kg/m³
Specific Heat	790 J/kg·°C
Coefficient of Linear Thermal Expansion	8.1×10^{-6} °C⁻¹
Thermal Conductivity	0.8 W/m·°C

A. 8.7×10^5 J   **B.** 7.4×10^3 J   **C.** 2.7×10^7 J   **D.** 4.3×10^4 J

69. What happens as a result of a temperature difference?

    A. No energy moves unless it is warm enough, at least above the freezing temperature
    B. Energy moves slowly from colder to warmer regions
    C. Energy moves from colder to warmer if the difference is less than 3%
    D. Energy moves from warmer to colder regions

70. How much heat must be removed from 435 g of water at 30 °C to change it into ice at –8 °C? (Use the specific heat of ice = 2,090 J/kg·K, the latent heat of fusion of water $L_f = 33.5 \times 10^4$ J/kg and the specific heat of water = 4,186 J/kg·K)

    A. 208 kJ   **B.** 420 kJ   **C.** 105 kJ   **D.** 145 kJ

71. How much heat is required to melt 400 g of ice? (Use the latent heat of fusion of ice $L_f = 80$ kcal/kg)

    A. 32 kcal   **B.** 16 kcal   **C.** 320 kcal   **D.** 7.7 kcal

72. A Carnot engine operates between a high-temperature reservoir at 420 K and a river with water at 270 K. If it absorbs 3,650 J of heat each cycle, how much work per cycle does the Carnot engine perform?

    A. 851 J   **B.** 1,846 J   **C.** 2,822 J   **D.** 1,303 J

73. If 800 kJ of heat is added to 800 g of water originally at 70 °C, how much water is left in the container? (Use a latent heat of vaporization of water $L_v = 22.6 \times 10^5$ J/kg and the specific heat of water $c = 4,186$ J/kg·K)

    A. 321 g   **B.** 490 g   **C.** 433 g   **D.** 253 g

74. When the first law of thermodynamics, $Q = \Delta U - W$, is applied to an ideal gas that is taken through an adiabatic process:

    A. $Q = 0$ **B.** $W > \Delta U$ **C.** $\Delta U = 0$ **D.** $W = 0$

75. A heat pump pumps heat into a greenhouse at a rate of 50 kW. If work is being done to run this heat pump at a rate of 7.5 kW, what is the coefficient of performance of the heat pump?

    A. 0.9   **B.** 1.7   **C.** 3.1   **D.** 6.7

76. Energy transfer by convection is primarily restricted to:

    I. liquids   II. gases   III. solids

    A. I only   **B.** II only   **C.** III only   **D.** I and II only

77. A 740 kg copper bar is put into a furnace for melting. The initial temperature of the copper is 250 K. How much heat must the furnace produce to melt the copper bar completely? (Use the specific heat of copper c = 386 J/kg·K, the heat of fusion of copper L_f = 205,000 J/kg, and the melting point of copper = 1,357 K)

    A. 3.5×10^7 kJ   **C.** 4.7×10^5 kJ
    B. 5.6×10^5 kJ   **D.** 3.3×10^{11} kJ

78. An investigator uses 8 grams of water which is initially at 100 °C. The water is poured into a cavity in a very large block of ice initially at 0 °C. How many grams of ice melt before thermal equilibrium is attained? (Use the latent heat of fusion for ice L_f = 80 kcal/kg)

    A. 80 g   **C.** 100 g
    B. 10 g   **D.** 800 g

79. A Carnot heat engine operating between a warmer unknown temperature and a reservoir of boiling helium at 1.9 K has an efficiency of 13%. What is the warmer temperature?

    A. 3.2 K   **B.** 0.2 K   **C.** 1.4 K   **D.** 2.2 K

80. A certain Carnot engine extracts 1,200 J of heat from a high-temperature reservoir and discharges 800 J of heat to a low-temperature reservoir. What is the efficiency of this engine?

    A. 18%   **B.** 74%   **C.** 33%   **D.** 44%

81. What is the rate of heat flow through a 35 × 55 cm glass pane that is 6 mm thick when the outside temperature is –10 °C and the inside temperature is 30 °C? (Use the specific heat of glass c = 0.180 cal/g·°C and the thermal conductivity of glass k = 0.105 W/m·K)

    A. 56 W   **B.** 135 W   **C.** 84 W   **D.** 96 W

82. A sphere, 0.3 m in radius, has a surface emissivity of 0.55 and is at a temperature of 500 K. The sphere is surrounded by a concentric spherical shell whose inner surface has a radius of 0.8 m and emissivity of 1. The temperature of the shell is 400 K. What is the rate at which heat is radiated in the space between the sphere and the shell? (Use the temperature of radiation T_H in K, the temperature of surrounding T_C in K, Stefan Boltzmann constant $\sigma = 5.67 \times 10^{-8}$ W/m^{2}K^4)

   A. 1.3 kW   **B.** 4.3 kW   **C.** 3.6 kW   **D.** 7.8 kW

83. 50 g of lead of specific heat 0.11 kcal/kg·°C at 100 °C, is put into 80 g of water at 0 °C. What is the final temperature of the mixture? (Use the specific heat of water = 1 kcal/kg·°C at 0 °C)

   A. 22.8 °C   **B.** 32.2 °C   **C.** 4.2 °C   **D.** 6.4 °C

84. A gas follows the PV trajectory shown in the figure. How much work is done per cycle by the gas if $P_0 = 4.8$ atm?

   A. 840 J
   B. 84 J
   C. 192 J
   D. 344 J

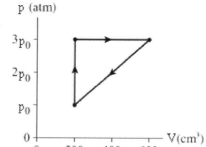

85. The water flowing over a large dam drops a distance of 60 m. If all the gravitational potential energy is converted to thermal energy, by what temperature does the water rise? (Use acceleration due to gravity $g = 10$ m/s^2 and specific heat of water = 4,186 J/kg·K)

   A. 0.34 °C   **B.** 0.44 °C   **C.** 0.09 °C   **D.** 0.14 °C

86. A lamp radiates 80 J/s when the room is set at 25 °C, but it radiates 95 J/s when the room temperature drops to 20 °C. What is the temperature of the lamp?

   A. 37 K   **B.** 48 °C   **C.** 101 °C   **D.** 84 °C

87. A Carnot heat engine receives 6,000 J of heat and loses 4,000 J in each cycle. What is the efficiency of this engine?

   A. 33%   **B.** 46%   **C.** 54%   **D.** 18%

88. A 40 m long steel pipe, installed when the temperature was 15 °C, is used to transport superheated steam at a temperature of 160 °C. The pipe is allowed to expand freely when the steam is transported. What is the increase in the length of the pipe? (Use a coefficient of linear expansion for steel $\alpha = 1.2 \times 10^{-5}$ K^{-1})

   A. 52 mm   **B.** 44 mm   **C.** 70 mm   **D.** 37 mm

89. When 2 kg of steam at 100 °C condenses to water at 100 °C, what is the change in entropy of the steam? (Use the latent heat of vaporization of water $L_v = 22.6 \times 10^5$ J/kg)

A. -6.1×10^3 J/K   **C.** 0 J/K

B. 12.1×10^3 J/K   **D.** -12.1×10^3 J/K

90. Change in internal energy is:

A. $Q + W$ **C.** Q / m

B. Q_{out} / W_{in} **D.** $1 - Q_{cold} / Q_{hot}$

91. On a cold winter day, the outside temperature is -20 °C and the inside temperature is maintained at 20 °C. There is a net heat flow to the outside through the home of 25 kW. What is the change of entropy of the air outside the house as a result of this heat flow?

A. 85 W/K   **B.** 99 W/K   **C.** 13 W/K   **D.** 25 W/K

92. A substance has a melting point of 20 °C and a heat of fusion of 3.6×10^4 J/kg. The boiling point is 150 °C, and the heat of vaporization is 7.2×10^4 J/kg at a pressure of one atmosphere. What is the quantity of heat released by 3.4 kg of the substance when it is cooled from 160 °C to 75 °C at a pressure of one atmosphere? (Use the specific heat for the solid phase = 600 J/kg·K, the specific heat for the liquid phase = 1,000 J/kg·K and the specific heat for the gaseous phase = 400 J/kg·K)

A. 448 kJ   **B.** 325 kJ   **C.** 249 kJ   **D.** 513 kJ

93. A mass of 0.2 kg ethanol, in the liquid state at its melting point of -114.4 °C, is frozen at atmospheric pressure. What is the change in the entropy of the ethanol as it freezes? (Use the heat of fusion of ethanol $L_f = 1.04 \times 10^5$ J/kg)

A. -360 J/K   **B.** 54 J/K   **C.** -131 J/K   **D.** -220 J/K

94. Isobaric work is

A. $Q - W$ **B.** $P\Delta V$ **C.** $P\Delta T$ **D.** $V\Delta P$

95. An adiabatic process is performed on 9 moles of an ideal gas. The initial temperature is 315 K, and the initial volume is 0.70 m^3. The final volume is 0.30 m^3. What is the amount of heat absorbed by the gas? (Use the adiabatic constant for the gas = 1.44)

A. -18 kJ   **B.** 32 kJ   **C.** 0 kJ   **D.** -32 kJ

96. An 80-gram aluminum calorimeter contains 360 g of water at an equilibrium temperature of 20 °C. A 180 g piece of metal, initially at 305 °C, is added to the calorimeter. The final temperature at equilibrium is 35 °C. Assume there is no external heat exchange. What is the specific heat capacity of the metal? (Use the specific heat capacity of aluminum = 910 J/kg·K and the specific heat of water = 4,190 J/kg·K)

    A. 260 J/kg·K   **B.** 324 J/kg·K   **C.** 488 J/kg·K   **D.** 410 J/kg·K

97. A chemist uses 120 g of water that is heated using 65 W of power with 100% efficiency. How much time is required to raise the temperature of the water from 20 °C to 50 °C? (Use the specific heat of water = 4.186 J/g·°C)

    A. 136 s   **B.** 182 s   **C.** 93 s   **D.** 232 s

98. The second law of thermodynamics leads to the following conclusion:

    A. the average temperature of the universe is increasing over time
    B. it is theoretically possible to convert heat into work with 100% efficiency
    C. disorder in the universe is increasing over time
    D. total energy of the universe remains constant

99. The statement that 'heat energy cannot be completely transformed into work' is a statement of which thermodynamic law?

    A. Third   **B.** Second   **C.** Zeroth   **D.** Fourth

100. What is the change in entropy when 20 g of water at 100 °C is turned into steam at 100 °C? (Use the latent heat of vaporization of water $L_v = 22.6 \times 10^5$ J/kg)

    A. −346 J/K   **B.** 346 J/K   **C.** −80.8 J/K   **D.** 121 J/K

101. A Carnot-efficiency engine is operated as a heat pump to heat a room in the winter. The heat pump delivers heat to the room at the rate of 32 kJ per second and maintains the room at a temperature of 293 K when the outside temperature is 237 K. The power requirement for the heat pump under these operating conditions is:

    A. 6,100 W   **B.** 3,400 W   **C.** 7,300 W   **D.** 14,300 W

102. Which of the following relationships is true for all types of Carnot heat engines?

    I. $\eta = 1 - T_C / T_H$
    II. $\eta = 1 - |Q_C / Q_H|$
    III. $T_C / T_H = Q_C / Q_H$

    A. I only   **B.** II only   **C.** III only   **D.** I, II and III

103. What is the change of entropy associated with 8 kg of water freezing to ice at 0 °C? (Use the latent heat of fusion $L_f = 80$ kcal/kg)

A. 1.4 kcal/K   C. –2.3 kcal/K

B. 0 kcal/K   D. –1.4 kcal/K

104. A Carnot-efficiency engine extracts 515 J of heat from a high-temperature reservoir during each cycle and ejects 340 J of heat to a low-temperature reservoir during the same cycle. What is the efficiency of the engine?

A. 34%   B. 21%   C. 53%   D. 17%

105. A glass beaker of unknown mass contains 65 ml of water. The system absorbs 1,800 cal of heat, and the temperature rises 20 °C. What is the mass of the beaker? (Use a specific heat of glass = 0.18 cal/g·°C and the specific heat of water = 1 cal/g·°C)

A. 342 g   B. 139 g   C. 546 g   D. 268 g

106. A 0.3 kg ice cube at 0 °C has sufficient heat added to result in total melting, and the resulting water is heated to 60 °C. How much total heat is added? (Use the latent heat of fusion for water $L_f = 334$ kJ/kg, the latent heat of vaporization for water $L_v = 2,257$ kJ/kg and the specific heat of water = 4.186 kJ/kg·K)

A. 73 kJ   B. 48 kJ   C. 176 kJ   D. 144 kJ

Thermodynamics – Answer Key

1: B	13: B	25: A	37: C	49: D	61: A	73: B	85: D	97: D
2: C	14: D	26: A	38: A	50: B	62: D	74: A	86: B	98: C
3: D	15: C	27: D	39: B	51: C	63: B	75: D	87: A	99: B
4: A	16: A	28: B	40: B	52: A	64: C	76: D	88: C	100: D
5: C	17: D	29: C	41: D	53: D	65: B	77: C	89: D	101: A
6: B	18: B	30: D	42: C	54: B	66: D	78: B	90: A	102: D
7: D	19: C	31: B	43: B	55: D	67: A	79: D	91: C	103: C
8: A	20: A	32: D	44: A	56: C	68: C	80: C	92: D	104: A
9: C	21: D	33: B	45: D	57: B	69: D	81: B	93: C	105: B
10: D	22: A	34: B	46: C	58: A	70: A	82: A	94: B	106: C
11: B	23: B	35: D	47: B	59: C	71: A	83: D	95: C	
12: A	24: D	36: A	48: A	60: B	72: D	84: C	96: C	

Fluid Statics and Dynamics

Questions **1-3** are based on the following:

A container has a vertical tube with an inner radius of 20 mm that is connected to the container at its side. An unknown liquid reaches level A in the container and level B in the tube. Level A is 5 cm higher than level B. The liquid supports a 20 cm high column of oil between levels B and C that has a density of 850 kg/m³. (Use the acceleration due to gravity g = 9.8 m/s²)

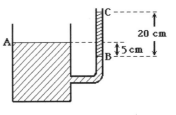

1. What is the density of the unknown liquid?

   A. 2,800 kg/m³   **B.** 2,100 kg/m³   **C.** 3,400 kg/m³   **D.** 3,850 kg/m³

2. The gauge pressure at level B is closest to:

   A. 1,250 Pa   **B.** 1,830 Pa   **C.** 340 Pa   **D.** 1,666 Pa

3. What is the mass of the oil?

   A. 210 g   **B.** 453 g   **C.** 620 g   **D.** 847 g

4. A cubical block of stone is lowered at a steady rate into the ocean by a crane, always keeping the top and bottom faces horizontal. Which of the following graphs best describes the gauge pressure P on the bottom of this block as a function of time *t* if the block just enters the water at time *t* = 0 s?

A.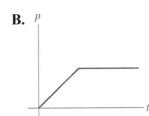

C.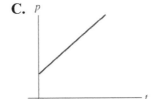

B.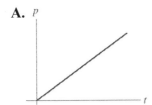

D.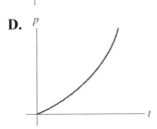

5. Consider a very small hole in the bottom of a tank that is 19 cm in diameter and is filled with water to a height of 80 cm. What is the speed at which the water exits the tank through the hole? (Use the acceleration due to gravity g = 9.8 m/s²)

   A. 8.6 m/s   **B.** 12 m/s   **C.** 14.8 m/s   **D.** 4 m/s

6. An ideal gas at standard temperature and pressure is compressed until its volume is half the initial volume, and then it is allowed to expand until its pressure is half the initial pressure. This is achieved while holding the temperature constant. If the initial internal energy of the gas is U, the final internal energy of the gas is:

    A. U/2   **B.** U/3   **C.** U   **D.** 2U

7. Ice has a lower density than water because ice:

    A. molecules vibrate at lower rates than water molecules
    B. is made of open-structured, hexagonal crystals
    C. is denser and therefore sinks when in liquid water
    D. molecules are more compact in the solid state

8. An object is sinking in a fluid. What is the weight of the fluid displaced by the sinking object when the object is completely submerged?

    A. Dependent on the viscosity of the liquid   **C.** Less than the weight of the object
    B. Equal to the weight of the object   **D.** Zero

9. A submarine in neutral buoyancy is 100 m below the surface of the water. For the submarine to surface, how much air pressure must be supplied to remove water from the ballast tanks? (Use the acceleration due to gravity $g = 9.8$ m/s^2 and density of water $\rho = 10^3$ kg/m^3)

    A. 9.8×10^5 N/m^2 **C.** 7.6×10^5 N/m^2
    B. 4.7×10^5 N/m^2 **D.** 5.6×10^5 N/m^2

10. When atmospheric pressure increases, what happens to the absolute pressure at the bottom of a pool?

    A. It does not change   **C.** It increases by the same amount
    B. It increases by double the amount   **D.** It increases by half the amount

11. When soup gets cold, it often tastes greasy because oil spreads out on the surface of the soup, instead of staying in small globules. This is explained in terms of the:

    A. increase in the surface tension of water with a decreasing temperature
    B. Archimedes' principle
    C. decrease in the surface tension of water with a decreasing temperature
    D. Joule-Thomson effect

12. A particular grade of motor oil, which has a viscosity of 0.3 N·s/m^2, is flowing through a 1 m long tube with a radius of 3.2 mm. What is the average speed of the oil, if the drop in pressure over the length of the tube is 225 kPa?

    A. 0.82 m/s   **B.** 0.96 m/s   **C.** 1.2 m/s   **D.** 1.4 m/s

13. An object whose weight is 60 N is floating at the surface of a container of water. How much of the object's volume is submerged? (Use acceleration due to gravity $g = 10$ m/s^2)

    A. 0.006 m^3 **B.** 0.06 m^3 **C.** 0.6 m^3 **D.** 6%

14. What is the volume flow rate of a fluid, if it flows at 2.5 m/s through a pipe of diameter 3 cm?

    A. 0.9 m^3/s   **C.** 5.7×10^{-4} m^3/s
    B. 1.8×10^{-3} m^3/s   **D.** 5.7×10^{-3} m^3/s

15. What is the specific gravity of a cork that floats with three-quarters of its volume in and one-quarter of its volume out of the water?

    A. 0.25   **B.** 0.5   **C.** 0.75   **D.** 2

16. What volume does 600 g of cottonseed oil occupy, if the density of cottonseed oil is 0.93 g/cm^3?

    A. 255 cm^3 **B.** 360 cm^3 **C.** 470 cm^3 **D.** 645 cm^3

17. The kinetic theory of a monatomic gas suggests the average kinetic energy per molecule is:

    A. 1/3 k_BT   **B.** 2 k_BT   **C.** 3/2 k_BT   **D.** 2/3 k_BT

18. An object is weighed in air, and it is also weighed while totally submerged in water. If it weighs 150 N less when submerged, find the volume of the object. (Use acceleration due to gravity $g = 10$ m/s^2 and density of water $\rho = 1,000$ kg/m^3)

    A. 0.0015 m^3 **B.** 0.015 m^3 **C.** 0.15 m^3 **D.** 1 m^3

19. When a container of water is placed on a laboratory scale, the scale reads 140 g. Now a 30 g piece of copper is suspended from a thread and lowered into the water without making contact with the bottom of the container. What does the scale read? (Use the acceleration due to gravity $g = 9.8$ m/s^2, density of water $\rho = 1$ g/cm^3 and density of copper $\rho = 8.9$ g/cm^3)

    A. 122 g   **B.** 168 g   **C.** 143 g   **D.** 110 g

20. An ideal, incompressible fluid flows through a 6 cm diameter pipe at 1 m/s. There is a 3 cm decrease in diameter within the pipe. What is the speed of the fluid in this constriction?

    A. 3 m/s   **B.** 1.5 m/s   **C.** 8 m/s   **D.** 4 m/s

21. Two blocks are submerged in a fluid. Block A has dimensions 2 cm high × 3 cm wide × 4 cm long and Block B is 2 cm × 3 cm × 8 cm. Both blocks are submerged with their large faces pointing up and down (i.e., the blocks are horizontal), and they are submerged to the same depth. Compared to the fluid pressure on the bottom of Block A, the bottom of Block B experiences:

A. equal fluid pressure

B. greater fluid pressure

C. exactly double the fluid pressure

D. less fluid pressure

22. A piece of thread of diameter d is in the shape of a rectangle (length l, width w) and is lying on the surface of the water in a beaker. If A is the surface tension of the water, what is the maximum weight that the thread can have without sinking?

A. $Ad(l + w) / \pi$ **B.** $A(l + w)$ **C.** $4A(l + w)$ **D.** $A(l + w) / 2$

23. What is the difference between the pressure inside and outside a tire called?

A. Absolute pressure

B. Fluid pressure

C. Atmospheric pressure

D. Gauge pressure

24. Which of the following is NOT a unit of pressure?

A. atm   **B.** $N \cdot m^2$ **C.** inches of mercury   **D.** Pascal

25. Which of the following is a dimensionless number?

    I. Reynolds number   II. specific gravity   III. shear stress

A. I only   **B.** II only   **C.** III only   **D.** I and II only

26. Water flows out of a large reservoir through a 5 cm diameter pipe. The pipe connects to a 3 cm diameter pipe that is open to the atmosphere, as shown.

What is the speed of the water in the 5 cm pipe? Treat the water as an ideal incompressible fluid. (Use the acceleration due to gravity g = 9.8 m/s²)

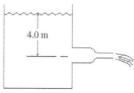

4.0 m

A. 2.6 m/s   **B.** 3.2 m/s   **C.** 4.8 m/s   **D.** 8.9 m/s

27. If the pressure acting on an ideal gas at constant temperature is tripled, what is the resulting volume of the ideal gas?

A. Increased by a factor of two

B. Remains the same

C. Reduced to one-third

D. Increased by a factor of three

28. A circular plate with an area of 1 m² covers a drain-hole at the bottom of a tank of water that is 1 m deep. Approximately how much force is required to lift the cover if it weighs 1,500 N? (Use the acceleration due to gravity $g = 10$ m/s²)

   A. 4,250 N   **B.** 9,550 N   **C.** 16,000 N   **D.** 11,500 N

29. A bowling ball that weighs 80 N is dropped into a swimming pool filled with water. If the buoyant force on the bowling ball is 20 N when the ball is 1 m below the surface (and sinking), what is the normal force exerted by the bottom of the pool on the ball when it comes to rest there, 4 m below the surface?

   A. 0 N   **B.** 60 N   **C.** 50 N   **D.** 70 N

30. A block of an unknown material is floating in a fluid, half-submerged. If the specific gravity of the fluid is 1.6, what is the block's density? (Use the specific gravity = ρ_{fluid} / ρ_{water} and the density of water $\rho = 1,000$ kg/m³)

   A. 350 kg/m³   **B.** 800 kg/m³   **C.** 900 kg/m³   **D.** 1,250 kg/m³

31. A solid sphere of mass 9.2 kg, made of metal whose density is 3,650 kg/m³, hangs by a cord. When the sphere is immersed in a liquid of unknown density, the tension in the cord is 42 N. What is the density of the liquid? (Use acceleration due to gravity $g = 9.8$ m/s²)

   A. 1,612 kg/m³   **C.** 1,950 kg/m³
   B. 1,468 kg/m³   **D.** 1,742 kg/m³

32. In a closed container of fluid, object A is submerged at 6 m from the bottom, and object B is submerged at 12 m from the bottom. Compared to object A, object B experiences:

   A. less fluid pressure   **C.** equal fluid pressure
   B. double the fluid pressure   **D.** triple the fluid pressure

33. Ideal, incompressible water flows at 14 m/s in a horizontal pipe with a pressure of 3.5 × 10⁴ Pa. If the pipe widens to twice its original radius, what is the pressure in the wider section? (Use the density of water $\rho = 1,000$ kg/m³)

   A. 7.6×10^4 Pa   **C.** 2×10^5 Pa
   B. 12.7×10^4 Pa   **D.** 11.1×10^3 Pa

34. Two kilometers above the surface of the Earth, the atmospheric pressure is:

   A. unrelated to the atmospheric pressure at the surface
   B. twice the atmospheric pressure at the surface
   C. triple the atmospheric pressure at the surface
   D. less than the atmospheric pressure at the surface

35. An 80 kg man would weigh 784 N if there were no atmosphere. By how much does the buoyancy due to air reduce the man's weight? (Use the density of the man = 1 g/cm^3, the density of the air = 1.2×10^{-3} g/cm^3, m = 80 kg and the acceleration due to gravity g = 9.8 m/s^2)

    A. 0.58 N   **B.** 0.32 N   **C.** 0.94 N   **D.** 2.8 N

36. Diffusion is described by which law?

    A. Dulong's   **B.** Faraday's   **C.** Kepler's   **D.** Graham's

37. An object has a volume of 4.2 m^3 and weighs 41,800 N. What is its apparent weight in water? (Use acceleration due to gravity g = 9.8 m/s^2 and density of water ρ = 1,000 kg/m^3)

    A. 1,140 N   **B.** 230 N   **C.** 800 N   **D.** 640 N

38. A pump uses a piston 12 cm in diameter that moves 3 cm/s. What is the fluid velocity in a tube that is 2 mm in diameter?

    A. 218 cm/s   **B.** 88 cm/s   **C.** 136 cm/s   **D.** 108 m/s

39. What is its specific gravity of an object floating with one-tenth of its volume out of the water?

    A. 0.3   **B.** 0.9   **C.** 1.3   **D.** 2.1

40. If each of the factors listed below was changed by 15%, which would have the greatest effect on the flow rate?

    A. Fluid density   **C.** Radius of the pipe
    B. Pressure difference   **D.** Fluid viscosity

41. A 680 g steel hammer (m_h) is tied to a string that is hung from a force meter. A 5 kg container of water (m_w) sits on a scale. The hammer is lowered completely into the water but above the bottom. What does the force meter read? (Use the density of steel ρ = 7.9 g/cm^3, density of water ρ = 1 g/cm^3 and acceleration due to gravity g = 10 m/s^2)

    A. 5.9 N   **B.** 8.4 N   **C.** 10.7 N   **D.** 5.2 N

42. An external pressure applied to an enclosed fluid that is transmitted unchanged to every point within the fluid is known as:

    A. Torricelli's law   **C.** Archimedes' principle
    B. Bernoulli's principle   **D.** Pascal's principle

43. A submarine rests on the bottom of the sea. What is the normal force exerted upon the submarine by the sea floor equal to?

    A. weight of the submarine
    B. weight of the submarine minus the weight of the displaced water
    C. buoyant force minus the atmospheric pressure acting on the submarine
    D. weight of the submarine plus the weight of the displaced water

44. Consider a brick that is totally immersed in water, with the long edge of the brick vertical. Which statement describes the pressure on the brick?

    A. Greatest on the sides of the brick
    B. Greatest on the top of the brick
    C. Smallest on the sides with largest area
    D. Greatest on the bottom of the brick

45. Water is flowing in a drainage channel of a rectangular cross-section. The width of the channel is 14 m, the depth of water is 7 m, and the speed of the flow is 3 m/s. What is the mass flow rate of the water? (Use the density of water $\rho = 1,000$ kg/m^3)

    A. 2.9×10^5 kg/s
    C. 6.2×10^5 kg/s
    B. 4.8×10^4 kg/s
    D. 9.3×10^4 kg/s

46. What is the magnitude of the buoyant force if a 3 kg object floats motionlessly in a fluid of specific gravity 0.8? (Use the acceleration due to gravity $g = 10$ m/s^2)

    A. 15 N
    B. 7.5 N
    C. 30 N
    D. 45 N

47. What is the pressure 6 m below the surface of the ocean? (Use density of water $\rho = 10^3$ kg/m^3, atmospheric pressure $P_{atm} = 1.01 \times 10^5$ Pa and acceleration due to gravity $g = 10$ m/s^2)

    A. 1.6×10^5 Pa
    B. 0.8×10^5 Pa
    C. 2.7×10^4 Pa
    D. 3.3×10^4 Pa

48. Density is:

    A. inversely proportional to both mass and volume
    B. proportional to mass and inversely proportional to the volume
    C. inversely proportional to mass and proportional to the volume
    D. proportional to both mass and volume

49. Which of the following would be expected to have the smallest bulk modulus?

    A. Solid plutonium
    B. Liquid water
    C. Helium vapor
    D. Liquid mercury

50. A 14,000 N car is raised using a hydraulic lift. The lift consists of a U-tube with arms of unequal areas, initially at the same level. The lift is filled with oil with a density of 750 kg/m³ with tight-fitting pistons at each end. The narrower arm has a radius of 6 cm, while the wider arm of the U-tube has a radius of 16 cm. The car rests on the piston on the wider arm of the U-tube. What is the force that must be applied to the smaller piston to lift the car after it has been raised 1.5 m? (Ignore the weight of the pistons and use the acceleration due to gravity $g = 9.8$ m/s²)

  A. 4,568 N   **B.** 3,832 N   **C.** 2,094 N   **D.** 1,379 N

51. A polar bear of mass 240 kg stands on a floating ice 100 cm thick. What is the minimum area of the ice that will just support the bear? (Use the specific gravity of ice = 0.98 and the specific gravity of saltwater = 1.03)

  A. 2.6 m²   **B.** 4.9 m²   **C.** 4.8 m²   **D.** 11.2 m²

52. If atmospheric pressure increases by an amount ΔP, which of the following statements about the pressure in a large pond is true?

  A. The gauge pressure increases by ΔP
  B. The absolute pressure increases by ΔP
  C. The absolute pressure increases, but by an amount less than ΔP
  D. The absolute pressure does not change

53. A cubical box with 25 cm sides is immersed in a fluid. The pressure at the top surface of the box is 108 kPa, and the pressure on the bottom surface is 114 kPa. What is the density of the fluid? (Use the acceleration due to gravity $g = 9.8$ m/s²)

  A. 980 kg/m³   **C.** 2,452 kg/m³
  B. 1,736 kg/m³   **D.** 2,794 kg/m³

54. Fluid is flowing through a 19 cm long tube with a radius of 2.1 mm at an average speed of 1.8 m/s. What is the viscosity of the fluid, if the drop in pressure is 970 Pa?

  A. 0.036 N·s/m²   **C.** 0.0044 N·s/m²
  B. 0.013 N·s/m²   **D.** 0.0016 N·s/m²

55. The pressure differential across the cross-section of a condor's wing due to the difference in air flow is explained by:

  A. Torricelli's law   **C.** Bernoulli's equation
  B. Poiseuille's law   **D.** Newton's First Law

56. An air bubble underwater has the same pressure as the water. As the air bubble rises toward the surface (with its temperature remaining constant), the volume of the air bubble:

    A. increases   **C.** remains constant

    B. decreases   **D.** depends on the rate it rises

57. At a depth of about 1,060 m in the ocean, the pressure has increased by 110 atmospheres (to about 10^7 N/m^2). By how much has 1 m^3 of water been compressed by this pressure? (Use the bulk modulus B of water = 2.3×10^9 N/m^2)

    A. 2.7×10^{-3} m^3 **C.** 5.2×10^{-3} m^3

    B. 4.3×10^{-3} m^3 **D.** 7.6×10^{-2} m^3

58. The hydraulic lift is a practical application of:

    A. Huygens' principle   **C.** Fermat's principle

    B. Pascal's principle   **D.** Kepler's law

59. What is the gauge pressure in the water at the deepest point of the Pacific Ocean which is 11,030 m? (Use the density of seawater $\rho = 1,025$ kg/m^3 and the acceleration due to gravity $g = 9.8$ m/s^2)

    A. 1.1×10^8 Pa   **B.** 3.1×10^8 Pa   **C.** 4.2×10^7 Pa   **D.** 7.6×10^7 Pa

60. A man is breathing through a snorkel while swimming in the ocean. When his chest is about 1 meter underwater, he has a difficult time breathing. What is the net pressure that his lungs must expand against for him to breathe? (Use the atmospheric pressure $P_{atm} = 1.01 \times 10^5$ Pa, the density of water $\rho = 10^3$ kg/m^3, the density of air $\rho = 1.2$ kg/m^3 and the acceleration due to gravity $g = 9.8$ m/s^2)

    A. 3.2×10^5 Pa   **B.** 1.1×10^5 Pa   **C.** 4.1×10^5 Pa   **D.** 1×10^4 Pa

61. What is the wall thickness of a hollow steel ball of diameter 3 m that barely floats in water? (Use the density of steel $\rho_{steel} = 7.87$ g/cm^3 and the density of water $\rho_{water} = 10^3$ kg/m^3)

    A. 3 cm   **B.** 18 cm   **C.** 7 cm   **D.** 26 cm

62. The Bernoulli effect describes the lift force on an airplane wing. Wings must be designed to ensure that air molecules:

    A. move more rapidly past the upper surface of the wing than past the lower surface

    B. flow around wings that are smooth enough for an easy flow of the air

    C. are deflected upward when they hit the wing

    D. are deflected downward when they hit the wing

63. Two horizontal pipes (A and B) are the same length, but pipe B has twice the diameter of pipe A. Water undergoes viscous flow in both pipes, subject to the same pressure difference across the lengths of the pipes. If the flow rate in pipe A is Q, what is the flow rate in pipe B?

A. 2Q   **B.** 4Q   **C.** 8Q   **D.** 16Q

Questions **64-66** are based on the following:

A pressurized cylindrical tank is 5 m in diameter. Water exits from the pipe at point C with a velocity of 13 m/s. Point A is 10 m above point B, and point C is 3 m above point B. The cross-sectional area of the pipe at point B is 0.08 m², and the pipe narrows to a cross-sectional area of 0.04 m² at point C. Assume an ideal fluid in laminar flow. The density of water is 1,000 kg/m³. (Use the acceleration due to gravity g = 9.8 m/s²)

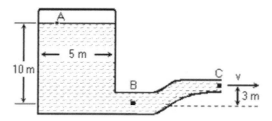

64. What is the mass flow rate in the pipe at point C?

A. 320 kg/s   **B.** 520 kg/s   **C.** 570 kg/s   **D.** 610 kg/s

65. What is the rate at which the water is falling in the tank?

A. 12 mm/s   **B.** 15 mm/s   **C.** 26 mm/s   **D.** 44 mm/s

66. What is the gauge pressure in the pipe at point B?

A. 82 kPa   **B.** 167 kPa   **C.** 71 kPa   **D.** 98 kPa

67. A closed cubical chamber resting on the floor contains oil and a piston. If the piston is pushed down hard enough to increase the pressure just below the piston by an amount ΔP, which of the following statements is correct?

A. The pressure at the top of the oil increases by less than ΔP
B. The increase in the force on the top of the chamber equals the increase in the force on the bottom of the chamber
C. The pressure in the oil increases by less than ΔP
D. The pressure at the bottom of the oil increases by more than ΔP

Fluid Statics and Dynamics – Answer Key

1: C	11: A	21: A	31: C	41: A	51: C	61: C
2: D	12: B	22: C	32: A	42: D	52: B	62: A
3: A	13: A	23: D	33: B	43: B	53: C	63: D
4: A	14: B	24: B	34: D	44: D	54: D	64: B
5: D	15: C	25: D	35: C	45: A	55: C	65: C
6: C	16: D	26: B	36: D	46: C	56: A	66: D
7: B	17: C	27: C	37: D	47: A	57: B	67: B
8: C	18: B	28: D	38: D	48: B	58: B	
9: A	19: C	29: B	39: B	49: C	59: A	
10: C	20: D	30: B	40: C	50: C	60: D	

Geometric and Physical Optics

1. What is the minimum thickness of a soap film that reflects a given wavelength of light?

  A. ¼ the wavelength   **C.** One wavelength

  B. ½ the wavelength   **D.** Two wavelengths

2. As the angle of an incident ray of light increases, the angle of the reflected ray:

  A. increases   **C.** stays the same

  B. decreases   **D.** increases or decreases

3. At what distance from a concave spherical mirror (with a focal length of 100 cm) must a woman stand to see an upright image of herself that is twice her actual height?

  A. 100 cm   **B.** 50 cm   **C.** 300 cm   **D.** 25 cm

4. If a person's eyeball is too long from front to back, what is the name of the condition that the person likely suffers?

  A. Hyperopia   **C.** Presbyopia

  B. Astigmatism   **D.** Myopia

5. According to the relationship between frequency and energy of light ($E = hf$), which color of light has more energy?

  A. Red   **B.** Yellow   **C.** Blue   **D.** Orange

6. A candle 18 cm tall sits 4 m away from a diverging lens with a focal length of 3 m. What is the size of the image?

  A. 6.3 cm   **B.** 7.7 cm   **C.** 2.9 cm   **D.** 13.5 cm

> Questions **7-8** are based on the following:

A tank holds a layer of oil 1.58 m thick that floats on a layer of syrup that is 0.66 m thick. Both liquids are clear and do not intermix. A ray, which originates at the bottom of the tank on a vertical axis (see figure), crosses the oil-syrup interface at a point 0.9 m to the right of the vertical axis. The ray continues and arrives at the oil-air interface, 2 m from the axis and at the critical angle. (Use the refractive index $n = 1$ for air)

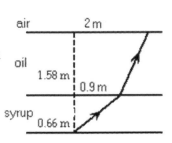

7. The index of refraction of the oil is closest to:

  A. 1.39   **B.** 1.56   **C.** 1.75   **D.** 1.82

8. What is the index of refraction of the syrup?

    A. 1.53   **B.** 1.46   **C.** 1.17   **D.** 1.24

9. Which of the following cannot be explained with the wave theory of light?

    A. Photoelectric effect   **C.** Polarization
    B. Interference   **D.** Diffusion

10. The use of wavefronts and rays to describe optical phenomena is known as:

    A. dispersive optics   **C.** wave optics
    B. reflector optics   **D.** geometrical optics

11. In the investigation of a new type of optical fiber (index of refraction $n = 1.26$), a laser beam is incident on the flat end of a straight fiber in air, as shown in the figure below. What is the maximum angle of incidence (θ_1) if the beam is not to escape from the fiber?

    A. 36°   **B.** 43°   **C.** 58°   **D.** 50°

12. An object is placed at a distance of 0.5 m from a converging lens with a power of 10 diopters. At what distance from the lens does the image appear?

    A. 0.13 m   **B.** 0.47 m   **C.** 0.7 m   **D.** 1.5 m

13. A virtual image is:

    I. produced by light rays
    II. the brain's interpretations of light rays
    III. found only on a concave mirror

    A. I only   **B.** II only   **C.** III only   **D.** I and II only

14. If Karen stands in front of a convex mirror, at the same distance from it as its radius of curvature:

    A. Karen does not see her image because it's focused at a different distance
    B. Karen sees her image, and she appears the same size
    C. Karen does not see her image, and she is not within its range
    D. Karen sees her image, and she appears smaller

15. An object is viewed at various distances using a mirror with a focal length of 10 m. If the object is 20 m away from the mirror, what best characterizes the image?

    A. Inverted and real   **C.** Upright and real
    B. Inverted and virtual   **D.** Upright and virtual

16. If an object is placed at a position beyond $2f$ of the focal point of a converging lens, the image is:

   A. real, upright and enlarged   **C.** virtual, upright and reduced

   B. real, inverted and reduced   **D.** real, inverted and enlarged

17. Which form of electromagnetic radiation has photons with the lowest energy?

   A. X-rays   **B.** Ultraviolet radiation   **C.** Radio waves   **D.** Microwaves

18. If the index of refraction of diamond is 2.43, a given wavelength of light travels:

   A. 2.43 times faster in diamond than it does in air

   B. 2.43 times faster in a vacuum than it does in diamond

   C. 2.43 times faster in diamond than it does in a vacuum

   D. 2.43 times faster in a vacuum than it does in air

19. An object is placed 15 cm to the left of a double-convex lens of focal length 20 cm. Where is the image of this object located?

   A. 15 cm to the left of the lens   **C.** 60 cm to the right of the lens

   B. 30 cm to the left of the lens   **D.** 60 cm to the left of the lens

20. A sheet of red paper appears black when it is illuminated with:

   A. orange light   **B.** cyan light   **C.** red light   **D.** yellow light

21. Where is an object if the image produced by a lens appears very close to its focal point?

   A. Near the center of curvature of the lens   **C.** Near the lens

   B. Far from the lens   **D.** Near the focal point

22. A light with the frequency 4.9×10^{14} Hz is produced by a source located 6 m from a converging lens with a focal length of 3 m. For a different frequency of light, the focal length of the lens is different from 3 m. This phenomenon is called:

   A. Dispersion   **B.** Incidence   **C.** Interference   **D.** Refraction

23. If an image appears at the same distance from a mirror as the object, the size of the image is:

   A. exactly quadruple the size of the object   **C.** the same size as the object

   B. exactly ¼ the size of the object   **D.** exactly twice the size of the object

24. When viewed straight down (90° to the surface), an incident light ray moving from water to air is refracted:

   A. 37° away from the normal   **C.** 28° toward the normal

   B. 37° toward the normal   **D.** 0°

25. Suppose that a beachgoer uses two lenses from a pair of disassembled polarized sunglasses and places one on top of the other. What would he observe if he rotates one lens 90° with respect to the normal position of the other lens and looks directly at the sun overhead?

    A. Light with an intensity reduced to about 50% of what it would be with one lens
    B. Light with an intensity that is the same of what it would be with one lens
    C. Complete darkness, since no light would be transmitted
    D. Light with an intensity reduced to about 25% of what it would be with one lens

26. A glass plate with an index of refraction of 1.45 is immersed in a liquid. The liquid is an oil with an index of refraction of 1.35. The surface of the glass is inclined at an angle of 54° with the vertical. A horizontal ray in the glass is incident on the interface of glass and liquid. The incident horizontal ray refracts at the interface. The angle that the refracted ray in the oil makes with the horizontal is closest to:

    A. 8.3°   **B.** 14°   **C.** 6°   **D.** 12°

27. Two plane mirrors make an angle of 30°. A light ray enters the system and is reflected once off each mirror. Through what angle is the ray turned?

    A. 60°   **B.** 90°   **C.** 120°   **D.** 160°

28. Which of the following statements about light is TRUE?

    A. A packet of light energy is known as a photon
    B. Color can be used to determine the approximate energy of visible light
    C. Light travels through space at a speed of 3.0×10^8 m/s
    D. All of the above

29. The angle of incidence:

    A. may be greater than, less than, or equal to the angle of refraction
    B. is always less than the angle of refraction
    C. must equal the angle of refraction
    D. is always greater than the angle of refraction

30. A 5-foot-tall woman stands next to a plane mirror on a wall. As she walks away from the mirror, her image:

    A. is always a real image, no matter how far she is from the mirror
    B. remains 5 feet tall
    C. has a height less than 5 feet
    D. may or may not get smaller, depending on where she is positioned

31. If a spherical concave mirror has a radius of curvature R, its focal length is:

    A. $2R$ **B.** R **C.** $R/2$ **D.** $R/4$

32. Let n_1 be the index of refraction of the incident medium, and let n_2 be the index of refraction of the refracting medium. Which of the following must be true if the angle that the refracted ray makes with the boundary (not with the normal) is less than the angle that the incident ray makes with the boundary?

A. $n_1 < n_2$ **B.** $n_1 > n_2$ **C.** $n_1 < 1$ **D.** $n_2 < 1$

33. If a person's eyeball is too short from front to back, the person is likely to suffer from:

A. nearsightedness   **B.** farsightedness   **C.** presbyopia   **D.** astigmatism

34. The shimmering that is observed over a hot surface is:

A. changing refraction from the mixing of warm and cool air
B. a mirage
C. heat rays
D. reflections from evaporating water vapor

35. When two parallel white rays pass through the outer edges of a converging glass lens, chromatic aberrations cause colors to appear on the screen in what order, from the top down?

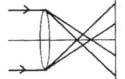

A. Blue, blue, red, red   **C.** Blue, red, red, blue
B. Red, blue, blue, red   **D.** Red, red, blue, blue

36. Two thin converging lenses are near each other so that the lens on the left has a focal length of 2 m and the one on the right has a focal length of 4 m. What is the focal length of the combination?

A. 1/4 m   **B.** 4/3 m   **C.** 3/4 m   **D.** 4 m

37. A cylindrical tank is 50 ft. deep, 37.5 ft. in diameter, and filled to the top with water. A flashlight shines into the tank from above. What is the minimum angle θ that its beam can make with the water surface if the beam is to illuminate part of the bottom? (Use the index of refraction $n = 1.33$ for water)

A. 25°   **B.** 31°   **C.** 37°   **D.** 53°

38. Which color of the visible spectrum has the shortest wavelength (400 nm)?

A. Violet   **B.** Green   **C.** Orange   **D.** Blue

39. An object is placed at a distance d in front of a plane mirror. The size of the image is:

A. dependent on where the observer is positioned when looking at the image
B. twice the size of the object
C. half the size of the object
D. the same as the object, independent of the position of the observer or distance d

40. If a single lens forms a virtual image of an object, then the:

    I. image must be upright

    II. lens must be a converging lens

    III. lens could be either diverging or converging

  A. I only   **B.** I and III only   **C.** III only   **D.** I and II only

41. When neon light passes through a prism, what is observed?

  A. White light   **C.** The same neon light

  B. Bright spots or lines   **D.** Continuous spectrum

42. The law of reflection holds for:

    I. plane mirrors   II. curved mirrors   III. spherical mirrors

  A. I only   **B.** II only   **C.** III only   **D.** I, II and III

43. The image formed by a single concave lens:

  A. can be real or virtual but is always real when the object is placed at the focal point

  B. can be real or virtual, depending on the object's distance compared to the focal length

  C. is always virtual

  D. is always real

44. A lens forms a virtual image of an object. Which of the following must be true of the image?

  A. It is inverted   **C.** It is larger than the object and upright

  B. It is upright   **D.** It is smaller than the object and inverted

45. Light with the lowest frequency (longest wavelength) detected by your eyes is perceived as:

  A. red   **B.** green   **C.** yellow   **D.** orange

46. A 0.1 m tall candle is observed through a converging lens that is 3 m away and has a focal length of 6 m. The resulting image is:

  A. 3 m from the lens on the opposite side of the object

  B. 6 m from the lens on the opposite side of the object

  C. 3 m from the lens on the same side as the object

  D. 6 m from the lens on the same side as the object

47. Which statement about thin lenses is correct when considering only a single lens?

  A. A diverging lens always produces a virtual, erect image

  B. A diverging lens always produces a real, erect image

  C. A diverging lens always produces a virtual, inverted image

  D. A diverging lens always produces a real, inverted image

48. A double-concave lens has equal radii of curvature of 15 cm. An object placed 14 cm from the lens forms a virtual image 5 cm from the lens. What is the index of refraction of the lens material?

A. 0.8 **B.** 1.4 **C.** 2 **D.** 2.6

49. The magnification m for an object reflected from a mirror is the ratio of what characteristic of the image to the object?

A. Center of curvature **B.** Distance **C.** Orientation **D.** Angular size

50. Suppose Mike places his face in front of a concave mirror. Which of the following statements is correct?

A. Mike's image is diminished in size
B. Mike's image is always inverted
C. No matter where Mike places himself, a virtual image is formed
D. If Mike positions himself between the center of curvature and the focal point of the mirror, he will not be able to see his image

51. Single-concave spherical mirrors produce images that:

A. are always smaller than the actual object
B. are always the same size as the actual object
C. are always larger than the actual object
D. could be smaller than, larger than, or the same size as the actual object, depending on the placement of the object

52. When two converging lenses of equal focal lengths are used together, the effective combined focal length is less than the focal length of either one of the individual lens. The combined power of the two lenses used together is:

A. greater than the power of either individual lens
B. the same as the power of either individual lens
C. less than the power of either individual lens
D. greater than the sum of the powers of both individual lens

53. The index of refraction is based on the ratio of the speed of light in:

A. water to the speed of light in the transparent material
B. a vacuum to the speed of light in the transparent material
C. two different transparent materials
D. air to the speed of light in the transparent material

54. An object is located 2.2 m in front of a plane mirror. The image formed by the mirror appears:

A. 4.4 m behind the mirror's surface   **C.** 4.4 m in front of the mirror's surface
B. 2.2 m in front of the mirror's surface   **D.** 2.2 m behind the mirror's surface

55. An upright object is 40 cm from a concave mirror with a radius of 50 cm. The image is:

A. virtual and inverted   **C.** real and inverted
B. virtual and upright   **D.** real and upright

56. In the figure, a ray in glass arrives at the glass-water interface at an angle of 48° with the normal. The refracted ray makes an angle of 68° with the normal. If another ray in the glass makes an angle of 29° with the normal, what is the angle of refraction in the water? (Use the index of refraction of water $n = 1.33$)

A. 29°   **C.** 31°
B. 37°   **D.** 46°

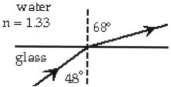

57. In a compound microscope:

A. the image of the objective serves as the object for the eyepiece
B. magnification is provided by the objective and not by the eyepiece. The eyepiece merely increases the brightness of the image viewed
C. magnification is provided by the objective and not by the eyepiece. The eyepiece merely increases the resolution of the image viewed
D. both the objective and the eyepiece form real images

58. Except for air, the refractive index of all transparent materials is:

A. equal to 1   **C.** less than 1
B. less than or equal to 1   **D.** greater than 1

59. The radius of curvature of the curved side of a plano-convex lens made of glass is 33 cm. What is the focal length of the lens? (Use the index of refraction for glass $n = 1.64$)

A. –28 cm   **B.** 28 cm   **C.** 38 cm   **D.** 52 cm

60. The part of the electromagnetic spectrum most absorbed by water is:

A. lower frequencies in the visible   **C.** infrared
B. higher frequencies in the visible   **D.** ultraviolet

61. A beam of light that is parallel to the principal axis strikes a concave mirror. Which statement is true about the reflected beam of light?

   A. It passes through the focal point of the mirror

   B. It passes through the center of curvature of the mirror

   C. It is perpendicular to the principal axis

   D. It is also parallel to the principal axis

62. The image of an object placed in front of a convex mirror is:

   A. real or virtual   **C.** real and upright

   B. virtual and upright   **D.** real and inverted

63. Which of the following cannot be explained with the particle theory of light?

     I. Polarization   II. Photoelectric effect   III. Quantization of energy

   A. I only   **B.** II only   **C.** III only   **D.** I and II only

64. If a person stands in front of a concave mirror exactly at its focal point:

   A. she sees her image at her actual height

   B. she sees her image, and she appears larger

   C. she will not see her image because none is formed

   D. she sees her image, and she appears smaller

65. An object is viewed at various distances using a mirror with a focal length of 16 m. If the object is an infinite distance away, where, relative to the mirror, is the image?

   A. 16 m behind   **C.** 8 m behind

   B. 16 m in front   **D.** 8 m in front

66. A convex lens has a focal length of f. If an object is placed at a distance of $2f$ from the lens on the principal axis, the image is located at a distance from the lens:

   A. between the lens and f **C.** between f and $2f$

   B. of f **D.** of $2f$

67. Which color of the visible spectrum has photons with the most energy?

   A. Violet   **B.** Green   **C.** Orange   **D.** Red

68. An index of refraction of less than one for a medium implies that:

    A. the speed of light in the medium is less than the speed of light in a vacuum
    B. refraction is not possible
    C. the speed of light in the medium is the same as the speed of light in a vacuum
    D. the speed of light in the medium is greater than the speed of light in a vacuum

69. The colors on an oil slick are caused by reflection and:

    A. refraction   **C.** diffraction
    B. polarization   **D.** interference

70. Which of the following describes the best scenario if a person wants to start a fire using sunlight and a mirror?

    A. Use a concave mirror with the object to be ignited positioned at the center of the curvature of the mirror
    B. Use a concave mirror with the object to be ignited positioned halfway between the mirror and its center of curvature
    C. Use a plane mirror
    D. Use a convex mirror

71. A lens has a focal length of 2 m. What lens could you combine with it to get a combination with a focal length of 3 m?

    A. A lens of power 1/6 diopters   **C.** A lens of power –6 diopters
    B. A lens of power 6 diopters   **D.** A lens of power –1/6 diopters

72. An incident ray traveling in the air makes an angle of 30° with the surface of a medium with an index $n = 1.73$. What is the angle that the refracted ray makes with the surface? (Use the index of refraction for air $n = 1$)

    A. 30°   **B.** $90 \sin^{-1}(0.5)$ **C.** 60°   **D.** $\sin^{-1}(0.5)$

73. A mirage is produced because:

    A. light travels faster through the air than through water
    B. images of water are reflected in the sky
    C. warm air has a higher index of refraction than cool air
    D. warm air has a lower index of refraction than cool air

74. An object is viewed at various distances using a concave mirror with focal length 14 m. What happens when a candle is placed at the focus?

   A. Light rays end up parallel going to infinity
   B. Light rays meet at the focus
   C. An image is formed 7 m in front of the mirror
   D. An image is formed 7 m behind the mirror

75. A material which has the ability to rotate the direction of polarization of linearly polarized light is said to be:

   A. diffraction limited
   B. optically active

   C. circularly polarized
   D. birefringent

76. When light enters a material of a higher index of refraction, its speed:

   A. increases
   B. stays the same

   C. first increases then decreases
   D. decreases

77. What is the correct order of the electromagnetic spectrum from shortest to longest wavelength?

   A. Radio waves → X-rays → Ultraviolet radiation → Visible light → Infrared radiation → Microwaves → Gamma rays
   B. Gamma rays → X-rays → Visible light → Ultraviolet radiation → Infrared radiation → Microwaves → Radio waves
   C. Gamma rays → X-rays → Ultraviolet radiation → Visible light → Infrared radiation → Microwaves → Radio waves
   D. Visible light → Infrared radiation → Microwaves → Radio waves → Gamma rays → X-rays → Ultraviolet radiation

78. The angle of incidence can vary between zero and:

   A. 2π radians
   B. π radians

   C. $\pi/2$ radians
   D. 1 radian

79. An amateur astronomer grinds a double-convex lens whose surfaces have radii of curvature of 40 cm and 60 cm. What is the focal length of this lens in the air? (Use the index of refraction for glass $n = 1.54$)

   A. 44 cm   **B.** 88 cm   **C.** 132 cm   **D.** 22 cm

80. When light reflects from a stationary surface, there is a change in its:

      I. frequency   II. speed   III. wavelength

A. I and II only   **C.** III only
B. I and III only   **D.** none of the above

81. If a distant galaxy is moving away from the Earth at 4,300 km/s, how do the detected frequency (f_{det}) and λ of the visible light detected on Earth compare to the f and λ of the light emitted by the galaxy?

A. The f_{det} is lower, and the λ is shifted towards the red end of the visible spectrum
B. The f_{det} is lower, and the λ is shifted towards the blue end of the visible spectrum
C. The f_{det} is the same, but the λ is shifted towards the red end of the visible spectrum
D. The f_{det} is the same, but the λ is shifted towards the blue end of the visible spectrum

Geometric and Physical Optics – Answer Key

1: A	11: D	21: B	31: C	41: B	51: D	61: A	71: D
2: A	12: A	22: A	32: B	42: D	52: A	62: B	72: A
3: B	13: D	23: C	33: B	43: C	53: B	63: A	73: D
4: D	14: D	24: D	34: A	44: B	54: D	64: C	74: A
5: C	15: A	25: C	35: C	45: A	55: C	65: B	75: B
6: B	16: B	26: C	36: B	46: D	56: B	66: D	76: D
7: C	17: C	27: A	37: C	47: A	57: A	67: A	77: C
8: D	18: B	28: D	38: A	48: C	58: D	68: D	78: C
9: A	19: D	29: A	39: D	49: B	59: D	69: D	79: A
10: D	20: B	30: B	40: B	50: D	60: C	70: B	80: D
							81: A

Atomic and Nuclear Physics

1. Which statement(s) about alpha particles is/are FALSE?

      I. They are a harmless form of radiation
      II. They have low penetrating power
      III. They have high ionization power

  A. I only   **B.** II only   **C.** III only   **D.** I and II only

2. What is the term for nuclear radiation that is identical to an electron?

  A. Positron   **C.** Beta minus particle
  B. Gamma ray   **D.** Alpha particle

3. Protons are being accelerated in a particle accelerator. When the speed of the protons is doubled, by what factor does their de Broglie wavelength change? Note: consider this situation non-relativistic.

  A. Increases by $\sqrt{2}$ **C.** Increases by 2
  B. Decreases by $\sqrt{2}$ **D.** Decreases by 2

4. The Bohr model of the atom was able to explain the Balmer series because:

  A. electrons were allowed to exist only in specific orbits and nowhere else
  B. differences between the energy levels of the orbits matched the differences between the energy levels of the line spectra
  C. smaller orbits require electrons to have more negative energy to match the angular momentum
  D. differences between the energy levels of the orbits were exactly half the differences between the energy levels of the line spectra

5. Radioactivity is the tendency for an element to:

  A. become ionized easily   **C.** emit radiation
  B. be dangerous to living things   **D.** emit protons

6. Which is the missing species in the nuclear equation: $^{100}_{44}\text{Ru} + ^{\ 0}_{-1}e^- \rightarrow$ ___?

  A. $^{100}_{45}\text{Ru}$ **B.** $^{100}_{43}\text{Ru}$ **C.** $^{101}_{44}\text{Ru}$ **D.** $^{100}_{43}\text{Tc}$

7. The term nucleon refers to:

  A. the nucleus of a specific isotope
  B. both protons and neutrons
  C. positrons that are emitted from an atom that undergoes nuclear decay
  D. electrons that are emitted from a nucleus in a nuclear reaction

8. An isolated ^{9}Be atom spontaneously decays into two alpha particles. What can be concluded about the mass of the ^{9}Be atom?

  A. The mass is less than twice the mass of the ^{4}He atom, but not equal to the mass of ^{4}He

  B. No conclusions can be made about the mass

  C. The mass is exactly twice the mass of the ^{4}He atom

  D. The mass is greater than twice the mass of the ^{4}He atom

9. Which of the following isotopes contains the most neutrons?

  A. $^{178}_{84}$Po   **B.** $^{178}_{87}$Fr   **C.** $^{181}_{86}$Rn   **D.** $^{170}_{83}$Bi

10. Which of the following correctly balances this nuclear fission reaction?

$$^1_0n + ^{235}_{92}U \rightarrow ^{131}_{53}I + \underline{\quad} + 3\,^1_0n$$

  A. $^{102}_{39}$Y   **B.** $^{102}_{36}$Kr   **C.** $^{104}_{39}$Y   **D.** $^{105}_{36}$Kr

11. What is the frequency of the light emitted by atomic hydrogen according to the Balmer formula where n = 12? (Use the Balmer series constant $B = 3.6 \times 10^{-7}$ m and the speed of light $c = 3 \times 10^8$ m/s)

  A. 5.3×10^6 Hz   **B.** 8.1×10^{14} Hz   **C.** 5.9×10^{13} Hz   **D.** 1.2×10^{11} Hz

12. Gamma rays require the heaviest shielding of all the common types of nuclear radiation because gamma rays have the:

  A. heaviest particles   **C.** most intense color

  B. lowest energy   **D.** highest energy

13. In making a transition from state n = 1 to state n = 2, the hydrogen atom must [ ] a photon of [ ]. (Use Planck's constant $h = 4.14 \times 10^{-15}$ eV·s, the speed of light $c = 3 \times 10^8$ m/s and the Rydberg constant $R = 1.097 \times 10^7$ m^{-1})

  A. absorb … 10.2 eV   **C.** emit … 8.6 eV

  B. absorb … 8.6 eV   **D.** emit … 10.2 eV

14. Rubidium $^{87}_{37}$Rb is a naturally-occurring nuclide which undergoes β^- decay. What is the resultant nuclide from this decay?

  A. $^{86}_{36}$Rb   **B.** $^{87}_{38}$Kr   **C.** $^{87}_{38}$Sr   **D.** $^{87}_{36}$Kr

15. Which of the following statements best describes the role of neutrons in the nucleus?

  A. The neutrons stabilize the nucleus by attracting protons

  B. The neutrons stabilize the nucleus by balancing charge

  C. The neutrons stabilize the nucleus by attracting other nucleons

  D. The neutrons stabilize the nucleus by repelling other nucleons

16. A Geiger–Muller counter detects radioactivity by:

  A. ionizing argon gas in a chamber which produces an electrical signal

  B. analyzing the mass and velocity of each particle

  C. developing film which is exposed by radioactive particles

  D. slowing the neutrons using a moderator and then counting the secondary charges produced

17. What percentage of the radionuclides in a given sample remains after three half-lives?

  A. 25%   **B.** 12.5%   **C.** 6.25%   **D.** 33.3%

18. The Lyman series is formed by electron transitions in hydrogen that:

  A. begin on the $n = 2$ shell   **C.** begin on the $n = 1$ shell

  B. end on the $n = 2$ shell   **D.** end on the $n = 1$ shell

19. Most of the volume of an atom is occupied by:

  A. neutrons   **B.** empty space   **C.** electrons   **D.** protons

20. Alpha and beta minus particles are deflected in opposite directions in a magnetic field because:

      I. they have opposite charges

      II. alpha particles contain nucleons, and beta minus particles do not

      III. they spin in opposite directions

  A. I only   **B.** II only   **C.** III only   **D.** I and II only

21. The conversion of mass to energy is measurable only in:

  A. chemiluminescent transformations   **C.** endothermic reactions

  B. spontaneous chemical reactions   **D.** nuclear reactions

22. What is the term given to the amount of a radioactive substance that undergoes 3.7×10^{10} disintegrations per second?

  A. Rem   **B.** Rad   **C.** Curie   **D.** Roentgen

23. An isolated ^{235}U atom spontaneously undergoes fission into two approximately equal-sized fragments. What is missing from the product side of the reaction:

$$^{235}U \rightarrow {}^{141}Ba + {}^{92}Kr + \underline{\quad}?$$

A. A neutron   **C.** Two protons and two neutrons

B. Two neutrons   **D.** Two protons and a neutron

24. How many protons and neutrons are in $^{34}_{16}S$?

A. 18 neutrons and 34 protons   **C.** 16 protons and 34 neutrons

B. 16 neutrons and 18 protons   **D.** 16 protons and 18 neutrons

25. The radioactive isotope Z has a half-life of 12 hours. What is the fraction of the original amount remaining after 2 days?

A. 1/16   **B.** 1/8   **C.** 1/4   **D.** 1/2

26. Which of the following nuclear equations correctly describes alpha emission?

A. $^{238}_{92}U \rightarrow {}^{242}_{94}Pu + {}^{4}_{2}He$ **C.** $^{238}_{92}U \rightarrow {}^{234}_{90}Th + {}^{4}_{2}He$

B. $^{238}_{92}U \rightarrow {}^{4}_{2}He$ **D.** $^{238}_{92}U \rightarrow {}^{235}_{90}Th + {}^{4}_{2}He$

27. A hydrogen atom makes a downward transition from the n = 20 state to the n = 5 state. Find the wavelength of the emitted photon. (Use Planck's constant $h = 4.14 \times 10^{-15}$ eV·s, the speed of light $c = 3 \times 10^8$ m/s and the Rydberg constant $R = 1.097 \times 10^7 \, m^{-1}$)

A. 1.93 μm   **B.** 2.82 μm   **C.** 1.54 μm   **D.** 2.43 μm

28. A nuclear equation is balanced when the:

A. same elements are found on both sides of the equation

B. sums of the atomic numbers of the particles and atoms are equal on both sides of the equation

C. sum of the mass numbers of the particles and the sum of atoms are the same on both sides of the equation

D. sum of the mass numbers and the sum of the atomic numbers of the particles and atoms are the same on both sides of the equation

29. A blackbody is an ideal system that:

A. absorbs 50% of the light incident upon it and emits 50% of the radiation it generates

B. absorbs 0% of the light incident upon it and emits 100% of the radiation it generates

C. absorbs 100% of the light incident upon it and emits 100% of the radiation it generates

D. emits 100% of the light it generates and absorbs 50% of the radiation incident upon it

30. Recent nuclear bomb tests have created an extra-high level of atmospheric ^{14}C. When future archaeologists date samples, without knowing of these nuclear tests, will the dates they calculate be correct?

   A. Correct, because biological materials do not gather ^{14}C from bomb tests
   B. Correct, since the ^{14}C decays within the atmosphere at the natural rate
   C. Incorrect, they would appear too old
   D. Incorrect, they would appear too young

31. When an isotope releases gamma radiation, the atomic number:

   A. and the mass number remain the same
   B. and the mass number decrease by one
   C. and the mass number increase by one
   D. remains the same and the mass number increases by one

32. If ^{14}Carbon is a beta emitter, what is the likely product of radioactive decay?

   A. ^{22}Silicon   **B.** ^{13}Boron   **C.** ^{14}Nitrogen   **D.** ^{12}Carbon

33. In a balanced nuclear equation, the:

      I. sum of the mass numbers on both sides must be equal
      II. sum of the atomic numbers on both sides must be equal
      III. daughter nuclide appears on the right side of the arrow

   A. I only   **B.** II only   **C.** III only   **D.** I, II and III

34. What is the term for the number that characterizes an element and indicates the number of protons found in the nucleus of the atom?

   A. Mass number   **C.** Atomic mass
   B. Atomic number   **D.** Neutron number

35. Hydrogen atoms can emit four spectral lines with visible colors from red to violet. These four visible lines emitted by hydrogen atoms are produced by electrons that:

   A. end in the ground state   **C.** end in the n = 2 level
   B. end in the n = 3 level   **D.** start in the ground state

36. The electron was discovered through experiments with:

   A. quarks   **B.** foil   **C.** light   **D.** electricity

Questions **37-39** are based on the following:

The image shows a beam of radiation passing between two electrically-charged plates.

 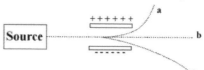

I. a

II. b

III. c

37. Which of the beams is due to an energetic light wave?

A. I only   **B.** II only   **C.** III only   **D.** I and II only

38. Which of the beams is/are composed of particles?

A. I only   **B.** II only   **C.** I, II and III   **D.** I and III only

39. Which of the beams is due to a positively-charged helium nucleus?

A. I only   **B.** II only   **C.** III only   **D.** I, II and III

40. Lithium atoms can absorb photons transitioning from the ground state (at –5.37 eV) to an excited state with one electron removed from the atom, which corresponds to the zero energy state. What is the wavelength of light associated with this transition? (Use Planck's constant $h = 4.14 \times 10^{-15}$ eV·s and the speed of light $c = 3 \times 10^8$ m/s)

A. 6.6×10^{-6} m   **C.** 3.6×10^{6} m
B. 2.3×10^{-7} m   **D.** 4.2×10^{5} m

41. All of the elements with atomic numbers of 84 and higher are radioactive because:

A. strong attractions between their nucleons make them unstable
B. their atomic numbers are larger than their mass numbers
C. strong repulsions between their electrons make them unstable
D. strong repulsions between their protons make their nuclei unstable

42. Which of the following statements about β particles is FALSE?

A. They have a smaller mass than α particles
B. They have high energy and a charge
C. They are created when neutrons become protons and vice versa
D. They are a harmless form of radioactivity

43. Which of the following provides the minimum amount of protection needed to block gamma radiation?

    A. Thick leather
    C. Lead suit

    B. T-shirt
    D. Suntan lotion

44. Which statement regarding Planck's constant is true?

    A. It relates mass to the amount of energy that can be emitted
    B. It sets a lower limit to the amount of energy that can be absorbed or emitted
    C. It sets an upper limit to the amount of energy that can be absorbed
    D. It sets an upper limit to the amount of energy that can be absorbed or emitted

45. The decay rate of a radioactive isotope will NOT be increased by increasing the:

    I. surface area   II. pressure   III. temperature

    A. I only   **B.** II only   **C.** III only   **D.** I, II and III

46. Why are some smaller nuclei such as ^{14}Carbon often radioactive?

    I. The attractive force of the nucleons has a limited range
    II. The neutron to proton ratio is too large or too small
    III. Most smaller nuclei are not stable

    A. I only   **B.** II only   **C.** III only   **D.** II and III only

47. Scandium ^{44}Sc decays by emitting a positron. What is the resultant nuclide which is produced by this decay?

    A. $^{43}_{21}$Sc   **B.** $^{45}_{21}$Sc   **C.** $^{44}_{20}$Ca   **D.** $^{43}_{20}$Ca

48. A scintillation counter detects radioactivity by:

    A. analyzing the mass and velocity of each electron
    B. ionizing argon gas in a chamber which produces an electrical signal
    C. emitting light from a NaI crystal when radioactivity passes through the crystal
    D. developing film which is exposed by radioactive particles

49. Which of the following is indicated by each detection sound by a Geiger counter?

    A. One half-life
    C. One neutron being emitted

    B. One nucleus decaying
    D. One positron being emitted

50. According to the Pauli Exclusion Principle, how many electrons in an atom may have a particular set of quantum numbers?

    A. 1   **B.** 2   **C.** 3   **D.** 4

51. The atomic number of an atom identifies the number of:

    A. excited states   **B.** electron orbits   **C.** neutrons   **D.** protons

52. Which of the following correctly characterizes gamma radiation?

    A. High penetrating power; charge $= -1$; mass $= 0$ amu
    B. Low penetrating power; charge $= -1$; mass $= 0$ amu
    C. High penetrating power; charge $= 0$; mass $= 0$ amu
    D. High penetrating power; charge $= 0$; mass $= 4$ amu

53. The rest mass of a proton is 1.0072764669 amu, and that of a neutron is 1.0086649156 amu. The ^{4}He nucleus weighs 4.002602 amu. What is the total binding energy of the nucleus? (Use the speed of light $c = 3 \times 10^8$ m/s and 1 amu $= 1.6606 \times 10^{-27}$ kg)

    A. 2.7×10^{-11} J   **C.** 1.6×10^{-7} J
    B. 4.4×10^{-12} J   **D.** 2.6×10^{-12} J

54. Which is the correct electron configuration for ground state boron ($Z = 5$)?

    A. $1s^2 1p^2 2s$ **B.** $1s^2 2p^2 3s$ **C.** $1s^2 2p^3$ **D.** $1s^2 2s^2 2p$

55. The Sun produces 3.85×10^{26} J each second. How much mass does it lose per second from nuclear processes alone? (Use the speed of light $c = 3 \times 10^8$ m/s)

    A. 9.8×10^1 kg   **B.** 2.4×10^9 kg   **C.** 4.3×10^9 kg   **D.** 1.1×10^8 kg

56. The damaging effects of radiation on the body are a result of:

    A. extensive damage to nerve cells
    B. transmutation reactions in the body
    C. the formation of radioactive particles in the body
    D. the formation of unstable ions or radicals in the body

57. How does the emission of a gamma ray affect the radioactive atom?

    I. The atomic mass increases
    II. The atom has a smaller amount of energy
    III. The atom gains energy for further radioactive particle emission

    A. I only   **B.** II only   **C.** III only   **D.** I and II only

58. The nuclear particle, which is described by the symbol ${}_{0}^{1}\text{n}$ is a(n):

A. neutron   **B.** gamma ray   **C.** beta particle   **D.** electron

59. Heisenberg's uncertainty principle states that:

A. at times a photon appears to be a particle and at other times it appears to be a wave
B. whether a photon is a wave or a particle cannot be determined with certainty
C. the position and the momentum of a particle cannot be simultaneously known with absolute certainty
D. the properties of an electron cannot be known with absolute certainty

60. The material used in nuclear bombs is ${}^{239}\text{Pu}$, with a half-life of about 20,000 years. What is the approximate amount of time that must elapse for a buried stockpile of this substance to decay to 3% of its original ${}^{239}\text{Pu}$ mass?

A. 0.8 thousand years   **C.** 90 thousand years
B. 65 thousand years   **D.** 101 thousand years

61. The emitted particle with the mass of an electron but carrying a +1 charge is a:

A. plusion   **C.** proelectron
B. positron   **D.** proton

62. Which type of nuclear radiation results in the release of particles that are identical to electrons and are deflected toward the positive electrode as they pass between electrically-charged plates?

A. Alpha   **C.** Beta
B. Gamma   **D.** Nuclide

63. The radial distance between the nucleus and the orbital shell in a hydrogen atom:

A. varies randomly with increasing values of n
B. remains constant for all values of n
C. decreases with increasing values of n
D. increases with increasing values of n

64. The first part of an atom to be discovered was the:

A. electron   **B.** nucleus   **C.** proton   **D.** neutron

65. Which is the best description of an alpha particle?

    A. Charge of –1; a mass of 0 amu; low penetrating power

    B. Charge of –2; a mass of 4 amu; medium penetrating power

    C. Charge of +2; a mass of 4 amu; low penetrating power

    D. Charge of +2; a mass of 4 amu; high penetrating power

66. Which isotope has the maximum binding energy per nucleon and therefore is represented as the maximum in the binding energy per nucleon curve?

    A. ^{56}Fe   **B.** ^{1}H   **C.** ^{251}Cf   **D.** ^{197}Au

67. In nuclear fusion:

    A. electrons and nuclei combine to form gamma rays

    B. several small nuclei combine to form an atom of an element with a greater atomic number

    C. an atomic nucleus emits alpha particles

    D. an atomic nucleus splits into two fragments, each forming an atom of an element with a smaller atomic number than the source nuclei

68. If the nucleus $^{15}_{7}$N is bombarded with a proton, one or more products are formed. Which of the following represents a possible set of products from this reaction?

    A. ^{16}N + γ   **B.** ^{14}B + ^{2}Li   **C.** ^{15}O + γ   **D.** ^{12}C + ^{4}He

69. Which is a common consumer item that utilizes the concept of radioactive decay?

    A. Carburetor   **C.** Furnace

    B. Smoke detector   **D.** Gas stove

70. What happens to the atomic number of a nucleus that undergoes β^{-} decay?

    A. It increases by two   **C.** It increases by one

    B. It decreases by one   **D.** It remains the same

71. Two radioactive nuclides I and II both decay to stable products. The half-life of I is about a day, while that of II is about a week. Suppose a radioactive sample consists of a mixture of these two nuclides. If the mixture is such that the radioactivity emitted from I and II are initially equal, then a few days later the radioactivity of the sample will be due:

    A. to nuclides I and II equally   **C.** predominantly to nuclide I

    B. entirely to nuclide II   **D.** predominantly to nuclide II

72. A metal surface is illuminated with blue light and electrons are ejected at a given rate, each with a certain amount of energy. If the intensity of the blue light is increased, electrons are ejected at:

  A. an increased rate with no change in energy per electron
  B. an increased rate with an increase in energy per electron
  C. the same rate, but with an increase in energy per electron
  D. the same rate, but with a decrease in energy per electron

73. How many $3d$ electron states can an atom have?

  A. 0   **B.** 4   **C.** 6   **D.** 10

74. Beyond which element in the periodic table (based on atomic number) are the successive elemental nuclei considered to be radioactive?

  A. Barium   **B.** Bismuth   **C.** Uranium   **D.** Radium

75. What is the term for a powerful type of nuclear radiation that has neither mass nor charge?

  A. Gamma ray   **B.** Positron   **C.** Alpha particle   **D.** Beta particle

76. To which of the following values of n does the shortest wavelength in the Balmer series correspond? (Use the Balmer series constant $B = 3.645 \times 10^{-7}$ m)

  A. 1   **B.** 5   **C.** 3   **D.** ∞

77. What is the name for the sum of the number of protons and neutrons in the nucleus of an atom?

  A. Atomic weight   **B.** Atomic number   **C.** Mass number   **D.** Atomic mass

78. Which of the following provides the minimum amount of protection needed to block beta radiation?

  A. Thin T-shirt   **C.** 1 m of water
  B. Thick leather   **D.** Thick lead shielding

79. What is the mass number of an alpha particle?

  A. 0   **B.** 1   **C.** 2   **D.** 4

80. What is the name of the particle having the following atomic notation: $_{-1}^{0}e^{-}$?

  A. Neutron   **B.** Gamma   **C.** Beta   **D.** Alpha

81. A common reaction in the Sun involves the encounter of two nuclei of light helium ($^3_2$He). If one ^{3}He nucleus encounters another, which products are possible?

A. ^{2}H + ^{2}H + ^{2}H

B. ^{7}Li + ^{1}H

C. ^{4}He + ^{1}H + ^{1}H

D. ^{4}He + ^{2}H

82. What is the term for the unit of biological radiation damage equivalent to 100 rems?

A. Gray   **B.** Becquerel   **C.** Rad   **D.** Sievert

83. Which statement about positron emission is FALSE?

I. It occurs with alpha and beta decay

II. The alternative symbol is β^+

III. It occurs when a proton is converted into a neutron and a positron

A. I only   **B.** II only   **C.** III only   **D.** I and II only

84. Why do heavy nuclei contain more neutrons than protons?

A. Neutrons are heavier than protons

B. Neutrons are repelled by the protons

C. Neutrons are radioactive, and so are heavy nuclei

D. Neutrons minimize the electric repulsion of the protons

85. Classical wave theory predicts that the photocurrent of the photoelectric effect is proportional to the:

A. intensity of light

B. magnitude of the electric field

C. frequency of light

D. wavelength of light

86. Suppose the half-life of some element is 2 days. 10 grams of this element is contained in a mixture produced by a laboratory 3 days ago. If the element is isolated from the mixture, how much of it would remain after 3 days from its separation from the mixture?

A. 0.75 grams

B. 1.25 grams

C. 2.5 grams

D. 4.5 grams

87. Nuclear fusion:

A. produces non-radioactive elements

B. is the energy source of the Sun and stars

C. releases a larger amount of heat than nuclear fission

D. all of the above

88. The type of nuclear radiation with the least penetrating ability is:

A. gamma radiation   **C.** alpha radiation

B. neutrons   **D.** beta radiation

89. Which of the following statements is true for the Bohr model of the atom?

A. As the electron shells increase, the shells get further apart, but the difference in the energy between them gets smaller

B. As electron shells increase, they get closer together, but the difference in energy between them gets greater

C. The energy difference between all the electron shells is the same

D. The spacing between all the electron shells is the same

90. A measure of radiation that takes into account the possible biological damage produced by different types of radiation is called a:

A. Roentgen   **B.** Curie   **C.** rem   **D.** rad

91. The accelerating voltage in an X-ray tube is doubled. Compared to the original value, what change occurs with respect to the minimum wavelength of the X-ray?

A. Remains the same   **C.** Doubles

B. Decreases to one half   **D.** Quadruples

92. Which nuclear process does not cause a change in the atomic number of the isotope undergoing the process?

A. Emission of a positron   **C.** Emission of a γ ray

B. Emission of a β particle   **D.** Emission of an α particle

93. Which is the product from the alpha decay of $^{235}_{92}\text{U}$?

A. $^{231}_{90}\text{Th}$ **B.** $^{233}_{80}\text{Ra}$ **C.** $^{235}_{93}\text{Np}$ **D.** $^{239}_{94}\text{Pu}$

94. The isotope $^{36}_{17}\text{Cl}$ most likely undergoes:

     I. α decay   II. β^- decay   III. β^+ decay

A. I only   **B.** II only   **C.** III only   **D.** I and II only

95. A positron is a particle emitted from the nucleus that has the same mass as a(n):

A. hydrogen atom   **B.** alpha particle   **C.** neutron   **D.** electron

96. Which of the following statements regarding radiation is FALSE?

   A. The time for half of the original sample to spontaneously decay is called the half-life

   B. All radioactive elements are spontaneously decaying toward the formation of a stable element

   C. All elements heavier than bismuth are radioactive

   D. All of the above are true

97. Isotopes are atoms of an element with similar chemical properties but with different:

   A. numbers of electrons   **C.** numbers of protons

   B. atomic numbers   **D.** masses

98. Which of the following statements regarding a nucleon is true?

   I. Attraction between nucleons changes their mass

   II. Some of the mass of a nucleon can be converted into energy by breaking certain nuclei

   III. The mass of a nucleon is different outside the nucleus

   A. I only   **B.** II only   **C.** III only   **D.** I, II and III

99. A nuclear power plant provides 10^{12} J of electrical power each day by using heat from the fission of ^{235}U to turn turbines. The mass deficit due to the fission of one ^{235}U atom is 3×10^{-25} grams. How much mass is converted to energy per day? (Use Planck's constant $h = 6.63 \times 10^{-34}$ J·s and the speed of light $c = 3 \times 10^8$ m/s)

   A. 10^{-22} g   **B.** 10^{-7} g   **C.** 10^{-2} g   **D.** 18 g

100. Which statement about a photon is true for a photon to eject an electron from a metal's surface in the photoelectric effect?

   A. Momentum must be zero

   B. Speed must be greater than a certain minimum value

   C. Polarization must have a component perpendicular to the surface

   D. Frequency must be greater than a certain minimum value

101. Which of the following correctly characterizes a beta particle β^-?

   A. Medium penetrating power; charge $= -1$; mass $= 0$ amu

   B. High penetrating power; charge $= -1$; mass $= 0$ amu

   C. High penetrating power; charge $= +2$; mass $= 4$ amu

   D. Low penetrating power; charge $= +2$; mass $= 4$ amu

102. The control rods of a nuclear reactor regulate the chain reaction because they:

A. produce positrons

B. absorb the neutrons

C. absorb the ^{235}U atoms

D. contain catalysts

103. What is the term for nuclear radiation that is identical to a ^4He nucleus?

A. Positron

B. Gamma ray

C. Beta particle

D. Alpha particle

104. The electron spin quantum number can have values of:

A. $-\frac{1}{2}$ and $\frac{1}{2}$

B. $-\frac{1}{2}, 0, +\frac{1}{2}$

C. $-\frac{1}{2}, -1, +1, +\frac{1}{2}$

D. $-\frac{1}{2}, -1, 0, +1, +\frac{1}{2}$

105. The nucleus was discovered through experiments with:

A. radio waves

B. cathode rays

C. radioactivity

D. light

106. Which of the following does NOT describe a nuclear fission reaction?

I. The energy released is proportional to the mass difference in the system

II. The number of nucleons in the products is different from the number of nucleons in the starting material

III. The mass of the products is less than the mass of the reactants

A. I only   **B.** II only   **C.** III only   **D.** I and II only

107. In the nuclear decay of a beta-emitter, the new nucleus may contain:

A. 4 fewer protons

B. 2 more protons

C. 2 fewer protons

D. 1 more proton

108. The nuclear particle which is represented by the symbol $_{+1}^{0}e$ is a(n):

A. neutron   **B.** positron   **C.** alpha particle   **D.** electron

109. Which statement describes an atom that loses an alpha particle?

A. Atomic number remains the same and the mass number decreases

B. Mass number decreases by 2, but its atomic number remains the same

C. Atomic number increases by 1, but its mass number remains the same

D. Atomic number decreases by 2, and its mass number decreases by 4

110. The radioactivity of a sample of ^{32}P was determined to be 400 mCi. How much time elapses before the radioactivity decreases to 25 mCi? (Use the half-life of ^{32}P = 14.3 days)

    A. 28.6 days   **B.** 42.9 days   **C.** 57.2 days   **D.** 114.4 days

111. The symbol $_{-1}^{0}e$ is used to represent a(n):

    A. alpha particle   **B.** beta particle   **C.** neutron   **D.** proton

112. For the atoms in a neon discharge tube to emit light characteristic of brilliant red color, it is necessary that:

    A. the electrons gain energy to be promoted from their ground state to an excited state
    B. the atoms are continually replaced with fresh atoms
    C. each atom carries a net electric charge
    D. there be no unoccupied energy levels in each atom

113. Increasing the brightness of a beam of light without changing its color increases the:

        I. speed of the photons
        II. energy of each photon
        III. number of photons emitted by light every second

    A. I only   **B.** II only   **C.** III only   **D.** I and II only

114. What is the term for the type of nuclear phenomenon in which a heavy nuclide attracts one of its inner core electrons into the nucleus?

    A. Nuclide decay   **C.** Beta decay
    B. Electron capture   **D.** Neutron reaction

115. The mass number of an atom is equal to the number of what particles in the atom?

    A. Electrons   **B.** Positrons   **C.** Neutrons   **D.** Nucleons

116. Neon has 10 electrons. What is the value for Z of the element with the next larger Z that has chemical properties very similar to those of neon?

    A. 10   **B.** 16   **C.** 18   **D.** 24

117. The binding energy per nucleon of a nucleus:

    A. has a maximum near iron in the periodic table and then decreases for heavier elements
    B. is approximately constant in the periodic table, except for very light nuclei
    C. decreases steadily in the progression towards heavier elements
    D. increases steadily in the progression towards heavier elements

118. Lithium atoms can absorb photons of frequency 2.01×10^{14} Hz transitioning from the ground state (at -5.37 eV) to an excited state. When one electron is completely removed from the atom, it corresponds to the zero energy state. Which statement is true about a photon that ionizes a lithium atom? (Use Planck's constant $h = 4.14 \times 10^{-15}$ eV·s and the speed of light $c = 3 \times 10^8$ m/s)

  A. It must have a frequency greater than 1.3×10^{15} Hz
  B. It must have a minimum frequency of 1.3×10^{15} Hz
  C. It must have a frequency less than 1.3×10^{15} Hz
  D. It must have a frequency greater than 2.6×10^{15} Hz

119. What percentage of a sample remains after 60 hours if the half-life of ^{24}Na is 15 hours?

  A. 0%   **B.** 2%   **C.** 6.25%   **D.** 8%

120. Observing the emission spectrum of a hypothetical atom, a line corresponding to a wavelength of 1.25×10^{-7} m is observed from the transition to the ground state. If the ground state has zero energy, what other energy level must exist in this atom? (Use Planck's constant $h = 6.63 \times 10^{-34}$ J·s and the speed of light $c = 3 \times 10^8$ m/s)

  A. -3.3×10^{-18} J   **C.** 1.6×10^{-18} J
  B. -1.6×10^{-18} J   **D.** 3.3×10^{-32} J

121. When a positron is emitted from the nucleus of an atom, what effect does this have on the nuclear mass?

  A. It increases by 1   **C.** It increases by 2
  B. It decreases by 2   **D.** It remains the same

122. An electron in a hydrogen atom is in its n = 2 excited state. What is the wavelength of photon needed to ionize this electron? (Use Planck's constant $h = 4.135 \times 10^{-15}$ eV·s and the speed of light $c = 3 \times 10^8$ m/s)

  A. 365 nm   **B.** 248 nm   **C.** 137 nm   **D.** 69 nm

123. The square of the wave function represents the:

  A. inertia of the particle   **C.** velocity of the particle
  B. probability density for finding the particle   **D.** momentum of the particle

124. A radioactive nuclide of atomic number Z emits an alpha particle, and the daughter nucleus then emits a beta-minus particle. What is the atomic number of the resulting nuclide?

   A. Z–1   **B.** Z+1   **C.** Z–2   **D.** Z–3

125. Which type of nuclear radiation is a helium nucleus and is deflected toward the negative electrode as it passes between electrically-charged plates?

   A. Gamma   **C.** Alpha
   B. Beta   **D.** Nuclide

126. In massive stars, three helium nuclei fuse, forming a carbon nucleus, and this reaction heats the core of the star. What is the net mass of the three helium nuclei?

   A. Same as the carbon nucleus because energy is always conserved
   B. Same as the carbon nucleus because mass is always conserved
   C. Less than that of the carbon nucleus
   D. Greater than the carbon nucleus

127. Why is the planetary model of an atom, with the nucleus playing the role of the Sun and the electrons playing the role of planets, flawed?

   A. The electrical attraction between a proton and an electron is too weak
   B. An electron is accelerating and loses energy
   C. The nuclear attraction between a proton and an electron is too strong
   D. An electron is accelerating and gains energy

128. Which of the following types of radiation might have the greatest application for medical imaging?

   A. Beta radiation would be best because it can be measured electrically
   B. X-rays would be best because they interact with the DNA in the cells
   C. Gamma radiation would be best because it penetrates the furthest
   D. Alpha radiation would be best because it penetrates the least and does the least damage

129. The type of nuclear radiation having particles with the greatest charge consists of:

   A. neutrons   **C.** beta particles
   B. gamma rays   **D.** alpha particles

130. All of the statements about nuclear reactions are true EXCEPT:

  A. they are not affected by the chemical state of the atoms involved
  B. they can have their rate increased by the addition of a catalyst
  C. they involve changes in the nucleus of an atom
  D. they have energy changes much greater than in ordinary chemical reactions

131. In a nuclear reaction, the mass of the products is less than the mass of the reactants. Why is this not observed in a chemical reaction?

  A. In chemical reactions, the mass is held constant by the nucleus
  B. In chemical reactions, the mass deficit is balanced by a mass surplus
  C. The mass deficit in chemical reactions is too small to be observed
  D. The mass does not convert to energy in chemical reactions

132. The isotope $^{13}_{7}N$ decays by positron emission to what isotope?

  A. $^{14}_{6}C$ **B.** $^{11}_{7}N$ **C.** $^{13}_{6}C$ **D.** $^{12}_{6}C$

133. The radioactive gas radon is:

  I. more hazardous to smokers than nonsmokers
  II. the single greatest source of human radiation exposure
  III. a product of the radioactive decay series of uranium

  A. I only   **B.** II only   **C.** III only   **D.** I, II and III

134. Which of the following statements best describes the strong nuclear force?

  A. The strength of the force increases with distance
  B. The force is very strong and is effective over a large range of distances
  C. The electrical force is stronger than the nuclear force
  D. The force is very strong but is effective only within a short range of distances

135. Natural line broadening can be understood in terms of the:

  A. Schrodinger wave equation   **C.** de Broglie wavelength
  B. Pauli exclusion principle   **D.** uncertainty principle

136. A blue photon has a:

  A. longer wavelength than a red photon and travels with a greater speed
  B. shorter wavelength than a red photon and travels with the same speed
  C. shorter wavelength than a red photon and travels with a greater speed
  D. longer wavelength than a red photon and travels with a lower speed

137. Which type of nuclear radiation is powerful light energy that is *not* deflected as it passes between electrically-charged plates?

    A. Gamma   **C.** Alpha

    B. Beta   **D.** Nuclide

138. The main reason that there is a limit to the size of a stable nucleus is the:

    A. weakness of the electrostatic force

    B. weakness of the gravitational force

    C. short-range effect of the strong nuclear force

    D. limited range of the gravitational force

139. Elements combine in fixed mass ratios to form compounds. This requires that elements:

    A. have unambiguous atomic numbers

    B. are always chemically active

    C. are composed of continuous matter without subunits

    D. are composed of discrete subunits called atoms

140. What is rem?

    A. A unit for measuring rapid electron motion

    B. A unit for measuring radiation exposure

    C. The number of radiation particles emitted per second

    D. The maximum exposure limit for occupational safety

141. The intensity of X-rays, gamma rays, or any other radiation is:

    A. inversely proportional to the square of the distance from the source

    B. inversely proportional to the distance from the source

    C. directly proportional to the square of the distance from the source

    D. directly proportional to the distance from the source

142. Ionizing radiation is:

    A. a neutron that has acquired a charge, resulting in the formation of an ion

    B. high-energy radiation that removes electrons from atoms or molecules

    C. radiation that only interacts with ions

    D. equivalent to a proton

143. What nucleus results when ^{55}Ni decays by positron emission?

    A. ^{55}Ca   **B.** ^{55}Ni   **C.** ^{55}Co   **D.** ^{55}Fe

144. Which of the following types of radiation has the highest energy?

    A. γ rays

    B. Visible light rays

    C. α particles

    D. β particles

145. If a star has a peak intensity at 580 nm, what is its temperature? (Use Wien's displacement constant $b = 2.9 \times 10^{-3}$ K·m)

    A. 5,000 °C   **B.** 2,000 °C   **C.** 5,000 °F   **D.** 5,000 K

Atomic, Nuclear and Quantum Physics – Answer Key

1: A	11: B	21: D	31: A	41: D	51: D	61: B	71: D
2: C	12: D	22: C	32: C	42: D	52: C	62: C	72: A
3: D	13: A	23: B	33: D	43: C	53: B	63: D	73: D
4: B	14: C	24: D	34: B	44: B	54: D	64: A	74: B
5: C	15: C	25: A	35: C	45: D	55: C	65: C	75: A
6: D	16: A	26: C	36: D	46: B	56: D	66: A	76: D
7: B	17: B	27: D	37: B	47: C	57: B	67: B	77: C
8: D	18: D	28: D	38: C	48: C	58: A	68: D	78: B
9: C	19: B	29: C	39: C	49: B	59: C	69: B	79: D
10: A	20: A	30: D	40: B	50: A	60: D	70: C	80: C

81: C	91: B	101: A	111: B	121: D	131: D	141: A
82: D	92: C	102: B	112: A	122: A	132: C	142: B
83: A	93: A	103: D	113: C	123: B	133: D	143: C
84: D	94: B	104: A	114: B	124: A	134: D	144: A
85: A	95: D	105: C	115: D	125: C	135: D	145: D
86: B	96: D	106: B	116: C	126: D	136: B	
87: D	97: D	107: D	117: A	127: B	137: A	
88: C	98: D	108: B	118: A	128: C	138: C	
89: A	99: C	109: D	119: C	129: D	139: D	
90: C	100: D	110: C	120: C	130: B	140: B	

Particle Physics

1. Which of the following statements about hadrons are correct?

   I. Hadrons are composed of leptons
   II. All hadrons are composed of quarks
   III. Protons and neutrons are hadrons, but electrons are not

   A. I only   **C.** II and III only
   B. III only   **D.** II and III only

2. Which of the following statements about hadrons are correct?

   I. All hadrons interact by the strong nuclear force
   II. Electrons, protons, and neutrons are commonly-occurring hadrons
   III. All hadrons are composed of quarks

   A. I only   **C.** I and II only
   B. II only   **D.** I and III only

3. Leptons can interact by which of the following forces?

   A. strong nuclear force and weak nuclear force
   B. weak nuclear force, electromagnetic force, and gravitation
   C. strong nuclear force, weak nuclear force and electromagnetic force
   D. strong nuclear force, weak nuclear force, electromagnetic force and gravitation

4. Which of the following particles do NOT contain any quarks?

   I. alpha particle   II. positron   III. neutron

   A. I only   **C.** I and III only
   B. II only   **D.** II and III only

5. What are the possible charges of a quark (not an antiquark)?

   A. $-2/3\ e, +1/3\ e$ **C.** $-e, 0, e$
   B. $-1/3\ e, +2/3\ e$ **D.** $-2/3\ e, -1/3\ e, +1/3\ e, +2/3\ e$

6. How many quarks are in a deuteron, $^{2}_{1}\text{H}$?
   A. 1   **B.** 3   **C.** 4   **D.** 6

135

7. How many quarks are in a tritium isotope, $^3_1$H?

   A. 1   **B.** 4   **C.** 5   **D.** 9

8. How does the range of an exchange force depend on the mass of the exchange particle?

    I. The range does not depend on the mass of the exchange particle

    II. The range is shorter for a massive exchange particle than for a light exchange particle

    III. The range is longer for a massive exchange particle than for a light exchange particle

   A. I only   **C.** III only

   B. II only   **D.** I and II only

9. An electron and a positron, both essentially at rest, annihilate each other, emitting two identical photons in the process. What is the wavelength of these photons? The mass of an electron or positron is 9.11×10^{-31} kg. (Use $h = 6.626 \times 10^{-34}$ J·s, $c = 3.00 \times 10^8$ m/s and $hc = 1240$ eV· nm)

   A. 2.42 pm   **C.** 1.21×10^{-12} pm

   B. 3.72 pm   **D.** 1.57 pm

10. A proton is a specific combination of three quarks. What are the electric charges on these quarks, expressed in terms of e?

   A. $+2/3\ e$, $+2/3\ e$, and $-1/3\ e$ **C.** $+2/3\ e$, $+2/3\ e$, and $+1/3\ e$

   B. $-2/3\ e$, $+2/3\ e$, and $-1/3\ e$ **D.** $-2/3\ e$, $-2/3\ e$, and $-1/3\ e$

11. A positron (or antielectron) is made to stop in a sample of matter. Soon after, how many gamma rays are observed and with what energy each?

   A. none   **C.** two, 0.511 MeV each

   B. one, 0.511 MeV each   **D.** one, 13.6 eV each

12. What is the minimum energy required to produce a proton-antiproton pair? (Use the rest mass of a proton = 938 MeV/c^2)

   A. 0 MeV   **C.** 1876 MeV

   B. 938 MeV   **D.** 2814 MeV

13. A η meson with rest energy of 548 MeV decays into two gamma rays. What is the wavelength of the gamma rays? (Use $h = 6.63 \times 10^{-34}$ J·s, $c = 3.0 \times 10^8$ m/s and $hc = 1{,}240$ eV nm).

    A. 2.3×10^{-15} m   **C.** 4.5×10^{-15} m

    B. 2.3×10^{-16} m   **D.** 4.5×10^{-16} m

14. What is the speed of a proton with kinetic energy equal to 2 GeV?

    A. $0.78\,c$ **B.** 0.84 c   **C.** $0.88\,c$ **D.** 0.95 c

15. What is the speed of a 2 MeV electron?

    A. 0.75 c   **B.** 0.84 c   **C.** $0.90\,c$ **D.** $0.97\,c$

16. What is the temperature corresponding to thermal energy of 50 GeV, the particle energy in the accelerator at SLAC?

    A. 3.9×10^{11} K   **C.** 7.8×10^{11} K

    B. 5.8×10^{14} K   **D.** 7.8×10^{14} K

17. How far is the galaxy from Earth if it recedes from Earth at a speed $v = 0.5\,c$? (Use $H_0 = 0.022$ m/s/lightyear for Hubble's constant).

    A. 22.7 lightyears   **C.** 2.3×10^5 lightyears

    B. 1.8×10^4 lightyears   **D.** 6.8×10^9 lightyears

18. A certain galaxy is 2.7×10^9 lightyears from Earth. How fast is it receding from Earth? (Use $H_0 = 0.022$ m/(s·lightyear) for Hubble's constant).

    A. 0.2 c   **B.** 0.3 c   **C.** 0.4 c   **D.** 0.5 c

19. What is the minimum energy required to produce an electron-positron pair? (Use the rest mass of an electron $= 0.511$ MeV/c^2).

    A. 0.511 MeV   **C.** 1.533 MeV

    B. 1.022 MeV   **D.** 2.044 MeV

20. The rest energy of π meson is about 140 MeV. Using the uncertainty principle, estimate the range of strong force. ($h = 6.63 \times 10^{-34}$ J·s, $hc = 1.24$ eV μm).

    A. 0.35×10^{-15} m   **C.** 1.4×10^{-15} m

    B. 0.7×10^{-15} m   **D.** 2.8×10^{-15} m

21. The rest energy of a Z^0 boson is 91 GeV. Using the uncertainty principle, what is the approximate interaction time when it mediates a weak interaction? (Use $h = 6.63 \times 10^{-34}$ J·s, and $hc = 1.24$ eV μm).

    A. 3.6×10^{-26} s   **C.** 7.2×10^{-27} s

    B. 2.6×10^{-27} s   **D.** 5.2×10^{-28} s

22. A μ^+ and μ^- at rest annihilate to produce two gamma rays that fly in opposite directions. What is the wavelength of each gamma ray? (Use the rest energy of a muon = 106 MeV, $h = 6.63 \times 10^{-34}$ J·s and $hc = 1.24$ eV μm).

    A. 1.17×10^{-14} m   **C.** 2.48×10^{-15} m

    B. 5.63×10^{-15} m   **D.** 1.24×10^{-15} m

23. The rest energy of W^+ boson is about 80 GeV. Using the uncertainty principle, estimate the range of weak interaction. (Use $h = 6.63 \times 10^{-34}$ J·s and $hc = 1.24$ eV μm).

    A. 1.3×10^{-15} m   **C.** 2.5×10^{-17} m

    B. 2.5×10^{-16} m   **D.** 2.5×10^{-18} m

Particle Physics – Answer Key

1: C	6: D	11: C	16: B	21: C
2: D	7: D	12: C	17: D	22: A
3: B	8: B	13: C	18: A	23: B
4: B	9: A	14: D	19: B	
5: B	10: A	15: D	20: C	

Electrostatics and Magnetism

1. A flat disk 1 m in diameter is oriented so that the area vector of the disk makes an angle of $\pi/6$ radians with a uniform electric field. What is the electric flux through the surface if the field strength is 740 N/C?

    A. 196π N·m^2/C   **B.** $250/\pi$ N·m^2/C   **C.** 644π N·m^2/C   **D.** 160π N·m^2/C

2. A positive charge $Q = 1.3 \times 10^{-9}$ C is located along the x-axis at $x = -10^{-3}$ m and a negative charge of the same magnitude is located at the origin. What is the magnitude and direction of the electric field at the point along the x-axis where $x = 10^{-3}$ m? (Use Coulomb's constant $k = 9 \times 10^9$ N·m^2/C^2 and to the right as the positive direction)

    A. 8.8×10^6 N/C to the left   **C.** 5.5×10^7 N/C to the right

    B. 3.25×10^7 N/C to the right   **D.** 2.75×10^6 N/C to the right

3. A proton is located at ($x = 1$ nm, $y = 0$ nm) and an electron is located at ($x = 0$ nm, $y = 4$ nm). Find the attractive Coulomb force between them. (Use Coulomb's constant $k = 9 \times 10^9$ N·m^2/C^2 and the charge of an electron $e = -1.6 \times 10^{-19}$ C)

    A. 5.3×10^8 N   **B.** 1.9×10^{-15} N   **C.** 9.3×10^4 N   **D.** 1.4×10^{-11} N

4. Which form of electromagnetic radiation has photons with the highest energy?

    A. Gamma rays   **C.** Microwaves

    B. Visible light   **D.** Ultraviolet radiation

Questions **5-6** are based on the following:

Two parallel metal plates separated by 0.01 m are charged to create a uniform electric field of 3.5×10^4 N/C between them, which points down. A small, stationary 0.008 kg plastic ball m is located between the plates and has a small charge Q on it. The only forces acting on it are the force of gravity and the electric field. (Use Coulomb's constant $k = 9 \times 10^9$ N·m^2/C^2, the charge of an electron $= -1.6 \times 10^{-19}$ C, the charge of a proton $= 1.6 \times 10^{-19}$ C, the mass of a proton $= 1.67 \times 10^{-27}$ kg, the mass of an electron $= 9.11 \times 10^{-31}$ kg and the acceleration due to gravity $g = 9.8$ m/s^2)

5. What is the charge on the ball?

    A. -250 C   **C.** 3.8×10^{-6} C

    B. 250 C   **D.** -2.2×10^{-6} C

6. How would the acceleration of an electron between the plates compare to the acceleration of a proton between the plates?

   A. One thousand eight hundred thirty times as large, and in the opposite direction
   B. The square root times as large, and in the opposite direction
   C. Twice as large, and in the opposite direction
   D. The same magnitude, but in the opposite direction

7. A positive charge $Q = 2.3 \times 10^{-11}$ C is 10^{-2} m away from a negative charge of equal magnitude. Point P is located equidistant between them. What is the magnitude of the electric field at point P? (Use Coulomb's constant $k = 9 \times 10^{9}$ N·m^2/C^2)

   A. 9.0×10^{3} N/C   **B.** 4.5×10^{3} N/C   **C.** 3.0×10^{4} N/C   **D.** 1.7×10^{4} N/C

8. Which statement is true for an H nucleus, which has a charge $+e$ that is situated to the left of a C nucleus, which has a charge $+6e$?

   A. The electrical force experienced by the H nucleus is to the right, and the magnitude is equal to the force exerted on the C nucleus
   B. The electrical force experienced by the H nucleus is to the right, and the magnitude is less than the force exerted on the C nucleus
   C. The electrical force experienced by the H nucleus is to the left, and the magnitude is greater than the force exerted on the C nucleus
   D. The electrical force experienced by the H nucleus is to the left, and the magnitude is equal to the force exerted on the C nucleus

9. Electrons move in an electrical circuit:

   A. because the wires are so thin   **C.** by colliding with each other
   B. by interacting with an established electric field   **D.** by being repelled by protons

10. If the number of turns on the secondary coil of a transformer is less than those on the primary, the result is a:

   A. 240 V transformer   **C.** step-up transformer
   B. 110 V transformer   **D.** step-down transformer

11. A light bulb is connected in a circuit and has a wire leading to it in a loop. What happens when a strong magnet is quickly passed through the loop?

   A. The brightness of the light bulb dims or gets brighter due to an induced emf produced by the magnet
   B. The light bulb's brightness remains the same although current decreases
   C. The light bulb gets brighter because more energy is being added to the system by the magnet inside the coil
   D. The light bulb gets brighter because there is an induced emf that drives more current through the light bulb

12. A loop of wire is rotated about a diameter (which is perpendicular to a given magnetic field). In one revolution, the induced current in the loop reverses direction how many times?

A. 2   **B.** 1   **C.** 0   **D.** 4

13. A solid aluminum cube rests on a wooden table in a region where a uniform external electric field is directed straight upward. What can be concluded regarding the charge on the top surface of the cube?

A. The top surface is neutral

B. The top surface is charged negatively

C. The top surface fluctuates between being charged neutral and positively

D. The top surface is charged positively

14. A point charge of $+Q$ is placed at the center of an equilateral triangle, as shown. When a second charge of $+Q$ is placed at one of the triangle's vertices, an electrostatic force of 5 N acts on it. What is the magnitude of the force that acts on the center charge when a third charge of $+Q$ is placed at one of the other vertices?

A. 0 N   **B.** 4 N   **C.** 5 N   **D.** 8 N

15. Which form of electromagnetic radiation has the highest frequency?

A. Gamma radiation   **C.** Visible light

B. Ultraviolet radiation   **D.** Radio waves

16. All of the following affect the electrostatic field strength at a point at a distance from a source charge, EXCEPT:

A. the sign of the source charge

B. the distance from the source charge

C. the magnitude of the source charge

D. the nature of the medium surrounding the source charge

17. A charged particle is observed traveling in a circular path in a uniform magnetic field. If the particle had been traveling twice as fast, the radius of the circular path would be:

A. three times the original radius   **C.** one-half of the original radius

B. twice the original radius   **D.** four times the original radius

18. What happens to the cyclotron frequency of a charged particle if its speed doubles?

A. It is ¼ as large   **C.** It doubles

B. It is ½ as large   **D.** It remains the same

19. If a value has SI units kg m^2/s^2/C, this value can be:

A. electric potential difference
C. electric field strength

B. resistance
D. Newton's forces

20. A circular loop of wire is rotated about an axis whose direction at constant angular speed can be varied. In a region where a uniform magnetic field points straight down, what orientation of the axis of the rotation guarantees that the emf will be zero (regardless of how the axis is aligned to the loop)?

A. It must be vertical

B. It must make an angle of 45° to the direction South

C. It could have any horizontal orientation

D. It must make an angle of 45° to the vertical

21. A proton, moving in a uniform magnetic field, moves in a circle perpendicular to the field lines and takes time T for each circle. If the proton's speed tripled, what would now be its time to go around each circle?

A. T/3
B. T
C. 6T
D. 3T

22. As measurements of the electrostatic field strength are taken at points that progressively approach a negatively-charged particle, the field vectors will point:

A. away from the particle and have a constant magnitude

B. away from the particle and have progressively decreasing magnitude

C. towards the particle and have progressively increasing magnitude

D. towards the particle and have progressively decreasing magnitude

23. Every proton in the universe is surrounded by its own:

    I. electric field   II. gravitational field   III. magnetic field

A. I only
B. II only
C. I and III only
D. I, II and III

24. In electricity, what quantity is analogous to the acceleration of gravity, g (i.e., a force per unit mass)?

A. Electric charge
C. Electric field

B. Electric current
D. Electromagnetic force

25. Which type of electromagnetic (EM) wave travels through space the slowest?

A. Visible light
C. Gamma rays

B. Ultraviolet light
D. All EM waves travel at the same speed

26. As a proton moves in the direction of the electric field lines, it is moving from:

A. high potential to low potential and losing electric potential energy
B. high potential to low potential and gaining electric potential energy
C. low potential to high potential and gaining electric potential energy
D. low potential to high potential and retaining electric potential energy

27. Which of the following requires a measure of time?

A. Joule   **B.** Watt   **C.** Volt   **D.** Coulomb

28. Two positive charges Q_1 and $Q_2 = 3.4 \times 10^{-10}$ C are located 10^{-3} m away from each other, and point P is exactly between them. What is the magnitude of the electric field at point P?

A. 0 N/C
B. 10^{-10} N/C
C. 6.8×10^{-7} N/C
D. 1.7×10^{-5} N/C

29. Which of the following is an accurate statement?

A. A conductor cannot carry a net charge
B. The electric field at the surface of a conductor is not necessarily parallel to the surface
C. If a solid metal sphere carries a net charge, the charge distributes uniformly throughout
D. If a solid metal sphere carries a net charge, the charge will move to the sphere surface

30. A charged particle moves and experiences no magnetic force. What can be concluded?

A. Either no magnetic field exists, or the particle is moving parallel to the field
B. No magnetic field exists in that region of space
C. The particle is moving at right angles to a magnetic field
D. The particle is moving parallel to a magnetic field

31. What is the electric field strength at ($x = 0$ m, $y = 0$ m) produced by two electrons, one at $x = 0.0001$ m, $y = 0$ m and the other at ($x = -0.0001$ m, $y = 0$ m)? (Use Coulomb's constant $k = 9 \times 10^9$ N·m^2/C^2)

A. 1.8×10^{-19} N/C
B. 7.9×10^{-19} N/C
C. 3.2×10^{-19} N/C
D. 0 N/C

32. The statement, 'the total electric flux at a closed surface is proportional to the charge enclosed by the surface' is known as:

A. Coulomb's law   **B.** Gauss's law   **C.** Raoult's law   **D.** Graham's law

33. Which one of the following statements is correct?

A. The north pole of a magnet points towards Earth's geographic North Pole

B. The north pole of a magnet points towards Earth's geographic South Pole

C. Earth's geographic North Pole is the north pole of Earth's magnetic field

D. None of the above

34. Two uncharged metal spheres, A and B, are mounted on insulating support rods. A third metal sphere, C, carrying a positive charge, is then placed near B. A copper wire is momentarily connected between A and B, and then removed. Finally, sphere C is removed. In this final state:

A. spheres A and B both carry equal positive charges

B. sphere A carries a negative charge and B carries a positive charge

C. sphere A carries a positive charge and B carries a negative charge

D. spheres A and B both carry positive charges, but B's charge is greater

35. A balloon after being rubbed on a wool rug can stick to a wall. This illustrates that the balloon has:

    I. magnetism

    II. net charge

    III. capacitance

A. I only   **B.** II only   **C.** III only   **D.** I, II and III

36. The diagram shows two unequal charges $+q$ and $-Q$, of opposite sign. Charge Q has a greater magnitude than charge q. Point X is midway between the charges.

In what section of the line is the point where the resultant electric field could equal zero?

A. VW   **B.** WX   **C.** XY   **D.** YZ

37. One coulomb of charge passes through a 6 V battery. Which of the following is the correct value for the increase of some property of the battery?

A. 6 watts   **B.** 6 ohms   **C.** 6 amps   **D.** 6 J

38. What travels through a conductor at near the speed of light when a current is established?

A. Protons   **C.** An electric field

B. Photons   **D.** Electrons

39. Which statement is accurate for a proton that moves in a direction perpendicular to the electric field lines?

   A. it is moving from high potential to low potential and gaining electric potential energy
   B. it is moving from high potential to low potential and losing electric potential energy
   C. it is moving from low potential to high potential and gaining electric potential energy
   D. both its electric potential and electric potential energy remain constant

40. When a current flows through a metal wire, the moving charges are:

     I. protons   II. neutrons   III. electrons

   A. I only   **B.** II only   **C.** III only   **D.** I and II only

41. A proton is traveling to the right and encounters a region S which contains an electric field or a magnetic field or both. The proton is observed to bend up the page. Which of the statements is true regarding region S?

        I. There is a magnetic field pointing into the page
        II. There is a magnetic field pointing out of the page
        III. There is an electric field pointing up the page
        IV. There is an electric field pointing down the page

   A. I only   **B.** II only   **C.** I and III   **D.** II and IV

42. An object with a 6 μC charge is accelerating at 0.006 m/s^2 due to an electric field. If the object has a mass of 2 μg, what is the magnitude of the electric field?

   A. 0.002 N/C   **B.** –0.005 N/C   **C.** 2 N/C   **D.** –2 N/C

43. Two Gaussian surfaces, A and B, enclose the same positive charge $+Q$. The Gaussian surface A has an area two times greater than surface B. Compared to the flux of the electric field through Gaussian surface B, the flux of the electric field through surface A is:

   A. two times smaller   **B.** equal   **C.** two times larger   **D.** four times larger

44. Which of these electromagnetic waves has the shortest wavelength?

   A. γ rays   **B.** Visible light   **C.** Radio waves   **D.** Infrared

45. With all other factors remaining constant, how does doubling the number of loops of wire in a coil affect the induced emf?

   A. The induced emf increases by a factor of $\sqrt{2}$
   B. The induced emf doubles
   C. There is no change in the induced emf
   D. The induced emf quadruples

46. A sphere with radius 2 mm carries a 1 μC charge. What is the potential difference, $V_B - V_A$, between point B 3.5 m from the center of the sphere and point A 8 m from the center of the sphere? (Use Coulomb's constant $k = 9 \times 10^9$ N·m^2/C^2)

    A. −485 V   **B.** 1,140 V   **C.** −140 V   **D.** 1,446 V

47. A proton with an initial speed of 1.5×10^5 m/s falls through a potential difference of 100 volts, gaining speed. What is the speed reached? (Use the mass of a proton $= 1.67 \times 10^{-27}$ kg and the charge of a proton $= 1.6 \times 10^{-19}$ C)

    A. 2×10^5 m/s   **C.** 8.6×10^5 m/s

    B. 4×10^5 m/s   **D.** 7.6×10^5 m/s

48. A positively-charged particle is at rest in an unknown medium. What is the magnitude of the magnetic field generated by this particle?

    A. Constant everywhere and dependent only on the mass of the medium

    B. Less at points near to the particle compared to a distant point

    C. Greater at points near to the particle compared to a distant point

    D. Equal to zero

49. An electron was accelerated from rest through a potential difference of 990 V. What is its speed? (Use the mass of an electron $= 9.11 \times 10^{-31}$ kg, the mass of a proton $= 1.67 \times 10^{-27}$ kg and the charge of a proton $= 1.6 \times 10^{-19}$ C)

    A. 0.8×10^7 m/s   **C.** 7.4×10^7 m/s

    B. 3.7×10^7 m/s   **D.** 1.9×10^7 m/s

50. Electromagnetic induction occurs in a coil when there is a change in the:

    A. coil's charge   **C.** magnetic field intensity in the coil

    B. current in the coil   **D.** electric field intensity in the coil

51. Consider the group of charges in this figure. All three charges have $Q = 3.8$ nC. What is their electric potential energy?

(Use Coulomb's constant $k = 9.0 \times 10^9$ N·m^2/C^2)

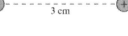

    A. 1.9×10^{-6} J   **C.** 8.8×10^{-6} J

    B. 7.4×10^{-5} J   **D.** 1.0×10^{-5} J

52. A positively-charged and negatively-charged particle are traveling on the same path perpendicular to a constant magnetic field. How do the forces experienced by the two particles differ, if the magnitudes of the charges are equal?

A. Differ in direction, but not in magnitude

B. Differ in magnitude, but not in direction

C. No difference in magnitude or direction

D. Differ in both magnitude and direction

53. An electron moves in a direction opposite to an electric field. The potential energy of the system:

A. decreases, and the electron moves toward a region of lower potential

B. increases, and the electron moves toward a region of higher potential

C. decreases, and the electron moves toward a region of higher potential

D. remains constant, and the electron moves toward a region of higher potential

54. A hydrogen atom consists of a proton and an electron. If the orbital radius of the electron increases, the absolute magnitude of the potential energy of the electron:

A. remains the same   **C.** increases

B. decreases   **D.** depends on the potential of the electron

55. The force on an electron moving in a magnetic field is largest when its direction is:

A. perpendicular to the magnetic field direction

B. at an angle greater than 90° to the magnetic field direction

C. at an angle less than 90° to the magnetic field direction

D. exactly opposite to the magnetic field direction

56. A proton with a speed of 1.7×10^5 m/s falls through a potential difference V and thereby increases its speed to 3.2×10^5 m/s. Through what potential difference did the proton fall? (Use the mass of a proton = 1.67×10^{-27} kg and the charge of a proton = 1.6×10^{-19} C)

A. 880 V   **B.** 1,020 V   **C.** 384 V   **D.** 430 V

57. Two isolated copper plates, each of area 0.6 m², carry opposite charges of magnitude 7.08 $\times 10^{-10}$ C. They are placed opposite each other in parallel alignment, with a spacing of 2 mm. What will be the potential difference between the plates when their spacing is increased to 6 cm? (Use the dielectric constant $k = 1$ in air and electric permittivity $\varepsilon_0 = 8.854 \times 10^{-12}$ F/m)

A. 8.0 V   **B.** 3.1 V   **C.** 4.3 V   **D.** 7.2 V

58. The metal detectors used to screen passengers at airports operate via:

A. Newton's Laws   **B.** Bragg's Law   **C.** Faraday's Law   **D.** Ohm's Law

59. A 7 μC negative charge is attracted to a large, well-anchored, positive charge. How much kinetic energy does the negatively-charged object gain if the potential difference through which it moves is 3.5 mV?

A. 0.86 J   **B.** 6.7 μJ   **C.** 36.7 μJ   **D.** 24.5 nJ

60. A charge $+Q$ is located at one of the corners of a square. The absolute potential at the center of a square is 3 V. If a second charge $-Q$ is placed at one of the other three corners, what is the absolute potential at the square's center?

A. –6 V   **B.** 12 V   **C.** 6 V   **D.** 0 V

61. A uniform electric field has a strength of 6 N/C. What is the electric energy density of the field? (Use the electric permittivity $\varepsilon_0 = 8.854 \times 10^{-12}$ F/m)

A. 1.5×10^{12} J/m^3 **B.** 1.6×10^{-10} J/m^3 **C.** 2.3×10^{12} J/m^3 **D.** 2.7×10^{-11} J/m^3

62. What is the potential energy of a $+2.4$ μC charge at a certain point in space where there is a potential of 320 V?

A. 368 J   **B.** 537 J   **C.** 826 J   **D.** 7.7×10^{-4} J

63. A proton with a speed of 1.8×10^5 m/s falls through a potential difference of 100 V, gaining speed. What is the speed reached? (Use the mass of a proton $m = 1.67 \times 10^{-27}$ kg and the charge of proton $= 1.6 \times 10^{-19}$ C)

A. 8.4×10^5 m/s   **B.** 5.2×10^5 m/s   **C.** 2.3×10^5 m/s   **D.** 4.6×10^5 m/s

64. A current of 5 A flows through an electrical device for 12 seconds. How many electrons flow through this device during this time? (Use the charge of an electron $= -1.6 \times 10^{-19}$ C)

A. 5.2×10^{18} electrons   **C.** 6.3×10^{19} electrons
B. 3.8×10^{20} electrons   **D.** 1.2×10^{8} electrons

65. A charged particle of mass 0.006 kg is subjected to a 6 T magnetic field, which acts at a right angle to its motion. If the particle moves in a circle of radius 0.1 m at a speed of 3 m/s, what is the magnitude of the charge on the particle?

A. 3 C   **B.** 30 C   **C.** 3.6 C   **D.** 0.03 C

Electrostatics and Magnetism – Answer Key

1: D	11: A	21: B	31: D	41: C	51: D	61: E
2: A	12: A	22: C	32: B	42: A	52: A	62: D
3: D	13: D	23: D	33: D	43: B	53: C	63: C
4: A	14: C	24: C	34: C	44: A	54: B	64: B
5: D	15: A	25: D	35: B	45: B	55: A	65: D
6: A	16: A	26: A	36: A	46: D	56: C	
7: D	17: B	27: B	37: D	47: A	57: A	
8: D	18: D	28: A	38: C	48: D	58: C	
9: B	19: A	29: D	39: D	49: D	59: D	
10: D	20: A	30: A	40: C	50: C	60: D	

DC and RC Circuits

1. Three 8 V batteries are connected in series to power light bulbs A and B. The resistance of light bulb A is 60 Ω and the resistance of light bulb B is 30 Ω. How does the current through light bulb A compare with the current through light bulb B?

   A. The current through light bulb A is less

   B. The current through light bulb A is greater

   C. The current through light bulb A is the same

   D. The current through light bulb A is exactly doubled that through light bulb B

2. Which of the following affect(s) capacitance of capacitors?

     I. material between the conductors

     II. distance between the conductors

     III. geometry of the conductors

   A. I only   **B.** II only   **C.** I and III only   **D.** I, II and III

3. The heating element of a toaster is a long wire of some metal, often a metal alloy, which heats up when a 120 V potential difference is applied across it. Consider a 300 W toaster connected to a wall outlet. Which statement would result in an increase in the rate by which heat is produced?

   A. Use a longer wire   **C.** Use a thicker and longer wire

   B. Use a thicker wire   **D.** Use a thinner and longer wire

4. A circular conducting loop with a radius of 0.5 m and a small gap filled with a 12 Ω resistor is oriented in the *xy*-plane. If a magnetic field of 1 T, making an angle of 30° with the *z*-axis, increases to 12 T, in 5 s, what is the magnitude of the current flowing in the conductor?

   A. 0.33 A   **B.** 0.13 A   **C.** 0.88 A   **D.** 1.5 A

5. A charged parallel-plate capacitor has an electric field E_0 between its plates. The bare nuclei of a stationary ^{1}H and ^{4}He are between the plates. Ignoring the force of gravity, how does the magnitude of the acceleration of the hydrogen nucleus a_H compare with the magnitude of the acceleration of the helium nucleus a_{He}? (Use mass of an electron = 9×10^{-31} kg, mass of a proton = 1.67×10^{-27} kg, mass of a neutron = 1.67×10^{-27} kg and charge of a proton = 1.6×10^{-19} C)

   A. $a_H = 2a_{He}$ **C.** $a_H = \frac{1}{4}a_{He}$

   B. $a_H = 4a_{He}$ **D.** $a_H = a_{He}$

6. Identical light bulbs are attached to identical batteries in three different ways (A, B, or C), as shown in the figure. What is the ranking (from lowest to highest) of the total power produced by the battery?

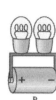

A. C, B, A   **C.** A, C, B

B. B, A, C   **D.** A, B, C

7. A parallel-plate capacitor consists of two parallel, square plates that have dimensions 1 cm by 1 cm. If the plates are separated by 1 mm, and the space between them is filled with Teflon, what is the capacitance? (Use the dielectric constant k for Teflon = 2.1 and the electric permittivity $\varepsilon_0 = 8.854 \times 10^{-12}$ F/m)

A. 0.83 pF   **B.** 2.2 pF   **C.** 0.46 pF   **D.** 1.9 pF

8. An alternating current is supplied to an electronic component with a rating that it be used only for voltages below 12 V. What is the highest V_{rms} that can be supplied to this component while staying below the voltage limit?

A. 6 V   **B.** 12 V   **C.** $3\sqrt{2}$ V   **D.** $6\sqrt{2}$ V

9. A generator produces alternating current electricity with a frequency of 40 cycles per second. What is the maximum potential difference created by the generator, if the rms voltage is 150 V?

A. 54 V   **B.** 91 V   **C.** 212 V   **D.** 141 V

10. Four identical capacitors are connected in parallel to a battery. If a total charge of Q flows from the battery, how much charge does each capacitor carry?

A. $Q/4$ **B.** Q **C.** $4Q$ **D.** $16Q$

11. Which statement is correct for two conductors that are joined by a long copper wire?

A. The electric field at the surface of each conductor is the same
B. Each conductor must be at the same potential
C. Each conductor must have the same resistivity
D. A free charge must be present on either conductor

12. Copper wire A has a length L and a radius r. Copper wire B has a length $2L$ and a radius $2r$. Which of the following is true regarding the resistances across the ends of the wires?

A. The resistance of wire A is one-half that of wire B
B. The resistance of wire A is four times higher than that of wire B
C. The resistance of wire A is twice as high as that of wire B
D. The resistance of wire A is equal to that of wire B

13. When a negative charge is free, it tries to move:

   A. toward infinity   **C.** from high potential to low potential

   B. away from infinity   **D.** from low potential to high potential

14. By what factor does the dielectric constant change when material is introduced between the plates of a parallel-plate capacitor if the capacitance increases by a factor of 4?

   A. ½   **B.** 4   **C.** 0.4   **D.** ¼

15. Two isolated copper plates, each of area 0.4 m², carry opposite charges of magnitude 6.8×10^{-10} C. They are placed opposite each other in parallel alignment. What is the potential difference between the plates when their spacing is 4 cm? (Use the dielectric constant $k = 1$ in air and the electric permittivity $\varepsilon_0 = 8.854 \times 10^{-12}$ F/m)

   A. 1.4 V   **B.** 4.1 V   **C.** 5.8 V   **D.** 7.7 V

16. Three capacitors are connected to a battery as shown. The capacitances are: $C_1 = 2C_2$ and $C_1 = 3C_3$. Which of the three capacitors stores the smallest amount of charge?

   A. C_1 **B.** C_2 **C.** C_3 **D.** The amount of charge is the same in all three capacitors

17. Two parallel plates that are initially uncharged are separated by 1.6 mm. What charge must be transferred from one plate to the other if 10 kJ of energy is to be stored in the plates? The area of each plate is 24 mm². (Use the dielectric constant $k = 1$ in air and the electric permittivity $\varepsilon_0 = 8.854 \times 10^{-12}$ F/m)

   A. 78 μC   **B.** 15 mC   **C.** 52 μC   **D.** 29 μC

18. When a proton is moving in the direction of the electric field, the potential energy of the system [   ] and it moves toward [   ] electric potential. (Use the dielectric constant $k = 1$ in air and the electric permittivity $\varepsilon_0 = 8.854 \times 10^{-12}$ F/m)

   A. increases ... increasing   **C.** increases ... decreasing

   B. decreases ... decreasing   **D.** decreases ... increasing

19. Each plate of a parallel-plate air capacitor has an area of 0.004 m², and the separation of the plates is 0.02 mm. An electric field of 8.6×10^6 V/m is present between the plates. What is the energy density between the plates? (Use the electric permittivity $\varepsilon_0 = 8.854 \times 10^{-12}$ F/m)

   A. 100 J/m³   **B.** 400 J/m³   **C.** 220 J/m³   **D.** 330 J/m³

20. Three capacitors are arranged as shown. C_1 has a capacitance of 9 pF, C_2 has a capacitance of 18 pF, and C_3 has a capacitance of 24 pF. What is the voltage drop across the entire system if the voltage drop across C_2 is 240 V?

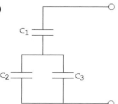

    A. 430 V   **B.** 870 V   **C.** 1,200 V   **D.** 1,350 V

21. Doubling the capacitance of a capacitor that is holding a constant charge causes the energy stored in that capacitor to:

    A. decrease to one-half   **C.** quadruple

    B. decrease to one-fourth   **D.** double

22. A charged parallel-plate capacitor has an electric field of 140 N/C between its plates. If a stationary proton is placed between the plates, what is its speed after 0.18 milliseconds? (Use the mass of a proton = 1.67×10^{-27} kg and the charge of a proton = 1.6×10^{-19} C)

    A. 3.7×10^1 m/s   **C.** 3.2×10^{-6} m/s

    B. 2.4×10^6 m/s   **D.** 3.2×10^{-8} m/s

23. In a parallel-plate capacitor, a positively-charged plate is on the left, and a negatively-charged plate is on the right. An electron is moving in between the plates to the right. Which statement is true?

    A. The PE of the electron decreases, and it moves to a region of higher potential

    B. The PE of the electron decreases, and it moves to a region of lower potential

    C. The PE of the electron increases, and it moves to a region of higher potential

    D. The PE of the electron increases, and it moves to a region of lower potential

24. If two identical storage batteries are connected in series ("+" to "−") and placed in a circuit, the combination provides:

    A. twice the voltage and the same current flows through each

    B. the same voltage and the same current flows through each

    C. zero volts and different currents flow through each

    D. the same voltage and different currents flow through each

25. An ideal parallel-plate capacitor consists of two parallel plates of area A separated by a distance d. This capacitor is connected across a battery that maintains a constant potential difference between the plates. What is the magnitude of the charge on the plates if the separation between the plates is doubled?

    A. reduced by half   **C.** doubled

    B. reduced by a fourth   **D.** quadrupled

26. Two parallel circular plates with radii 7 mm carrying equal-magnitude surface charge densities of ± 3 $\mu C/m^2$ are separated by a distance of 1 mm. How much stored energy do the plates have? (Use dielectric constant $k = 1$ and electric permittivity $\varepsilon_0 = 8.854 \times 10^{-12}$ F/m)

   A. 226 nJ   **B.** 17 nJ   **C.** 127 nJ   **D.** 78 nJ

27. The potential difference between the plates of a parallel plate capacitor is 75 V. The magnitude of the charge on each plate is 3.5 μC. What is the capacitance of the capacitor?

   A. 116×10^{-6} F   **C.** 0.7×10^{-6} F

   B. 37×10^{-6} F   **D.** 4.7×10^{-8} F

28. 1 mm separates two parallel plates. If the potential difference between them is 3 V, what is the magnitude of their surface charge densities? (Use the electric permittivity $\varepsilon_0 = 8.854 \times 10^{-12}$ F/m)

   A. 64×10^{-9} C/m^2 **C.** 27×10^{-9} C/m^2

   B. 33×10^{-9} C/m^2 **D.** 16×10^{-9} C/m^2

29. Each plate of a parallel-plate air capacitor has an area of 0.005 m^2, and the separation of the plates is 0.08 mm. What is the potential difference across the capacitor when an electric field of 5.6×10^6 V/m is present between the plates?

   A. 367 V   **B.** 578 V   **C.** 448 V   **D.** 227 V

30. When the frequency of the AC voltage across a capacitor is doubled, the capacitive reactance of that capacitor will:

   A. become zero   **C.** increase to 4 times its original value

   B. decrease to ½ its original value   **D.** decrease to ¼ its original value

DC and RC Circuits – Answer Key

1: C	11: B	21: A
2: D	12: C	22: B
3: B	13: D	23: D
4: B	14: B	24: A
5: A	15: D	25: A
6: B	16: D	26: D
7: D	17: C	27: D
8: D	18: B	28: C
9: C	19: D	29: C
10: A	20: D	30: B

Quantum Mechanics

1. The work function of a certain metal is 1.90 eV. What is the longest wavelength of light that can cause photoelectron emission from this metal?

A. 64 nm
B. 98 nm

C. 247 nm
D. 653 nm

2. Which of the following statements is correct if the frequency of the light in a laser beam is doubled while the number of photons per second in the beam is fixed?

    I. The power in the beam does not change
    II. The intensity of the beam doubles
    III. The energy of individual photons does not change

A. I only
B. II only

C. III only
D. I and II only

3. Upon being struck by 240 nm photons, a material ejects electrons with a maximum kinetic energy of 2.58 eV. What is the work function of this material?

A. 1.17 eV
B. 2.04 eV

C. 2.60 eV
D. 3.26 eV

4. A high energy photon collides with matter and creates an electron-positron pair. What is the minimum frequency of the photon? (Use the $m_{electron} = 9.11 \times 10^{-31}$ kg, $c = 3.00 \times 10^8$ m/s, and $h = 6.626 \times 10^{-34}$ J·s)

A. greater than 1.24×10^{12} Hz
B. greater than 2.47×10^{16} Hz

C. greater than 2.47×10^{20} Hz
D. greater than 2.47×10^{22} Hz

5. What is the longest wavelength of light that can cause photoelectron emission from a metal that has a work function of 2.20 eV?

A. 216 nm
B. 372 nm

C. 484 nm
D. 564 nm

6. In 1932, C. D. Anderson:

A. set the limits on the probability of measurement accuracy
B. predicted the positron from relativistic quantum mechanics
C. discovered the positron using a cloud chamber
D. was the first to produce diffraction patterns of electrons in crystals

7. What is the energy of an optical photon of frequency 6.43×10^{14} Hz (Use $h = 6.626 \times 10^{-34}$ J·s and 1 eV $= 1.60 \times 10^{-19}$ J)

    A. 1.04 eV   **B.** 1.86 eV   **C.** 2.66 eV   **D.** 3.43 eV

8. A photocathode has a work function of 2.4 eV. The photocathode is illuminated with monochromatic radiation whose photon energy is 3.4 eV. What is the maximum kinetic energy of the photoelectrons produced? (Use 1 eV $= 1.60 \times 10^{-19}$ J)

    A. 3.4×10^{-20} J   **B.** 1.6×10^{-19} J   **C.** 4.6×10^{-19} J   **D.** 5.8×10^{-19} J

9. A photocathode whose work function is 2.9 eV is illuminated with white light that has a continuous wavelength band from 400 nm to 700 nm. What is the range of the wavelength band in this white light illumination for which photoelectrons are NOT produced?

    A. 360 to 440 nm   **C.** 430 to 500 nm

    B. 400 to 480 nm   **D.** 430 to 700 nm

10. Photon A has twice the momentum of photon B as both travel in a vacuum. Which of the following statements about these photons is correct?

    A. Both photons have the same speed

    B. Both photons have the same wavelength

    C. Photon A is traveling twice as fast as photon B

    D. The energy of photon A is half as great as the energy of photon B

11. What is the energy of the photon emitted when an electron drops from the n = 20 state to the n = 7 state in a hydrogen atom?

    A. 0.244 eV   **B.** 0.288 eV   **C.** 0.336 eV   **D.** 0.404 eV

12. Protons are being accelerated in a particle accelerator. What is the de Broglie wavelength when the energy of the protons is doubled if the protons are non-relativistic (i.e., their kinetic energy is much less than mc^2)?

    A. increases by a factor of 2   **C.** decreases by a factor of 2

    B. increases by a factor of 3   **D.** decreases by a factor of $\sqrt{2}$

13. A certain photon, after being scattered from a free electron that was at rest, moves at an angle of 120° with respect to the incident direction. If the wavelength of the incident photon is 0.591 nm, what is the wavelength of the scattered photon? (Use $m_{electron} = 9.11 \times 10^{-31}$ kg, $c = 3.00 \times 10^8$ m/s and $h = 6.626 \times 10^{-34}$ J·s)

    A. 0.0 nm   **B.** 0.180 nm   **C.** 0.252 nm   **D.** 0.595 nm

14. Increasing the *brightness* of a beam of light without changing its color, increases the:

    A. speed of the photons

    B. frequency of the light

    C. number of photons per second traveling in the beam

    D. energy of each photon

15. What is the frequency of the light emitted by atomic Hydrogen according to the Balmer formula with $m = 4$ and $n = 9$?

    A. 820 Hz   **C.** 1,820 Hz

    B. 1.65×10^{14} Hz   **D.** 1,640 Hz

16. One of the emission lines described by the original version of the Balmer formula has wavelength 377 nm. What is the value of n in the Balmer formula that gives this emission line?

    A. 5   **B.** 7   **C.** 9   **D.** 11

17. What is the wavelength of the most intense light emitted by a giant star of surface temperature 5000 K? (Use the constant in Wien's law = 0.00290 m·K)

    A. 366 nm   **C.** 580 nm

    B. 448 nm   **D.** 490 nm

18. In 1928, Paul Dirac:

    A. set the limits on the probability of measurement accuracy

    B. developed a wave equation for matter waves

    C. suggested the existence of matter waves

    D. predicted the positron from relativistic quantum mechanics

19. A photocathode has a work function of 2.4 eV. The photocathode is illuminated with monochromatic radiation whose photon energy is 3.4 eV. What is the maximum kinetic energy of the photoelectrons produced?

    A. 0.9×10^{-19} J   **C.** 2.8×10^{-19} J

    B. 1.6×10^{-19} J   **D.** 4.2×10^{-19} J

20. In a Compton scattering experiment, which scattering angle produces the greatest change in wavelength?

    A. 0°   **C.** 90°

    B. 45°   **D.** 180°

21. A photocathode has a work function of 2.4 eV. The photocathode is illuminated with monochromatic radiation whose photon energy is 3.5 eV. What is the wavelength of the illuminating radiation?

A. 280 nm   **C.** 350 nm

B. 325 nm   **D.** 395 nm

22. If the wavelength of a photon is doubled, what happens to its energy?

A. It is reduced to one-half of its original value

B. It stays the same

C. It is doubled

D. It is increased to four times its original value

23. A photocathode has a work function of 2.8 eV. The photocathode is illuminated with monochromatic radiation. What is the threshold frequency for the monochromatic radiation required to produce photoelectrons?

A. 1.2×10^{14} Hz   **C.** 4.6×10^{14} Hz

B. 2.8×10^{14} Hz   **D.** 6.8×10^{14} Hz

24. If the de Broglie wavelength of an electron is 380 nm, what is the speed of this electron? (Use $m_{electron} = 9.11 \times 10^{-31}$ kg and $h = 6.626 \times 10^{-34}$ J·s)

A. 0.6 km/s   **C.** 3.4 km/s

B. 1.9 km/s   **D.** 4.6 km/s

25. What is the wavelength of the scattered photon if a photon of wavelength 1.50×10^{-10} m is scattered at an angle of 90° in the Compton effect?

A. 1.29×10^{-10} m   **C.** 1.84×10^{-10} m

B. 1.52×10^{-10} m   **D.** 2.42×10^{-10} m

26. When the surface of a metal is exposed to blue light, electrons are emitted. Which of the following increases if the intensity of the blue light increases?

     I. the maximum kinetic energy of the ejected electrons

     II. the number of electrons ejected per second

     III. the time lag between the onset of the absorption of light and the ejection of electrons

A. I only   **C.** III only

B. II only   **D.** I and II only

27. A proton has a speed of 7.2×10^4 m/s. What is the energy of a photon that has the same wavelength as the de Broglie wavelength of this proton? (Use $m_{\text{proton}} = 1.67 \times 10^{-27}$ kg and $c = 3.00 \times 10^8$ m/s)

    A. 80 keV   **C.** 160 keV

    B. 120 keV   **D.** 230 keV

28. In the Compton effect, as the scattering angle increases monotonically from 0° to 180°, the frequency of the X-rays scattered at that angle:

    A. decreases by the $\sqrt{2}$ **C.** increases by the $\sqrt{2}$

    B. decreases monotonically   **D.** increases monotonically

29. In the spectrum of Hydrogen, the lines obtained by setting m = 1 in the Rydberg formula is referred to as the Lyman series. What is the wavelength of the spectral line of the 15th member of the Lyman series?

    A. 91.6 nm   **C.** 244.6 nm

    B. 126.2 nm   **D.** 368.2 nm

30. If the frequency of the light in a laser beam is doubled while the number of photons per second in the beam is fixed, which of the following statements is correct?

    I. The energy of individual photons doubles

    II. The wavelength of the individual photons doubles

    III. The intensity of the beam doubles

    A. I only   **C.** III only

    B. II only   **D.** I and III only

31. The spacing of the surface planes of a crystal is 159.0 pm. A beam directed normally at the surface of the crystal undergoes first order diffraction at an angle of 58° from the normal. What is the energy of the neutrons if the diffraction is done with a beam of monenergistic neutrons? (Use 1.67×10^{-27} kg for the mass of a neutron)

    A. 0.0155 eV   **C.** 0.0909 eV

    B. 0.0106 eV   **D.** 0.1450 eV

32. A photocathode whose work function is 2.5 eV is illuminated with white light that has a continuous wavelength band from 360 nm to 700 nm. What is the stopping potential for this white light illumination?

    A. 0.95 V   **C.** 1.90 V

    B. 1.45 V   **D.** 2.6 V

33. If the momentum of an electron is 1.95×10^{-27} kg·m/s, what is its de Broglie wavelength? (Use $h = 6.626 \times 10^{-34}$ J·s)

A. 86.2 nm

B. 130.6 nm

C. 240.8 nm

D. 340.0 nm

34. A Hydrogen atom is excited to the n = 9 level. Its decay to the n = 6 level is detected on a photographic plate. What is the frequency of the light photographed?

A. 3,810 Hz

B. 7,240 Hz

C. 5.08×10^{13} Hz

D. 3.28×10^{-9} Hz

35. How much energy is carried by a photon of light having frequency 110 GHz? (Use $h = 6.626 \times 10^{-34}$ J·s)

A. 7.3×10^{-23} J

B. 2.9×10^{-25} J

C. 1.7×10^{-26} J

D. 1.1×10^{-21} J

36. How many of the infinite number of Balmer spectrum lines are in the visible spectrum range?

A. 0

B. 2

C. 4

D. 6

37. Each photon in a beam of light has an energy of 4.20 eV. What is the wavelength of this light? ($c = 3.00 \times 10^8$ m/s, $h = 6.626 \times 10^{-34}$ J·s and 1 eV = 1.60×10^{-19} J)

A. 118.0 nm

B. 296.0 nm

C. 365.0 nm

D. 462.0 nm

38. Electrons are emitted from a surface when a light of wavelength 500.0 nm is shone on the surface, but electrons are not emitted for longer wavelengths of light. What is the work function of the surface?

A. 0.5 eV

B. 1.6 eV

C. 2.5 eV

D. 3.8 eV

39. In the Bohr theory, the orbital radius depends upon the principal quantum number in what way?

A. n

B. 1/n

C. n^2

D. n^3

40. The uncertainty in the position of a proton is 0.053 nm. What is the minimum uncertainty in its speed? (Use 1.67×10^{-27} kg as the proton mass)

A. 0.6×10^3 m/s

B. 1.2×10^3 m/s

C. 2.4×10^3 m/s

D. 3.6×10^3 m/s

41. What is the wavelength of the light emitted by atomic Hydrogen according to the Balmer formula with m = 9 and n = 11?

   A. 8,500 nm   **C.** 22,300 nm
   B. 14,700 nm   **D.** 31,900 nm

42. A certain particle's energy is known within 10^{-18} J. What is the minimum uncertainty in its arrival time at a detector?

   A. 5.08×10^{-12} s   **B.** 4.25×10^{-13} s   **C.** 3.88×10^{-14} s   **D.** 1.05×10^{-16} s

43. Upon being struck by 240.0 nm photons, a material ejects electrons with a maximum kinetic energy of 2.58 eV. What is the work function of this material?

   A. 1.20 eV   **B.** 2.82 eV   **C.** 2.60 eV   **D.** 3.46 eV

44. What is the de Broglie wavelength of a 1.30 kg missile moving at 28.10 m/s. (Use $h = 6.626 \times 10^{-34}$ J·s)

   A. 1.85×10^{-37} m   **C.** 1.81×10^{-35} m
   B. 2.40×10^{-36} m   **D.** 3.37×10^{-35} m

45. A beam of light falling on a metal surface is causing electrons to be ejected from the surface. If the frequency of the light now doubles, which of the following statements is always true?

   A. The number of electrons ejected per second doubles
   B. Twice as many photons hit the metal surface as before
   C. The kinetic energy of the ejected electrons doubles
   D. None of the above statements is always true

46. What is the longest wavelength of a photon that can be emitted by a hydrogen atom, for which the initial state is n = 3?

   A. 486 nm   **C.** 540 nm
   B. 510 nm   **D.** 656 nm

47. Which of the following always increases if the brightness of a beam of light is increased without changing its color?

     I. the speed of the photons
     II. the average energy of each photon
     III. the number of photons

   A. I only   **B.** II only   **C.** III only   **D.** I and II only

48. In a particular case of Compton scattering, a photon collides with a free electron and scatters backward. The wavelength after the collision is exactly double the wavelength before the collision. What is the wavelength of the incident photon? (Use $m_{electron} = 9.11 \times 10^{-31}$ kg, $c = 3.00 \times 10^8$ m/s and $h = 6.626 \times 10^{-34}$ J·s)

A. 3.4×10^{-12} m   **C.** 5.6×10^{-12} m

B. 4.8×10^{-12} m   **D.** 6.8×10^{-12} m

49. Two sources emit beams of microwaves. The microwaves from source A have a frequency of 15 GHz, and the microwaves from source B have a frequency of 30 GHz. This is all the information available for the two beams. Which of the following statements about these microwave beams must be correct?

A. The intensity of beam B is twice as great as the intensity of beam A

B. A photon in beam B has the same energy as a photon in beam A

C. Beam B carries twice as many photons per second as beam A

D. A photon in beam B has twice the energy of a photon in beam A

50. What is the shortest wavelength of a photon that can be emitted by a hydrogen atom, for which the initial state is n = 3?

A. 102.6 nm   **B.** 97.3 nm   **C.** 820.0 nm   **D.** 121.6 nm

51. The radius of a typical nucleus is about 5.0×10^{-15} m. Assuming this to be the uncertainty in the position of a proton in the nucleus, what is the uncertainty in the proton's energy? (Use 1.67×10^{-27} kg as the proton mass)

A. 0.06 MeV   **C.** 0.4 MeV

B. 0.25 MeV   **D.** 0.8 MeV

52. A photocathode has a work function of 2.4 eV. The photocathode is illuminated with monochromatic radiation and electrons are emitted with a stopping potential of 1.1 volt. What is the wavelength of the illuminating radiation? (Use $c = 3.00 \times 10^8$ m/s, $h = 6.626 \times 10^{-34}$ J·s and 1 eV = 1.60×10^{-19} J)

A. 300 nm   **B.** 350 nm   **C.** 390 nm   **D.** 420 nm

53. The Compton effect directly demonstrated which property of electromagnetic radiation?

     I. energy content
     II. particle nature
     III. momenta

A. I only   **B.** II only   **C.** I and II only   **D.** II and III only

54. What is the wavelength of the matter wave associated with an electron moving with a speed of 2.5×10^7 m/s? (Use $m_{electron} = 9.11 \times 10^{-31}$ kg and $h = 6.626 \times 10^{-34}$ J·s)

A. 17 pm	**C.** 39 pm
B. 29 pm	**D.** 51 pm

55. A laser produces a beam of 4000 nm light. A shutter allows a pulse of light, for 30.0 ps, to pass. What is the uncertainty in the energy of a photon in the pulse? ($h = 6.626 \times 10^{-34}$ J·s and 1 eV $= 1.60 \times 10^{-19}$ J)

A. 2.6×10^{-2} eV	**C.** 6.8×10^{-4} eV
B. 4.2×10^{-3} eV	**D.** 2.2×10^{-5} eV

Quantum Mechanics – Answer Key

1: D	11: A	21: C	31: B	41: C	51: D
2: B	12: D	22: A	32: A	42: D	52: B
3: C	13: D	23: D	33: D	43: C	53: B
4: C	14: C	24: B	34: C	44: C	54: B
5: D	15: B	25: B	35: A	45: D	55: D
6: C	16: D	26: B	36: C	46: D	
7: C	17: C	27: D	37: B	47: C	
8: B	18: D	28: B	38: C	48: B	
9: D	19: B	29: A	39: C	49: D	
10: A	20: D	30: D	40: B	50: A	

Diagnostic Tests

Explanations

Diagnostic Test #1 – Explanations

1. C is correct. Heat transfer between two materials occurs until both materials reach the same temperature, so the colder material gains the amount of heat lost by the hotter material.

2. A is correct.

$$F_B = V\rho g$$

where F_B = buoyant force upward, V = volume of fluid that the object displaces, ρ = density of the fluid, g = acceleration due to gravity

The lead weight starts in the air above the water so at its origin it is experiencing zero buoyant force from the water.

As the weight breaks the surface of the water and sinks, the buoyant force increases until the weight is fully submerged, after which the force remains constant since the density of water is uniform.

3. D is correct. Calculate the focal length:

$$1/f = 1/d_i + 1/d_o$$

where f is focal length d_o is the distance to the object and d_i is the distance to the image

$$1/f = 1/2 \text{ m} + 1/4 \text{ m}$$

$$1/f = 2/4 \text{ m} + 1/4 \text{ m}$$

$$1/f = 3/4 \text{ m}$$

$$f = 4/3 \text{ m}$$

4. B is correct. $\quad {}^A_Z n + e^- \rightarrow {}^A_{Z-1}(n-1) + v_e$

A proton captures an electron and transforms it into a neutron. Therefore, the atomic number Z decreases by 1 because the nucleus contains one less proton.

The $(n-1)$ signifies the new element name (since the atomic number changed), and v_e is the release of an electron neutrino.

5. A is correct.

A moving charge experiences a magnetic force from a magnetic field, but the force is perpendicular to the velocity (as well as the magnetic field), so the speed does not change.

$$F_B = qvB \sin \theta$$

F_B is perpendicular to both v and B

6. C is correct.

When a copper wire joins two conductors they must have the same potential because the wire allows for a charge to flow. Any potential difference is neutralized by charge flow.

7. B is correct.

Enthalpy of fusion

As a solid undergoes a phase change, the temperature will always stay constant until the phase change is complete.

To calculate the amount of heat absorbed to completely melt the solid, multiply the heat of fusion by the mass undergoing the phase change.

Heat needed to melt a solid:

$$q = m\Delta H_f$$

8. B is correct.

The expression for mechanical stress:

$$\sigma = F / A$$

Stress is simply the load per unit area (force per cross-sectional area).

9. C is correct.

Snell's Law:

$$n_g / n_w = (\sin \phi) / (\sin \theta)$$

Find the index of refraction for glass:

$$n_g / 1.33 = (\sin 61°) / (\sin 48°)$$

$$n_g / 1.33 = (0.875) / (0.743)$$

$$n_g / 1.33 = 1.18$$

$$n_g = (1.18){\cdot}(1.33)$$

$$n_g = 1.57$$

Solve for the new angle of refraction after the angle of incidence has changed:

$$1.57 / 1.33 = (\sin \phi) / (\sin 25°)$$

$$1.18 = (\sin \phi) / (0.423)$$

$$(1.18){\cdot}(0.423) = \sin \phi$$

$$\sin \phi = 0.5$$

$$\phi = 30°$$

10. A is correct.

Gamma radiation is high energy electromagnetic rays and not particles. As such its notation contains zero in the subscript and zero in the superscript.

11. C is correct.

Perpendicular magnetic and electric fields are required for a mass spectrometer.

12. D is correct.

$$C = 1 / (2\pi R f)$$
$$C = 1 / (2\pi \times 4{,}000 \ \Omega \times 600 \ \text{Hz})$$
$$C = 6.6 \times 10^{-8} \ \text{F}$$

Because the answers are in the micro-Faradays, divide by 10^{-6} to find proper units (μFaradays)

$$C = 6.6 \times 10^{-8} \ \text{F} / (10^{-6})$$
$$C = 0.066 \ \mu\text{F}$$

13. D is correct.

$$\text{KE}_{avg} = (3/2)kT$$
$$\text{KE}_{avg} = (3/2) \cdot (1.38 \times 10^{-23} \ \text{J/K}) \cdot (740 \ \text{K})$$
$$\text{KE}_{avg} = 1.5 \times 10^{-20} \ \text{J}$$

14. A is correct.

$$\text{mass} = \text{density} \times \text{volume}$$
$$m = \rho V$$
$$m = (1 \times 10^{18} \ \text{kg/m}^3) \cdot (1.76 \times 10^{-6} \ \text{m})^3$$
$$m = 5.45 \ \text{kg} \approx 5.5 \ \text{kg}$$

15. A is correct.

When an atom absorbs energy their valence electrons move to higher "orbits." As the electrons fall back to their original (ground state), they emit the absorbed energy as light.

16. A is correct.

Sievert (Sv) is the standard SI unit that measures a low radiation dose and is equivalent to the biological effect of one joule of x-rays per kilogram of recipient mass. The average person receives about 0.002-0.003 Sieverts per year from naturally occurring radiation in the environment.

17. D is correct.

None of the choices are correct for the differences between a conductor and an insulator.

18. D is correct.

If one mass is halved, then the gravitational attraction between them is halved.

For equilibrium, the electrostatic repulsion must also be halved.

$F_e = F_g$

$F_e = kQ_1Q_2 \, / \, r^2$

$F_g = Gm_1m_2 \, / \, r^2$

$kQ_1Q_2 \, / \, r^2 = Gm_1m_2 \, / \, r^2$

$kQ_1Q_2 = Gm_1m_2$, k and G are constants and cannot be manipulated.

If the mass of object 1 is halved, while equilibrium is maintained:

$G(m_1 \, / \, 2)m_2 = (Gm_1m_2) \, / \, 2$

If the electrostatic force is halved, the charge of one of the objects must be halved:

$(kQ_1Q_2) \, / \, 2 = kQ_1(Q_2 \, / \, 2)$

19. D is correct.

For materials with a positive coefficient of thermal expansion, a hole drilled in the material expands as temperature increases. Regardless of the surrounding metal's expansion, the hole's diameter always increases with higher temperature.

20. C is correct.

Young's Modulus is expressed as:

$E = \sigma$ (stress) $/ \, \varepsilon$ (strain)

$E = (F \, / \, A) \, / \, (\Delta L \, / \, L)$

$E = (FL) \, / \, (\Delta LA)$

Solve for E:

$E = (8.8 \text{ kg}) \cdot (9.8 \text{ m/s}^2) \cdot (4.4 \text{ m}) \, / \, (0.0033 \text{ m}) \cdot (\pi \, / \, 4) \cdot (0.0016 \text{ m})^2$

$E = 5.7 \times 10^{10} \text{ N/m}^2$

21. A is correct. Car mirrors are convex because they offer a wider field of view than plane mirrors.

Convex mirrors compress images to create this wider field of view. Thus, the image on the mirror looks smaller than what a plane mirror would show. Because of this, the objects in a car mirror are closer than what the small image would lead the viewer to believe.

22. D is correct.

An alpha particle is composed of two neutrons and two protons and can be represented by a helium nucleus:

$$^4_2\text{He}$$

23. D is correct.

A: it is possible to convert work entirely into heat, but heat cannot be converted entirely into work.

B: heat can be transferred from a cooler body to a hotter body (e.g., refrigeration), but the process is not spontaneous and requires work.

C: the second law of thermodynamics is not a consequence of the first law and goes beyond the limitations imposed by the first law.

24. A is correct.

Volume flow rate (Q) is how much water is flowing per second.

Find the cross-sectional area of the pipe and multiply the area with the velocity of the water.

$$Q = \text{A}_{\text{pipe}}v$$
$$Q = \pi(0.03 \text{ m})^2 \times (4 \text{ m/s})$$
$$Q = 0.0113 \text{ m}^3/\text{s}$$
$$Q = 1.1 \times 10^{-2} \text{ m}^3/\text{s}$$

25. B is correct. The power of the combination is:

$P = P_1 + P_2$

Since power is the reciprocal of the focal length (in meters),

$$f_1 = 10 \text{ cm} = 1 / 10 \text{ m}$$
$$P_1 = 1 / f_1$$
$$P_1 = 1 / (1 / 10 \text{ m})$$
$$P_1 = 10 \text{ D}$$
$$f_2 = 20 \text{ cm} = 1 / 5 \text{ m}$$
$$P_2 = 1 / f_2$$
$$P_2 = 1 / (1 / 5 \text{ m})$$
$$P_2 = 5 \text{ D}$$
$$P = P_1 + P_2$$
$$P = 10 \text{ D} + 5 \text{ D} = 15 \text{ D}$$

26. B is correct.

$_0^0\gamma$ is a gamma particle, so the atomic mass and atomic number do not change.

Alpha decay: during alpha decay, the parent nuclide sheds two protons and two neutrons which is identical to the nucleus of ^{4}He.

$$_Z^A X \rightarrow {_{Z-2}^{A-4}}Y + {_2^4}\alpha$$

Beta Decay (minus): during beta minus decay, the parent nuclide sheds an electron and electron antineutrino. However, in the process, a neutron converts to a proton, so the mass number remains the same but the atomic number increases by 1.

$$_Z^A X \rightarrow {_{Z+1}^A}Y + {_{-1}^0}e^- + {_0^0}v_e$$

Beta Decay (plus): during beta plus decay, the parent nuclide sheds a positron and neutrino. However, in the process, a proton converts to a neutron, so the mass number remains the same, but the atomic number decreases by 1.

$$_Z^A X \rightarrow {_{Z-1}^A}Y + {_{+1}^0}e^+ + {_0^0}v_e$$

27. D is correct.

$$E = F\,/\,q$$

$$F = Eq_{proton}$$

$$F = (4 \times 10^4 \text{ N/C}) \cdot (1.6 \times 10^{-19} \text{ C})$$

$$F = 6.4 \times 10^{-15} \text{ N}$$

28. A is correct.

Capacitance:

$$C = Q\,/\,V$$

$$Q = CV$$

$$V = IR$$

$$Q = C \times (IR)$$

$$Q = (12 \times 10^{-6} \text{ F}) \cdot (33 \times 10^{-6} \text{ A}) \cdot (8.5 \times 10^6 \text{ } \Omega)$$

$$Q = 0.0034 \text{ C}$$

Divide by 10^{-6} to determine micro-coulombs:

$$Q = (0.0034 \text{ C})\,/\,10^{-6}$$

$$Q = 3,400 \text{ } \mu\text{C}$$

29. D is correct.

$Q = mc\Delta T$, where ΔT is constant

If $m = 4$ times increase and $c = 3$ times increase

$Q = (4){\cdot}(3)\Delta T$

$Q = (12)\Delta T$

$Q_1 / 12 = \Delta T$

30. B is correct.

Output pressure (P_2) = input pressure (P_1)

$P_2 = P_1$

$(F_2 / A_2) = (F_1 / A_1)$

$F_1 = (A_1 / A_2)F_2$

$F_1 = [\pi(3 \text{ cm})^2 / \pi(12.5 \text{ cm})^2]{\cdot}(12{,}000 \text{ N})$

$F_1 = (9 \text{ cm} / 156.25 \text{ cm}){\cdot}(12{,}000 \text{ N})$

$F_1 = 691 \text{ N}$

31. C is correct.

The plane mirror is double the distance from an object, so $\tfrac{1}{2}h$ is required for the minimum length.

Law of reflection: $\theta_1 = \theta_2$

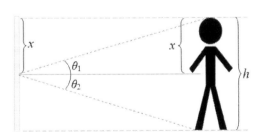

$h = 2x$

$x = \tfrac{1}{2}h$

32. C is correct.

Fission occurs when an atom with a larger atomic number is struck by a free neutron and splits.

For example:

$$^{235}_{92}U + ^{1}_{0}n \rightarrow ^{92}_{36}Kr + ^{141}_{56}Ba + 3^{1}_{0}n$$

33. B is correct.

The Carnot cycle is an idealized thermodynamic cycle consisting of two isothermal processes and two adiabatic processes. It is the most efficient heat engine operating between two temperatures.

34. B is correct.

The nucleus of an atom consists of protons and neutrons held together by the strong nuclear force. This force counteracts the electrostatic force of repulsion between the protons in the nucleus.

The gravitational and weak nuclear forces are negligible when discussing the nucleus and the force acting within it.

35. A is correct.

Conduction occurs through microscopic diffusion and collision of particles with a material. It transfers energy from molecule to molecule through their collision. Example: a spoon that gets warmer from being submerged into a cup of hot coffee.

Convection is the concerted, collective movement of groups of molecules within fluids (e.g., liquids and gases). It does not occur in solids because neither bulk current flows nor significant diffusion can occur. Example: heat leaves a hot cup of coffee as the current of steam and air rise.

36. B is correct.

Buoyancy force:

$$F_B = \rho gh\text{A}$$

$$F_B = \rho g\text{V}$$

Because the cube is lowered at a constant rate the volume of the cube underwater increases linearly and thus the F_B increases linearly.

After the cube is submerged, F_B stays constant because the volume of displaced water is constant.

Thus, a linearly increasing line then steady flat slope of zero describes the buoyant force vs. time graph.

37. C is correct.

$d = 130$ m

$f = 3.6$ MHz

$\theta = ?$

velocity = frequency × wavelength

$\lambda = c / f$

$\lambda = (3 \times 10^8 \text{ m/s}) / (3.6 \times 10^6 \text{ Hz})$

$\lambda = 83.3$ m

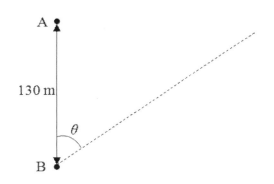

The condition for constructive interference is:

$m\lambda = d \cos \theta$

or

$\cos \theta = m\lambda / d$

The value of cosine gets closer to 1.0 as the angle gets *smaller*. Thus, to find the smallest angle, find the largest possible value of cos θ, as long as the value does not exceed 1.0.

With $m = 1$:

$\theta = \cos^{-1}(83.3 \text{ m} / 130 \text{ m})$

$\theta = \cos^{-1}(0.641)$

$\theta = 50°$

With $m = 2$:

$\theta = \cos^{-1}(2 \times 83.3 \text{ m} / 130 \text{ m})$

$\theta = \cos^{-1}(1.281)$, which has no solution.

Therefore, the smallest angle for which constructive interference occurs is 50°.

38. A is correct.

The magnetic quantum number is an interval from $-\ell$ to $+\ell$ (includes zero and an allowable value). The total amount of magnetic quantum numbers possible is:

$2(\ell) + 1$

For example:

$\ell = 2$

$m_\ell = -2, -1, 0, 1, 2$

$m_{\ell \text{ total possible}} = 2(2) + 1 = 5$

In the range from $-\ell$ to $+\ell$, there are 5 possible magnetic quantum numbers.

Verification through the equation:

$m_{\ell \text{ tot possible}} = 2(\ell) + 1$

---

39. A is correct. Charged objects always interact with other charged objects.

If electric charge is conserved, by definition charge cannot be created or destroyed.

Electrons and protons are the fundamental particles that carry a charge.

Therefore, the charge of an object is a whole-number multiple of an electron ($Q = ne^-$).

The electric charge of an object can be infinitely large, so there are infinite whole-number multiples of an electron's charge.

Because the charge is a whole-number multiple of an electron's charge, it cannot have a value that is not a whole-number multiple, and therefore it occurs in restricted quantities.

40. D is correct.

$$P = IV$$

$$P = (2 \text{ A}){\cdot}(120 \text{ V})$$

$$P = 240 \text{ W}$$

41. D is correct.

2 (10 cm aluminum rods) + 5 (8 cm steel rods) = 20 cm + 40 cm = 60 cm

$\Delta L = L\alpha\Delta T$, where α is the coefficient of linear expansion

$$\Delta L_{alum} = (20 \text{ cm}){\cdot}(2.4 \times 10^{-5} \text{ K}^{-1}){\cdot}(80 \text{ °C} - 5 \text{ °C})$$

$$\Delta L_{alum} = 3.6 \times 10^{-2} \text{ cm} = 0.36 \text{ mm}$$

$$\Delta L_{steel} = (40 \text{ cm}){\cdot}(1.2 \times 10^{-5} \text{ K}^{-1}){\cdot}(80 \text{ °C} - 5 \text{ °C})$$

$$\Delta L_{steel} = 3.6 \times 10^{-2} \text{ cm} = 0.36 \text{ mm}$$

The change in length of the composite rod is the sum of these: 0.72 mm

42. C is correct.

The pressure in the hose depends on the height of the water above it and the pressure in the atmosphere. So, the pressure in the hose is given by:

$$P = \rho gh + P_{atm}$$

where h = height of water

The 12 m water tank is 25 m above the ground, so $h = 37$ m

So, the water pressure in the hose is:

$$P = (1{,}000 \text{ kg/m}^3){\cdot}(9.8 \text{ m/s}^2){\cdot}(37 \text{ m}) + 101{,}325 \text{ N/m}^2$$

$$P = 362{,}600 \text{ N/m}^2 + 101{,}325 \text{ N/m}^2$$

$$P = 4.6 \times 10^5 \text{ N/m}^2$$

43. A is correct. Optical density is related to the index of refraction of material and describes how electromagnetic waves travel in a medium.

The optical density of a material is not related to its mass (physical) density.

44. B is correct.

Beta radiation is more powerful than alpha radiation but less powerful than gamma rays.

Beta radiation can penetrate the skin, paper or even a light layer of clothing.

45. C is correct.

The process whereby heat flows by the mass movement of molecules from one place to another is known as convection.

Convection is the concerted, collective movement of groups of molecules within fluids (e.g., liquids and gases). It does not occur in solids because neither bulk current flows nor significant diffusion can occur. Example: heat leaves a hot cup of coffee as the current of steam and air rise.

Radiation is a form of heat transfer in which electromagnetic waves carry energy from the emitting object and deposit the energy to the object that absorbs the radiation.

Conduction occurs through microscopic diffusion and collision of particles with a material. It transfers energy from molecule to molecule through their collision. Example: a spoon that gets warmer from being submerged into a cup of hot coffee.

46. C is correct.

$$P = IV$$

$$I = P / V$$

$$I = (1 \times 10^{-3} \text{ W}) / (9 \text{ V})$$

$$P = 0.00011 \text{ A} = 0.11 \text{ mA}$$

47. D is correct.

Diverging mirrors (i.e., convex mirrors) are curved outward toward the light source and therefore have a focal point *behind* the mirror, so the focal length f is a negative value.

Using the equation for focal length:

$$1 / f = 1 / d_o + 1 / d_i$$

where d_o is the distance to the light source, and d_i is the distance to the image.

$$-1 / 6 \text{ m} = 1 / 12 \text{ m} + 1 / d_i$$

$$1 / d_i = -1 / 4 \text{ m}$$

$$d_i = -4 \text{ m}$$

48. D is correct.

In the photoelectric effect, photons from a light source are absorbed by electrons on a metal surface and cause them to be ejected. The energy of the ejected electrons is only dependent upon photon frequency and is found by:

$$KE = hf - \phi$$

where h = Planck's constant, f = frequency and ϕ = stopping potential

Increasing the intensity of the light only increases the number of photons incident upon the metal and thus the number of ejected electrons, but their KE does not change.

49. D is correct.

Series: R_1 R_2 R_3 $R_{tot} = R_1 + R_2 + R_3$

Parallel: R_1 R_2 R_3 $1 / R_{tot} = 1 / R_1 + 1 / R_2 + 1 / R_3$

50. A is correct.

The velocity of light in a medium is:

$$v = c / n$$

where c is the speed of light in a vacuum and n is the refractive index.

Thus, light travels slower in glass because its refraction index is higher than that of air.

Diagnostic Test #2 – Explanations

1. D is correct.

The rate of heat transfer:

$$Q/t = kA\Delta T/d$$

where k is the thermal conductivity of the wall material, A is the surface area of the wall, d is the wall's thickness, and ΔT is the temperature difference on either side.

Therefore, if thickness d is doubled, the rate is halved.

2. C is correct.

Hydrostatic equilibrium:

$$P_{bottom} = P_{atm} + \rho g(h_3 - h_1)$$

Absolute pressure:

$$P = P_{atm} + \rho g(h_3 - h_1)$$

Gauge pressure:

$$P = \rho g(h_3 - h_1)$$

3. C is correct.

Ultraviolet radiation has the highest frequency among the choices.

Energy is related to frequency by:

$$E = hf$$

Thus, ultraviolet light has the most energy per photon because it has the highest frequency which is directly proportional to energy.

4. A is correct.

This is an example of a β^- decay.

A neutron converts to a proton and an electron (e^-) along with an electron neutrino (v_e).

5. D is correct.

The Earth's magnetic field is thought to be created by circulating electric currents in the Earth's mantle (liquid portion). These charges move slowly due to the convection currents in the mantle and create the magnetic field through a large number of charges present.

6. B is correct. Voltage results in a current but not vice versa.

Voltage is a potential difference across a circuit but does not flow through it.

7. A is correct.

$$Q = c_p m \Delta T$$

$$c_{p1} m_w \Delta T = c_{p2} m \Delta T$$

$$c_{p2} = (c_{p1} m_w \Delta T_w) / (m_2 \Delta T_2)$$

$$c_{p2} = (1 \text{ kcal/kg·°C}) \cdot (0.2 \text{ kg}) \cdot (40 \text{ °C}) / (0.06 \text{ kg}) \cdot (60 \text{ °C})$$

$$c_{p2} = 2.2 \text{ kcal/kg·°C}$$

8. A is correct.

Pressure is given as:

$$P = F / A$$

$$F = PA$$

As the tire leaks, the pressure decreases resulting in an increase in surface area with the road.

The force remains constant if pressure decreases and area increases at a constant rate.

9. B is correct.

A blue object illuminated with yellow light appears black because it absorbs the yellow light and reflects none.

10. C is correct.

$$^{A}_{Z}X \rightarrow \, ^{A-4}_{Z-2}Y + \, ^{4}_{2}\alpha$$

Alpha decay: the parent nuclide ejects two protons and two neutrons as $^{4}_{2}$He (essentially a helium nucleus). The daughter nucleus has an atomic number of two less than the parent nucleus and an atomic weight of four less than the parent nucleus.

11. B is correct.

Magnetic moment of a circular loop:

$$\mu = IA$$

$$A = (\pi r^2)$$

$$\mu = I(\pi r^2)$$

If r is doubled:

$$\mu = I\pi(2r)^2$$

$$\mu = I\pi(4r^2)$$

The magnetic moment increases by a factor of 4.

12. B is correct.

Polarity switches twice per wavelength. There are 60 λ per second.

$2 \times f = \#$ polarity switches

$2 \times 60 = 120$ times/s

13. A is correct.

From the Second Law of Thermodynamics: it is not possible to extract heat from a hot reservoir and convert it all into useful work.

The maximum efficiency is that of a Carnot cycle given as:

$\eta = (Q_H - Q_C) / Q_H$

14. D is correct.

gauge pressure $= \rho g h$

gauge pressure $= (1,000 \text{ kg/m}^3) \cdot (10 \text{ m/s}^2) \cdot (110 \text{ m})$

gauge pressure $= 1.1 \times 10^6$ Pa

15. A is correct.

A simple compound microscope normally uses a short focal length objective and a long focal length eyepiece.

16. B is correct. De Broglie equation:

$\lambda = h / mv$

If velocity increases, then λ decreases because they are inversely proportional.

17. B is correct.

Before the switch is closed, there is no current and no magnetic field in either solenoid. After the switch is closed, current in the first solenoid begins to flow from positive to negative, and a magnetic field is created pointing to the right (according to the solenoid right-hand rule).

According to Lenz's Law, an EMF is induced in the second solenoid to oppose the change in magnetic flux. Since the field from the first solenoid points to the right, the induced current in the second solenoid must induce a current pointing to the left to oppose it.

By the right-hand solenoid rule, the current in the galvanometer must flow from right to left to create a temporary magnetic field in the direction opposite to the original field.

18. A is correct.

An electric current measures the amount of charge passing a point in the circuit per unit of time. In a flow of water, the analogous parameter is the volume (i.e., amount) of water passing a point per unit of time (i.e., volume flow rate).

By analogy, the current is the same for resistors in series, and the volume flow rate is constant (absent any branching) along a flow, which is not true of flow velocity.

19. C is correct.

$\Delta E = E_2 - E_1$

$\Delta E = 110 \text{ J} - 40 \text{ J}$

$\Delta E = 70 \text{ J}$

20. D is correct. The flow rate must be equal in both parts of the pipe:

$A_1 v_1 = A_2 v_2$

$(\pi / 4)D_1^2 v_1 = (\pi / 4)D_2^2 v_2$, cancel $(\pi / 4)$ from both sides of the expression

$D_1^2 v_1 = D_2^2 v_2$

$v_2 = (D_1^2 v_1) / D_2^2$

$v_2 = [(0.2 \text{ m})^2 / (0.004 \text{ m})^2] \cdot (0.03 \text{ m/s})$

$v_2 = (2{,}500) \cdot (0.03 \text{ m/s})$

$v_2 = 75 \text{ m/s}$

21. D is correct. A plane mirror has a magnification of m = 1.

$m = -d_i / d_o$

$m = h_i / h_o$

$1 = -d_i / d_o$

$1 = h_i / h_o$

$-d_i = d_o$

$h_i = h_o$

The negative image distance indicates that the image is virtual and the positive image height indicates that the image is erect.

22. B is correct. Beta (β^-) decay: the parent nuclide ejects an electron and electron antineutrino. However, in the process, a neutron converts to a proton, so the mass number remains the same but the atomic number increases by 1.

$$_Z^A X \rightarrow _{Z+1}^{A} Y + _{-1}^{0} e^- + _0^0 v_e$$

23. B is correct.

Boltzmann's constant (k) relates energy at the individual particle level to temperature. $k =$ gas constant (R) divided by Avogadro's constant (N_A).

$$k_B = R / N_A$$

where $k_B = 1.381 \times 10^{-23}$ J/K

Boltzmann's constant has the same dimensions as entropy (energy / temperature).

24. A is correct.

The buoyant force is given by:

$$F_B = \rho V g$$

ρ = density of fluid, V = volume of fluid displaced, g = acceleration due to gravity

To calculate how much the brick *appears* to weigh, subtract the buoyant force from the force due to gravity, where m is the *actual* mass of the brick:

$$F_{apparent} = F_{gravity} - F_{buoyant}$$

$$F_{apparent} = mg - \rho V g$$

The *actual* mass of the brick can be calculated as density × volume

$$V_{brick} = (2 \text{ in} \times 4 \text{ in} \times 6 \text{ in})$$

$$V_{brick} = 48 \text{ in}^3$$

$$V_{brick} = (48 \text{ in}^3) \cdot (16.4 \text{ cm}^3/1 \text{ in}^3)$$

$$V_{brick} = 787 \text{ cm}^3$$

$$\text{mass} = \text{density} \times \text{volume}$$

$$m = (11.4 \text{ g/cm}^3) \cdot (787 \text{ cm}^3)$$

$$m = 8{,}972 \text{ g}$$

To get the apparent *mass*, divide the apparent force by g:

$$m_{apparent} = F_{apparent} / g$$

$$m_{apparent} = (m_{brick}g - \rho V g) / g$$

$$m_{apparent} = m_{brick} - \rho V$$

$$m_{apparent} = 8{,}972 \text{ g} - [(0.92 \text{ g/cm}^3) \cdot (787 \text{ cm}^3)]$$

$$m_{apparent} = (8{,}972 \text{ g} - 724 \text{ g})$$

$$m_{apparent} = 8.2 \text{ kg}$$

25. B is correct.

$$v = c / n$$

$$v = 3 \times 10^8 \text{ m/s} / 2$$

$$v = 1.5 \times 10^8 \text{ m/s}$$

26. D is correct.

Photon energy:

$$E = hf$$
$$f = c / \lambda$$
$$f = (3 \times 10^8 \, \text{m/s}) / (6.5 \times 10^{-6} \, \text{m})$$
$$f = 4.6 \times 10^{13} \, \text{Hz}$$
$$E = (4.136 \times 10^{-15} \, \text{eV·s}) \cdot (4.6 \times 10^{13} \, \text{Hz})$$
$$E = 0.19 \, \text{eV}$$

27. A is correct.

The magnetic force on a charged particle can change the velocity and direction of the particle but cannot change its speed.

Kinetic energy is calculated using the square of speed:

$$KE = \frac{1}{2}mv^2$$

Thus, if speed does not change the energy of the charge does not change.

28. A is correct.

Resistance in a wire:

$R = (\rho L) / A$

where ρ = resistivity, L = length of wire and A = cross-sectional area of wire

Cross-sectional area of a wire:

$$A = \pi r^2$$
$$A = \pi D^2 / 4$$

If D is doubled:

$$A = \pi (2D)^2 / 4$$
$$A = \pi (4D^2) / 4$$

The area is increased by a factor of 4.

The new resistance if D is doubled and L is doubled:

$$R = (\rho \times 2L) / (4A)$$
$$R = \frac{1}{2}(\rho L / A)$$

29. B is correct. Heat conduction follows the equation:

$$\Delta Q / \Delta t = kA\Delta T / d$$

Assuming all other values are constant, the equation can be written as:

$$\Delta Q / \Delta t = (1 / d)x$$

where x is a constant.

The rate of heat loss is inversely proportional to the thickness, so by increasing d, the slope of the curve is negative.

30. C is correct. Under one meter of water the gauge pressure is:

$$P = \rho g h$$

Jack's lungs are open to atmospheric pressure due to the snorkel, so he only needs to overcome the gauge pressure.

The force needed is:

$$P = F / A$$

$$F = PA$$

$$F = (\rho g h)A$$

The area is the area of his chest as this is what the pressure acts against.

$$F = (\text{gauge pressure}) \cdot (\text{chest area})$$

31. B is correct. For the critical angle, the refracted angle is 90°.

$$n_{water} \sin \theta_{crit} = n_{air} \sin 90°$$

$$\sin \theta_{crit} = (n_{air} / n_{water}) \sin 90°$$

$$\theta_{crit} = \sin^{-1} [(1 / 1.33) \cdot (1)]$$

$$\theta_{crit} = \sin^{-1} (3/4)$$

32. C is correct.

Energy needed to change hydrogen from one state to another:

$$E = -13.6 \text{ eV}[(1 / n_1^2) - (1 / n_2^2)]$$

To ionize hydrogen, the electron must be removed to the $n = \infty$ state.

Energy needed to change from the ground state:

$$E = -13.6[(1 / 1) - (1 / \infty)]$$

$$E = -13.6 \text{ eV}$$

Energy is expressed as a negative number to indicate that this much energy is needed to be input to the atom.

33. A is correct.

Kelvin is calculated as 273.15 more than the temperature in Celsius.

$0\ °C = 273\ K$

For example:

$23\ °C = 23 + 273.15 = 296.15\ K$

Kelvin is measured in Kelvin, so there is no ° symbol as in °C

34. A is correct.

$F_B = mg$

$F_B = \rho Vg$

$\rho Vg = mg$, cancel g from both sides of the expression

$m = \rho V$

$m = (\pi r^2 h)\cdot(1\ g/cm^3)$

$m = \pi(1\ cm)^2\cdot(14\ cm)\cdot(1\ g/cm^3)$

$m = 14\pi\ g$

$m = 44\ g$

35. A is correct.

Magnification is defined as:

$m = -d_i\ /\ d_o$

For a mirror:

$1\ /\ f = 1\ /\ d_i + 1\ /\ d_o$

Multiplying both sides by d_o gives:

$d_o\ /\ f = d_o\ /\ d_i + 1$

$d_o\ /\ f = -(1\ /\ m) + 1$

Or:

$1\ /\ m = 1 - d_o\ /\ f$

$m = 1\ /\ (1 - d_o\ /\ f)$

$m = 1\ /\ (1 - 5\ m\ /\ 10\ m)$

$m = +2$

The magnification is positive, so the image is upright, and twice as large.

36. C is correct.

Background radiation is the energy source that provides most of a person's annual exposure to radiation.

37. B is correct.

Magnetics are materials that produce magnetic fields and can, therefore, exert a magnetic force.

The field surrounds the magnet as shown:

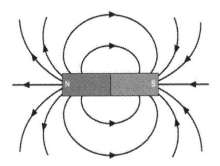

38. C is correct.

$$V = IR$$

Resistivity is the measure of resistance along the length of a given material:

$$R = \rho L \, / \, A$$

where ρ is resistivity

$$\rho = RA \, / \, L$$

$$\rho = (\Omega) \cdot (m^2) \, / \, (m)$$

$$\rho = \Omega \cdot m$$

39. C is correct.

Although an iceberg has a much lower temperature than hot coffee, it contains far more thermal energy due to its much greater mass.

For example, assume coffee at 90 °C goes to 80 °C:

$$Q = mc\Delta T$$

$$Q = (1 \text{ kg}) \cdot (4.2 \text{ kJ/kg} \cdot \text{K}) \cdot (90 \text{ °C} - 80 \text{ °C})$$

where specific heat for water = 4.2 kJ/kg·K

$$Q = 42 \text{ kJ were released during temperature change}$$

If a 10,000 kg iceberg (very small iceberg) were to go from 0 °C to –10 °C:

$$Q = mc\Delta T$$

$$Q = (10,000 \text{ kg}) \cdot (2.05 \text{ kJ/kg} \cdot \text{K}) \cdot (0 \text{ °C} - (-10 \text{ °C}))$$

where specific heat for ice = 2.05 kJ/kg·K

$$Q = 205,000 \text{ kJ were released during temperature change}$$

Therefore, even a small iceberg at a much lower temperature contains more thermal energy due to its far greater mass.

40. A is correct.

Flow velocity:

$$v = f / A$$

where flow rate $f = 0.04 \text{ m}^3/\text{s}$

$$v = f / (\pi r^2)$$
$$v = (0.04 \text{ m}^3/\text{s}) / [\pi(0.06 \text{ m})^2]$$
$$v = 3.5 \text{ m/s}$$

41. D is correct.

The magnification:

$$m = -d_i / d_o$$
$$m = -3 \text{ m} / 6 \text{ m}$$

$m = -\frac{1}{2}$, where the negative sign indicates that the image is inverted

42. D is correct.

Uranium decays because the electromagnetic repulsion of the protons overcomes the strong nuclear force due to its limited range and the massive size of the uranium nucleus.

43. B is correct.

The equation for the magnetic field of an infinitely long straight wire is given as:

$$B = \mu I / 2\pi r$$

Where μ = permittivity of free space, I = current and r is the radial distance from the wire

When r doubles, B decreases by a factor of $\frac{1}{2}$.

44. A is correct.

B and C only have circuit elements in series.

In D, the resistor is in series with one of the batteries.

A correctly has the resistor and capacitor in parallel, which is between the two batteries.

45. A is correct.

Use SI units for consistency.

Express the specific heat in SI units:

$c = 108$ cal/kg/°C

$c = 108$ cal/kg/°C (4.186 J/cal)

$c = 450.09$ J/kg/°C

Calculate ΔT:

$\Delta T = Q/(mc) = (1/2 \ mv^2) / (mc) = v^2/(4c)$

$\Delta T = (1{,}250 \text{ m/s})^2 / [4 \ (450.09 \text{ J/kg/°C})]$

$\Delta T = 1728$ °C

Note that the temperature increase is independent of the mass of the meteorite.

46. A is correct.

The 400 m distance between the aircraft (i.e., source) and the observer remains constant.

Since there is no relative motion between the source and the detector, f_d equals f_s.

47. B is correct.

The equation for focal length is:

$1 / f = 1 / d_o + 1 / d_i$

where d_o is object distance and d_i is image distance

$1 / f = 1 / d_o + 1 / d_i$

$1 / f = 1 / 24$ cm $+ 1 / 3$ cm

$1 / f = 1 / 24$ cm $+ 8 / 24$ cm

$1 / f = 0.375$ cm

$f = 2.7$ cm

48. C is correct.

Heavy nuclides with atomic numbers greater than 83 almost always undergo alpha decay to reduce the number of neutrons and protons in the nucleus.

49. B is correct.

According to the Lorentz force law for a charged particle in a magnetic field, the magnetic force on a particle acts in a direction given by the right-hand rule.

For particles with a velocity perpendicular to the field (as in this case), the magnitude of the force is:

$$F_B = qvB$$

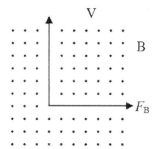

The centripetal force F_C on the proton is the magnetic force F_B:

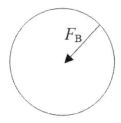

$$F_B = F_C$$

$$qvB = (mv^2) / r$$

Therefore:

$$r = (mv) / (qB)$$

The values for m, q, and B are fixed.

If the speed is increased by a factor of three, so is the radius.

Thus, the time needed to complete one circular path is:

$$t = 2\pi(3r) / 3v$$

$t = 2\pi r / v$, unchanged from the original time.

50. B is correct.

The magnetic force on an object changes the direction of the charge and thus the velocity. However, the speed does not change.

Kinetic energy is calculated using speed.

Thus, if the magnetic force does not change the speed it does not change its kinetic energy.

Diagnostic Test #3 – Explanations

1. B is correct.

Heat conduction equation:

$$Q / t = (kA\Delta T) / d$$

where k is the thermal conductivity of the wall material, A is the surface area of the wall, d is the wall's thickness, and ΔT is the temperature difference on either side.

Assume heat flow is lengthwise so barrier distance:

$$d = 2d_0$$

The important value here is A (A = πr^2), which is the surface area of the object with respect to the direction of heat flow and d, which is barrier thickness.

The surface area with respect to heat flow:

$$A_0 = (\pi / 4)D_0{}^2$$
$$A = (\pi / 4)\cdot(2D_0)^2$$
$$A = 4(\pi / 4) D_0{}^2$$
$$A = 4A_0$$

Substitute values into original equation:

$$Q / t = (k\Delta T)\cdot(4A_0 / 2d_0)$$
$$Q / t = 2(kA_0\Delta T / d_0)$$
$$Q / t = 2(Q_0 / t)$$
$$Q / t = 2(30 \text{ W})$$
$$Q / t = 60 \text{ W}$$

2. D is correct.

The weight of the piston surface area is a ratio:

$$F_1 / A_1 = F_2 / A_2$$
$$F_2 = F_1 \times A_2 / A_1$$
$$F_2 = (600 \text{ N})\cdot(50 \text{ cm}^2) / 5 \text{ cm}^2$$
$$F_2 = 6,000 \text{ N}$$

3. B is correct.

The resolution is the smallest distance between two objects where they are still capable of being distinguished as separate objects.

Therefore, the light with a shorter wavelength gives a smaller distance between peaks and therefore a higher resolution.

4. D is correct. The photoelectric effect is the phenomenon where light incident upon a metallic surface causes electrons to be emitted.

The photoelectric effect is described by the equation:

$KE_{max} = hf - \phi$

where h = Planck's constant, f = frequency and ϕ = work function.

If light of a threshold frequency such that $hf > \phi$ shines upon a metallic surface, the electrons will be ejected with KE. Increasing frequency increases the KE.

Note: hf is the energy carried by one incident photon. Since the incident intensity remains constant, but the energy per photon has increased, the rate of incident photons must decrease, resulting in a decrease in the rate of ejection events.

5. D is correct. Equation for potential energy:

$\Delta PE = q\Delta V$

Note: q is negative because electrons are negatively charged

$\Delta PE = (-1.6 \times 10^{-19}\ C) \cdot (-500\ V - 500\ V)$

$\Delta PE = (-1.6 \times 10^{-19}\ C) \cdot (-1,000\ V)$

$\Delta PE = 1.6 \times 10^{-16}\ J$

Moving this electron increases its PE energy.

6. B is correct.

Calculate impedance for each circuit element.

Resistor:

$Z_r = 30\ \Omega$

Inductor:

$Z_i = j2\pi fL$

where j is an imaginary number used in calculating complex impedance.

$Z_i = j2\pi(50\ Hz) \cdot (0.4\ H)$

$Z_i = j125.6\ \Omega$

Capacitor:

$Z_c = -j / (2\pi fC)$

$Z_c = -j / [2\pi(50\ Hz) \cdot (50 \times 10^{-6}\ F)]$

$Z_c = -j63.7\ \Omega$

Adding in series:

$Z_{total} = 30\ \Omega + j(125.6\ \Omega - 63.7\ \Omega)$

To find magnitude, use Pythagorean Theorem:

$$|Z| = \sqrt{[(30\ \Omega)^2 + (61.9\ \Omega)^2]}$$

$$|Z| = 68.79\ \Omega$$

$$V = IR$$

Using impedance (Z) as resistance:

$$V = (1.8\ A){\cdot}(68.79\ \Omega)$$

$$V = 124\ V$$

7. C is correct. Foods with high specific heat capacities tend to burn more than foods with lower specific heat capacities. This is because specific heat is a measure of how much thermal energy a material can absorb (or loose) before changing temperature.

Thus, high specific heat foods can deliver more energy and burn a person's mouth before cooling down (compared to low specific heat foods).

8. C is correct.

First, find the total mass of the mixture once the ethanol has been added to the chloroform:

Total Mass = $x + 5$ grams

where x is the mass of the ethanol added.

Then, find the volume of the resulting mixture. Volume is found using the specific gravity formula:

Volume (mL) = Mass (g) / SG

Therefore:

$$V_e = x\ /\ 0.8$$

$$V_c = 5\ g\ /\ 1.5$$

Total Volume = $V_e + V_c$

Total Volume = $(x\ /\ 0.8) + (5\ g\ /\ 1.5)$

Total Volume = $1.25x + 3.33$ mL

Find the mass of added ethanol using the given specific gravity of the mixture:

$SG_{mixture}$ = Total Mass / Total Volume

$$1.2 = (x + 5\ g)\ /\ (1.25x + 3.33\ mL)$$

$$(1.2){\cdot}(1.25x + 3.33\ mL) = (x + 5\ g)$$

$$1.5x + 3.96\ g = x + 5\ g$$

$$0.5x = 1.04\ g$$

$$x = 2.08\ g \approx 2\ g$$

9. C is correct.

First, assume that the distance of the Moon from the lens is ∞.

$$d_o = \infty$$

Next, assume d_i is the distance from the lens where the image forms.

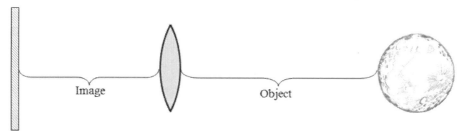

By the thin lens equation:

$$1 / d_i + 1 / d_o = 1 / f$$
$$1 / d_i + 1 / \infty = 1 / f$$
$$1 / d_i + 0 = 1 / f$$
$$1 / d_i = 1 / f$$
$$d_i = f$$

10. D is correct.

The superscript is the mass number (# protons and # neutrons).

The subscript is the atomic number (# protons).

Thus, $_1^1 \text{H}$ depicts a hydrogen atom with 1 proton, 1 electron, and 0 neutrons.

11. D is correct.

The centripetal force F_C on a charged particle in a magnetic field is the magnetic Lorentz force:

$$F_M = qvB$$

Therefore:

$$F_C = F_M$$
$$mv^2 / r = qvB$$

or

$$r = mv / qB$$

Increasing the speed by a factor of two increases the radius by a factor of two.

12. C is correct.

$$P = IV$$

Voltage is considered potential in a DC circuit.

Slope = Voltage / Power

Slope = V / IV

Slope = 1 / I

Slope = 1 / current

13. B is correct. Heat can never flow from a cold body to a hot body without some other change. This violates the Clausius Statement of the Second Law of Thermodynamics.

14. A is correct. The reading on the meter is the net force between the necklace weight and buoyant force.

$$F_{total} = F_O - F_B$$

$$F_{total} = mg - \rho Vg$$

$$F_{total} = g(m - \rho V)$$

$$F_{total} = (9.8 \text{ m/s}^2) \cdot [(0.06 \text{ kg}) - (1 \text{ g/cm}^3) \cdot (5.7 \text{ cm}^3) \cdot (1 \text{ kg/1,000 g})]$$

$$F_{total} = 0.53 \text{ N}$$

15. C is correct. According to the law of reflection, the angle of incidence is always equal to the angle of reflection.

$$\theta_{incidence} = \theta_{reflection}$$

16. D is correct. The sum of subscripts and superscripts must be balanced:

$$_{7}^{14}\text{N} + _{0}^{1}\text{n} \rightarrow _{6}^{14}\text{C} + _{1}^{1}\text{p}$$

A proton is necessary to balance the subscripts to 7 and the superscripts to 15 on each side of the expression.

17. B is correct. The equation for force in a magnetic field (B):

$$F = qv \times B$$

The direction of B is given by the right-hand rule.

If the thumb is oriented upward as shown for F, the magnetic field B points into the page.

18. C is correct.

Resistance = resistivity × (length / area)

$A = \pi r^2$

$R = (1.68 \times 10^{-8} \ \Omega \cdot m) \cdot [(57 \ m) / \pi (5.7 \times 10^{-3} \ m)^2]$

$R = 9.4 \times 10^{-3} \ \Omega$

$V = IR$

$I = V / R$

$I = 70 \ V / 9.4 \times 10^{-3} \ \Omega$

$I = 7{,}447 \ A$

19. C is correct. Solve for heat required:

$Q = cm\Delta T$

$Q = (113 \ cal/kg \cdot °C) \cdot (1.14 \ kg) \cdot (90 \ °C - 18 \ °C)$

$Q = 9{,}275 \ cal$

Convert to Joules:

$Q = (9{,}275 \ cal / 1) \cdot (4.186 \ J / cal)$

$Q = 38{,}825 \ J$

20. A is correct. The gauge pressure is referenced at ambient air pressure thus:

$P = \rho g h$

$P = (1{,}000 \ kg/m^3) \cdot (9.8 \ m/s^2) \cdot (6 \ m + 22 \ m)$

$P = 2.7 \times 10^5 \ N/m^2$

21. A is correct.

$m = -d_i / d_o$

$m = -(-6 \ m) / (2 \ m)$

$m = 3$

Positive magnification means an upright image.

22. C is correct. Energy needed to change hydrogen from one state to another:

$E = -13.6 \ eV[(1 / n_1^2) - (1 / n_2^2)]$

To ionize hydrogen, the electron must be removed to the $n = \infty$ state.

Energy needed to change from the ground state:

$$E = -13.6[(1 / 1) - (1 / \infty)]$$

$$E = -13.6 \text{ eV}$$

Energy is expressed as a negative number to indicate that this much energy is needed to be input to the atom.

23. D is correct. Heat required to melt a solid:

$$Q = mL_f$$

$$Q = (70 \text{ kg}) \cdot (334 \times 10^3 \text{ J/kg})$$

$$Q = 2.3 \times 10^4 \text{ kJ}$$

24. B is correct. Atmospheric pressure is not taken into account because it acts at the surface of the water and all around Mike's finger, so it cancels.

$$P_{water} = \rho g h$$

$$P_{water} = (10^3 \text{ kg/m}^3) \cdot (10 \text{ m/s}^2) \cdot (1 \text{ m})$$

$$P_{water} = 10^4 \text{ N/m}^2$$

Area of hole:

$$A = (0.01 \text{ m}) \cdot (0.01 \text{ m })$$

$$A = 10^{-4} \text{ m}^2$$

$$F = PA$$

$$F = (10^4 \text{ N/m}^2) \cdot (10^{-4} \text{ m}^2)$$

$$F = 1 \text{ N}$$

25. D is correct.

$$\text{Critical angle} = \sin^{-1} (n_2 / n_1)$$

$$\text{Critical angle} = \sin^{-1} (1.3 / 1.6)$$

$$\text{Critical angle} = \sin^{-1} (0.81)$$

$$\text{Critical angle} = 54°$$

26. A is correct. Beam A is due to high energy electrons because it deflects towards the positive plate indicating attraction.

27. A is correct.

$$F = qE$$

where q is the charge and E is the electric field

They both act in the same direction because they have a positive charge and are moving opposite the negative charge generated by the plates.

Since E is constant, and q is twice as large for the α particle (He has two protons and two neutrons), the charge is multiplied by +2.

$$F \propto q$$

F is twice as large.

28. B is correct. A graph with a negative slope is representative for a semiconductor material, where R = resistivity (along y-axis) and T = temperature (along the x-axis).

29. B is correct. The sun warms the Earth only through radiation because space is a vacuum and contains no matter to transfer heat through convection or conduction.

30. C is correct. To calculate the buoyant force due to the water:

$$F_B = 7.86 \text{ N} - 6.92 \text{ N}$$

$$F_B = 0.94 \text{ N}$$

Volume of displaced water is equal to volume of object:

$$F_B = \rho g V$$

$$V = F_B / \rho g$$

$$V = 0.94 \text{ N} / (1,000 \text{ kg/m}^3) \cdot (9.8 \text{ m/s}^2)$$

$$V = 9.6 \times 10^{-5} \text{ m}^3$$

Mass of the object:

$$m = W / g$$

$$m = 7.86 \text{ N} / 9.8 \text{ m/s}^2$$

$$m = 0.8 \text{ kg}$$

$$\rho = \text{mass} / \text{volume}$$

$$\rho = 0.8 \text{ kg} / 9.6 \times 10^{-5} \text{ m}^3$$

$$\rho = 8,333 \text{ kg/m}^3$$

31. A is correct.

$$n_1 \sin \theta_1 = n_2 \sin \theta_2$$

$$1.33 \sin 42° = 1 \sin \theta_2$$

$$1.33 \times (0.67) = 1 \sin \theta_2$$

$$\sin \theta_2 = 0.89$$

$$\theta_2 = \sin^{-1}(0.89)$$

$$\theta_2 = 63°$$

32. B is correct. Half-life is the time it takes for ½ of the quantity to decay.

1st half-life: 3,200 μg / 2 = 1,600 μg

2nd half-life: 1,600 μg / 2 = 800 μg

If two periods took 24.6 years, then one cycle takes 12.3 years.

Mathematically solving for half-life:

$A_{final} = A_{initial} \times (½)^{t/h}$

where t = time and h = half-life

$800 \text{ μg} = (3,200 \text{ μg}) \cdot (½)^{24.6 \text{ yr}/h}$

$(800 \text{ μg}) / (3,200 \text{ μg}) = (½)^{24.6 \text{ yr}/h}$

$0.25 = (½)^{24.6 \text{ yr}/h}$

$\ln(0.25) = (24.6 \text{ yr}/h) \ln(½)$

$h = 12.3 \text{ yr}$

33. B is correct. Solve for heat required:

$Q = cm\Delta T$

$Q = (92 \text{ cal/kg·°C}) \cdot (0.5 \text{ kg}) \cdot (70 \text{ °C} - 20 \text{ °C})$

$Q = 2,300 \text{ cal}$

Convert to Joules:

$Q = (2,300 \text{ cal} / 1 \text{ J}) \cdot (4.186 \text{ J/cal})$

$Q = 9,628 \text{ J}$

34. D is correct. The elastic modulus is calculated as stress divided by strain.

$E = \sigma / \varepsilon$

Stress is measured in N/m^2, the strain is unitless, and work is measured in Joules, so the other choices are incorrect based upon the units being dissimilar.

35. C is correct.

$1/f = 1/d_o + 1/d_i$

$1/d_i = 1/f - 1/d_o$

Since $d_o > f$,

$1/f - 1/d_o$ is always positive, so the image is real.

$m = -d_i/d_o$

Since i is positive, $m = -(+i/o)$ is negative, so the image is inverted.

If the resulting magnification is positive, the image is upright. If the magnification is negative, the image is inverted (upside down).

36. D is correct. The effect of nuclear radiation on living tissue is measured by biological radiation units.

Gray (Gy) is the SI unit of biological radiation effect and one gray corresponds to the transfer of one joule of energy to one kilogram of tissue.

The rad is an older unit not in use today and equals 0.01 Gy.

Another the older unit of roentgen (R) is still commonly used and was originally devised as a measurement unit for use with X-rays or gamma rays. Roentgen is the quantity of radiation that generates 2.1×10^9 ion pairs per 1 cm^3 of dry air. It is also 1.8×10^{12} ion pairs per gram of tissue. 1 R roentgen = 0.0096 Gy ≈ 1 rad.

37. D is correct. According to Coulomb's Law, like charges repel with equal and opposite force:

$$F_1 = F_2 = kq_1q_2 \, / \, r^2$$

38. A is correct. The resistance of a wire is given by:

$R = \rho L \, / \, A$

where ρ = resistivity, L = length and A = cross-sectional area

Resistance of thin wire:

$R_0 = \rho L \, / \, A_0$

Resistance of thicker wire:

$A = 2A_0$

$R = \rho L \, / \, 2A_0$

$R = \frac{1}{2}R_0$

The thicker wire has ½ the resistance of the thinner wire.

39. B is correct.

$\Delta L \, / \, L = \alpha \Delta T$

where α is the coefficient of linear expansion

$\Delta L = \alpha \Delta T L$

Using $3L$ for L:

$\Delta L = \alpha \Delta T (3L)$

$\Delta L = 3(\alpha \Delta T L)$

ΔL is 3 times larger

40. C is correct. As the block just enters the water, the total pressure will be the sum of atmospheric pressure and the pressure produced by submersion.

$$P_{total} = P_{atmosphere} + \rho g h$$

When the block just enters the water:

$$P_{total} = P_{atmosphere} + 0$$

Graph C depicts the scenario as the block will experience an initial pressure of $P_{atmosphere}$ and this will linearly increase (from $\rho g h$) as the block is lowered further into the water.

41. D is correct. Virtual images can be seen (image in a plane mirror) but cannot be projected onto a screen.

42. C is correct. Beta Decay (plus): the parent nuclide ejects a positron and neutrino. However, in the process, a proton converts to a neutron, so the mass number remains the same, but the atomic number decreases by 1.

$$^A_Z X \rightarrow ^{\ \ A}_{Z-1} Y + ^{\ 0}_{+1} e^+ + ^0_0 v$$

43. C is correct. As the copper sheet is quickly passed through the magnetic field eddy currents form.

According to Lenz's Law, the eddy currents rotate in such a way to produce magnetic fields that oppose the changing magnetic flux. This opposing magnetic force acts to impede the motion of the copper sheet.

44. A is correct. Height determines the energy per mass required to position the water at a particular point.

This is analogous to an electric potential, as a measure of energy per charge required to position the charge at a particular point.

45. A is correct.

$$Q = m_s c_p \Delta T$$

$$Q = (70 \text{ g}) \cdot (0.11 \text{ cal/g} \cdot ^\circ C) \cdot (450 \ ^\circ C - 100 \ ^\circ C)$$

$$Q = 2{,}695 \text{ cal}$$

$$Q = m_w c_p \Delta T$$

$$m_w = Q / c_p \Delta T$$

$$m_w = 2{,}695 \text{ cal} / [(1 \text{ cal/g} \cdot ^\circ C) \cdot (100 \ ^\circ C - 25 \ ^\circ C)]$$

$$m_w = 36 \text{ g}$$

46. A is correct.

$$F_B = \rho g V$$

Buoyant force is directly proportional to volume.

Volume of a sphere is given as:

$$V = 4 / 3\pi r^3$$

If radius doubles:

$$V = 4 / 3\pi(2r)^3$$

$$V = (8)\cdot(4 / 3\pi r^3)$$

Therefore, when r doubles, F_B increase by a factor of 8 times.

47. D is correct.

$$n_1 \sin \theta_1 = n_2 \sin \theta_2$$

When the critical angle is reached:

$$\theta_2 = 90°$$

$$\sin \theta_C = (n_2 / n_1)$$

For this statement to be valid:

$$n_1 > n_2$$

48. B is correct.

The orbital angular momentum is given by:

$$L = \sqrt{[\ell(\ell + 1)]} \, h$$

Allowable angular momentum quantum numbers: $\ell = 0, 1, 2 \ldots n - 1$

49. C is correct. A volt is equal to the difference in electric potential between two points of a conductor and is also defined as the potential difference between two parallel infinite plates with an electric field between them.

50. D is correct.

$$Q = mc_p\Delta T$$

$$c_p = Q / m\Delta T$$

$$c_p = (14 \text{ J}) / (0.185 \text{ kg})\cdot(10 \text{ °C})$$

$$c_p = 7.6 \text{ J/kg·C}$$

$$1 \text{ °C} = 1 \text{ K}$$

$$c_p = 7.6 \text{ J/kg·K}$$

Diagnostic Test #4 – Explanations

1. C is correct.

$Q = 9$ kJ

$W = -5$ kJ

By the first law of thermodynamics:

$\Delta U = Q + W$

$\Delta U = 9$ kJ $- 5$ kJ

$\Delta U = 4$ kJ

2. A is correct.

Young's Modulus (E) is given as:

$E = FL\ /\ A\Delta L$

where $F = mg$

$E = mgL\ /\ A\Delta L$

Rearranging for m:

$m = EA\Delta L\ /\ gL_i$

$A = \pi r^2$

$m = E\pi r^2 \Delta L\ /\ gL_i$

$m = [(2 \times 10^{11}\ \text{N/m}^2) \cdot \pi (0.9 \times 10^{-3}\ \text{m})^2 \cdot (1.8 \times 10^{-3}\ \text{m})]\ /\ (9.8\ \text{m/s}^2) \cdot (4.2\ \text{m})$

$m = 916.8\ \text{kg} \cdot \text{m}^2\ /\ 41.2\ \text{m}^2/\text{s}^2$

$m = 22$ kg

3. B is correct.

A diverging thin lens always produces images that are virtual, erect and reduced in size.

A converging thin lens produces images that are real or virtual, erect or inverted and reduced or magnified.

4. A is correct.

Beta Decay (plus): the parent nuclide ejects a positron and neutrino. However, in the process, a proton converts to a neutron, so the mass number remains the same, but the atomic number decreases by 1.

$$^A_Z X \rightarrow\ ^A_{Z-1} Y + ^0_{+1} e^+ + ^0_0 v_e$$

---

5. D is correct. Parallel to the field direction.

Faraday's Law (induced emf in a coil with changing magnetic flux):

$$V_{generated} = -N\Delta(BA) / \Delta t$$

where N = number of turns, B = magnetic field, A = area of coil and t = time

Positioning the loop such that the area vector is parallel to the magnetic field maximizes the flux through the loop (BA) and maximizes $V_{generated}$.

6. A is correct.

$$V_{rms} = V_{max} / \sqrt{2}$$

$$V_{rms} = 200 \text{ V} / 1.41$$

$$V_{rms} = 142 \text{ V}$$

7. A is correct.

$$PE = mgh$$

Energy used in one repetition:

$$PE = (2) \cdot (3 \text{ kg}) \cdot (9.8 \text{ m/s}^2) \cdot (0.5 \text{ m})$$

$$PE = 29.4 \text{ J}$$

Convert 19kcal to joules:

$$PE = (19 \text{ kcal} / 1) \cdot (1,000 \text{ cal} / \text{kcal}) \cdot (4.186 \text{ J} / \text{cal})$$

$$PE = 79,534 \text{ J}$$

Divide by 29.4 J to find the # of repetitions

$$\# = (79,534 \text{ J}) / (29.4 \text{ J})$$

$$\# = 2,705 \text{ repetitions}$$

8. C is correct.

$$P = F / A$$

$$F = PA$$

$$F = (3 \text{ atm}) \cdot (1.01 \times 10^5 \text{ Pa}/1 \text{ atm}) \cdot (0.2 \text{ m})^2$$

$$F = 12,120 \text{ N} = 1.2 \times 10^4 \text{ N}$$

9. C is correct. In the situation of a diverging lens, the image is always located on the same side as the object.

The equation is:

$$1 / f = 1 / d_i + 1 / d_o$$

For a diverging lens, the focal length is negative by convention.

$$-1 / 3 \text{ m} = 1 / d_i + 1 / 4 \text{ m}$$

$$1 / d_i = -1 / 3 \text{ m} - 1 / 4 \text{ m}$$

$$1 / d_i = -4 / 12 \text{ m} - 3 / 12 \text{ m}$$

$$1 / d_i = -7 / 12 \text{ m}$$

$$d_i = -12 / 7 \text{ m}$$

For a diverging lens, the image distance is always negative.

For a concave or diverging lens, the focal length is negative because the focus used in the ray diagram is located on the left side (*x*- and *y*-axis coordinate system) of the lens.

The image distance will be negative because it is also formed on the left-hand side.

10. D is correct.

The transition from level 3 to 2 produces a wavelength λ so that wavelength has energy of:

$$E_{3,2} = hf$$

$$f = c / \lambda$$

$$E_{3,2} = h(c / \lambda)$$

$$E_{3,2} = (1 / \lambda) \cdot (hc)$$

Then the energy from 2 to 1 is:

$$E_{2,1} = 2E_{3,2}$$

Then the energy from 3 to 1 is:

$$E_{3,1} = 3E_{3,2}$$

Because the energy and wavelength are inversely related, the transition from 2 to 1 must have ½ λ and the transition from 3 to 1 must have 1/3 λ.

11. C is correct.

The nuclei have the same charge because each has one proton.

Therefore, the forces are the same.

12. D is correct.

Faraday's Law states that a voltage will be induced in a coil exposed to a magnetic field:

$$V = -N\Delta(BA) / \Delta t$$

All three choices are correct because options I and III would increase the rate of change of the magnetic field (B) and thereby increase the voltage. Option II is correct because it would increase the number of turns (N) and therefore increase the induced voltage.

13. D is correct.

Stefan-Boltzmann Law:

$$P = A\varepsilon\sigma T^4$$

Temperature is doubled:

$$P = A\varepsilon\sigma(2T)^4$$

$$P = A\varepsilon\sigma(16)T^4$$

The power increases by a factor of 16.

$$P_2 = P(16)$$

$$P_2 = (15\ W)\cdot(16)$$

$$P_2 = 240\ W$$

14. B is correct.

The equation of continuity:

$$f = Av\ \text{remains constant.}$$

$$A_2V_2 = A_1V_1$$

$$V_2 = A_1V_1 / A_2$$

$$V_2 = \pi(16\ cm)^2\cdot(V_1) / \pi(4\ cm)^2$$

$$V_2 = 16V_1$$

If the radius decreases by a factor of 4 then the velocity increases by a factor of 16.

15. B is correct.

Linear magnification of lens:

$$m = -d_i / d_o$$

The negative in the image distance is because all real images are inverted.

If the image distance value is negative, the image is virtual, m is positive and the image is erect:

m	Image	Inverted / Erect
+	virtual	erect
−	real	inverted

16. C is correct.

All the masses of the elements are determined relative to ^{12}C (Carbon-12), which is defined as an exact number 12 amu. Elements exist as a variety of isotopes, and two major isotopes of carbon are ^{12}C and ^{13}C. Each carbon atom has the same number of protons and electrons − 6. ^{12}C has 6 neutrons, ^{13}C has 7 neutrons.

17. A is correct. Force from a magnetic field on a charged particle equals the electric field force on the charged particle.

For an electromagnetic wave:

$B = E / c$

$B = (1{,}200 \text{ V/m}) / (3 \times 10^8 \text{ m/s})$

$B = 4 \times 10^{-6} \text{ T}$

18. B is correct.

In a current-carrying wire, the magnetic field circles the wire in closed loops in the direction according to the right-hand rule.

19. D is correct.

Isometric refers to constant volume. Since the container does not expand when heat energy is added, it undergoes an isometric process.

20. B is correct. Boltzmann's constant relates energy at the individual particle level with temperature. Where N is the number of molecules of gas.

21. A is correct.

Angular magnification equation:

$M_\alpha = NP / f$

where NP = near point

$M_\alpha = (250 \text{ mm} / 50 \text{ mm})$

$M_\alpha = 5$

22. C is correct. Because protons are positively charged they repel each other in the nucleus due to the forces from electrostatic repulsion. The strong nuclear force keeps the protons together because it overcomes the electrostatic repulsion and thus binds the nucleus together.

23. D is correct.

$10 \,^\circ\text{C} = 10 \text{ K}$

$Q = mc\Delta T$

$Q = (0.3 \text{ kg}) \cdot (128 \text{ J/kg·K}) \cdot (10 \text{ K})$

$Q = 384 \text{ J}$

24. A is correct.

Volumetric flow rate:

$$V_f = Av$$

$$A = \pi d^2 / 4$$

So, for the original pipe:

$$V_f = (\pi d^2 / 4) \cdot v$$

If diameter is doubled:

$$V_f = [\pi\ (2d)^2 / 4]\ v$$

$$V_f = (\pi / 4) \cdot (4d^2)\ v$$

$$V_f = 4\ [(\pi d^2 / 4)\ v]$$

where the term in square brackets is identical to the original flow rate. Thus, the flow rate increases by a factor of 4.

25. C is correct.

Among the choices listed, radio waves have the lowest frequency.

$$f_{radio} < f_{microwave} < f_{infrared} < f_{X\text{-}ray} < f_{\gamma\ rays}$$

26. C is correct.

Heavy nuclei tend to have more neutrons than protons because neutrons contribute to the nuclear strong force but do not contribute to the electrostatic repulsion (i.e., protons) because of their neutral charge.

Thus, an excess of neutrons help keep the nuclei together without adding repulsion forces within the nuclei.

27. B is correct.

Particle 1 is negative because it is deflected in the magnetic field but goes in the opposite direction of the right-hand rule.

Particle 2 is neutral because it is unaffected by the magnetic field.

Particle 3 is positive because it is deflected in the presence of the magnetic field and obeys the right-hand rule.

28. A is correct.

The volt is expressed in Joules per Coulomb:

$$1\ V = 1\ J / 1\ C$$

Thus, 120 V is 120 J per Coulomb of charge.

29. C is correct.

Linear expansion:

$$\Delta L = L_i \alpha \Delta T$$

Total linear expansion of two rods:

$$\Delta L_{total} = \Delta L_A + \Delta L_S$$

$$\Delta L_{total} = L_{iA}\alpha_A\Delta T + L_{iS}\alpha_S\Delta T$$

$$\Delta L_{total} = \Delta T(L_{iA}\alpha_A + L_{iS}\alpha_S)$$

$$\Delta L_{total} = (90\ °C - 15\ °C)\cdot[(0.1\ m)\cdot(2.4 \times 10^{-5}\ K^{-1}) + (0.8\ m)\cdot(1.2 \times 10^{-5}\ K^{-1})]$$

$$\Delta L_{total} = 9 \times 10^{-4}\ m$$

Convert to mm:

$$\Delta L_{total} = (9 \times 10^{-4}\ m/1)\cdot(1,000\ mm/1\ m)$$

$$\Delta L_{total} = 0.9\ mm$$

30. C is correct.

Both the solid circle and wire circle have the same diameters, but the wire has two surface areas exposed to the water (i.e., inner and outer circumference) where the difference in circumference length is assumed to be negligible. The solid circle only has the outer edge exposed to the water's surface (i.e., circumference).

$L_{wire} = 2(2\pi r) =$ the relevant length for the wire circle

$2\pi r =$ the relevant length for the solid circle

Solid circle on water:

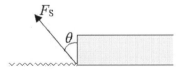

$$F_{s1} = y \cos \theta\, L$$

Wire on water:

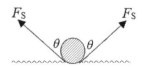

$$F_{s2} = 2y \cos \theta\, L$$

$$F_{s2} = 2F_{s1}$$

Balance weight vs. surface tension where F_s point up and F_w points down.

For solid circle:

$$F_{w1} = F_{s1}$$

For wire circle:

$$F_{w2} = F_{s2}$$
$$F_{w2} = 2F_{s1}$$
$$F_{w2} = 2F_{w1}$$

The wire circle can have double the mass without sinking.

31. A is correct.

A convex mirror always produces an image that is upright, virtual and smaller regardless of object location.

32. C is correct.

According to the de Broglie hypothesis, the idea of matter waves describes the wave-like behavior of particles that are moving.

33. A is correct.

Graham's Law:

$$\text{rate}_1 / \text{rate}_2 = \sqrt{(m_2 / m_1)}$$

34. A is correct.

Bernoulli's Equation:

$$P_1 + \tfrac{1}{2}\rho v_1^2 + \rho g h_1 = P_2 + \tfrac{1}{2}\rho v_2^2 + \rho g h_2$$

When simplifying Bernoulli's Equation, both the top opening and the bottom opening experience atmospheric pressure, so P_1 and P_2 cancel.

Likewise, $v_1 << v_2$ so it can be assumed to be negligible and go to zero.

Finally, $h_2 = 0$ because it is at the bottom of the tank and is the reference for all further heights in the problem

This results in the simplified expression:

$\rho g h_1 = \tfrac{1}{2}\rho v_2^2$, cancel ρ from both sides of the expression

$gh_1 = \tfrac{1}{2}v_2^2$

$v_2 = \sqrt{(2gh_1)}$

$v_2 = \sqrt{[(2) \cdot (9.8 \text{ m/s}^2) \cdot (0.5 \text{ m})]}$

$v_2 = 3.1$ m/s

35. D is correct.

When a wave enters a different medium, both its speed and wavelength change.

An electromagnetic wave always transports its energy in a vacuum at a speed of approximately 3.00×10^8 m/s (speed of light or c).

The frequency remains constant and is related to wavelength by:

$$\lambda = c / f$$
$$\lambda = (3 \times 10^8 \text{ m/s}) / (1.8 \times 10^{14} \text{ Hz})$$
$$\lambda = 1.667 \times 10^{-6} \text{ m} = 1,667 \text{ nm}$$

36. C is correct.

Wavelength relates to photon energy:

$$E = hc / \lambda$$
$$E = [(6.626 \times 10^{-34} \text{ J·s}) \cdot (3 \times 10^8 \text{ m/s})] / (580 \times 10^{-9} \text{ m})$$
$$E = 3.4 \times 10^{-19} \text{ J}$$

37. A is correct.

According to the right-hand rule for a negative charge, the magnetic field causes the electron to curve by path X.

If the charge were positive, the charge would curve by path Z.

38. C is correct.

Current:

$$6 \text{ mA} = 0.006 \text{ A}$$
$$0.006 \text{ A} = 0.006 \text{ Coulombs/sec}$$

During 1 minute (60 sec), calculate the charge that has flowed:

$$0.006 \text{ C/s} \times 60 \text{ s} = 0.36 \text{ C}$$

Each electron carries: 1.602×10^{-19} C

Calculate the # of electrons:

$$(0.36 \text{ C}) \cdot (1 \text{ electron} / 1.602 \times 10^{-19} \text{ C}) = 2.25 \times 10^{18} \text{ electrons}$$

39. D is correct.

Heat required to melt a solid:

$$Q_1 = mL_f$$
$$Q_1 = (0.4 \text{ kg}) \cdot (334 \times 10^3 \text{ J/kg})$$

$Q_1 = 133.6$ kJ

Heat required to raise temperature of water from 0 °C to 60 °C:

$Q_2 = mc\Delta T$

$Q_2 = (0.4$ kg)$\cdot(4.186 \times 10^3$ J/Kg·°C)$\cdot(60$ °C)

$Q_2 = 100.5$ kJ

Total heat added:

$Q_1 + Q_2 = Q_{total}$

$Q_{total} = (133.6$ kJ $+ 100.5$ kJ)

$Q_{total} = 234.1$ kJ

40. B is correct.

The flow rate must be constant along the flow because water is incompressible.

Volumetric Flow Rate is:

$\upsilon = Av$

Volumetric Flow Rate at different points in a pipe with different areas:

$A_1v_1 = A_2v_2$

Thus, the Volumetric Flow Rate at one point must match that of the other.

$A_2v_2 = 0.09$ m^3/s

41. C is correct.

Relationship between lens power and focal length:

$P = 1 / f$, with f expressed in meters

$f = 1 / P$

$f = 1/4$ m

The lens is a converging lens because the focal length of ¼ m is more than 0.

42. D is correct.

An alpha particle is more massive than a beta particle and thus has more inertia.

An alpha particle deflects less in a magnetic field because its extra inertia requires more force to change it from its path.

43. C is correct.

For the magnetic field around a current-carrying wire, the magnetic field strength is:

$B = (\mu_0 I) / (2\pi r)$

where B is the magnetic field strength, μ_0 is the magnetic constant, I is the current in the wire and r is the distance of the particle from the wire.

According to the equation for magnetic field strength, there are two ways to increase B:

  1) increase the current I through the wire, or

  2) decrease the distance r from the wire

Changing the particle's charge does not affect the field, nor does changing the particle's speed. The field becomes weaker as the particle moves away from the wire (r increases).

44. D is correct.

Resistance in a wire:

  $R = (\rho L) / A$

  where ρ = resistivity, L = length of wire and A = cross-sectional area of wire

  If the first wire has resistance R_1:

  $R_1 = \rho L_1 / A_1$

  The second wire has:

  $L_2 = 2L_1$

  $A_2 = 2A_1$

  $R_2 = \rho 2L_1 / 2A_1$

  $R_2 = \rho L_1 / A_1$

  $R_2 = R_1$

The resistances are equal.

45. A is correct. Stefan-Boltzmann Law:

  $P = \varepsilon A \sigma T^4$

  $P = (1) \cdot (1.25 \text{ m}^2) \cdot (5.67 \times 10^{-8} \text{ W/m}^2\text{K}^4) \cdot (100 + 273 \text{ K})^4$

  $P = 1{,}371.9 \text{ W} \approx 1.4 \text{ kW}$

46. B is correct. Archimedes Principle:

  $\rho_{object} / \rho_{fluid} = W_{object} / W_{fluid}$

  $\rho_{object} / \rho_{fluid} = (11.3 \text{ g/cm}^3) / (13.6 \text{ g/cm}^3)$

  $\rho_{object} / \rho_{fluid} = 0.83$

83% of the lead ball is below the surface by weight. The ball has 17% above the surface because the density is assumed to be consistent throughout the sphere.

The weight is directly correlated to volume.

47. D is correct.

Lens equation:

$$1/f = 1/d_i + 1/d_o$$

$$1/20 \text{ cm} = 1/d_i + 1/10 \text{ cm}$$

$$-1/20 \text{ cm} = 1/d_i$$

$$d_i = -20 \text{ cm}$$

The negative sign indicates the image should be on the object side of the mirror.

By the sign convention for mirrors, a negative value places the image behind the mirror.

48. C is correct.

Positron: $^{0}_{1}\beta^{+}$

The atomic mass remains the same, but the atomic number decreases.

49. A is correct.

$$W = Q\Delta V \text{ (for work or energy with charges)}$$

The charge transferred is:

$$Q = 10^{-10} \text{ C}$$

A positive charge moving from 8,000 V to –8,000 V is a negative sign.

$$W = (10^{-10} \text{ C}) \cdot (-8,000 \text{ V} - 8,000 \text{ V})$$

$$W = (10^{-10} \text{ C}) \cdot (-1.6 \times 10^{4} \text{ V})$$

$$W = -1.6 \times 10^{-6} \text{ J}$$

56. B is correct.

The Carnot cycle is an example of a reversible process.

Topical Practice Questions

Explanations

Thermodynamics – Explanations

1. B is correct. Ideal gas law:

$$PV = nRT$$

$$P_0 = nRT / V_0$$

If isothermal expansion, then n, R and T are constant

$$P = nRT / (1/3\ V_0)$$

$$P = 3(nRT / V_0)$$

$$P = 3P_0$$

2. C is correct. Area expansion equation:

$$\Delta A = A_0(2\alpha\Delta T)$$

$$\Delta A = (\pi / 4)\cdot(1.2\ cm)^2\cdot(2)\cdot(19 \times 10^{-6}\ K^{-1})\cdot(200\ °C)$$

$$\Delta A = 8.6 \times 10^{-3}\ cm^2$$

$$\Delta A = A_f - A_0$$

$$8.6 \times 10^{-3}\ cm^2 = (\pi / 4)\cdot[d_f^2 - (1.2\ cm)^2]$$

$$d_f = 1.2\ cm$$

3. D is correct.

$$1\ Watt = 1\ J/s$$

$$Power \times Time = Q$$

$$Q = mc\Delta T$$

$$P \times t = mc\Delta T$$

$$t = (mc\Delta T) / P$$

$$t = (90\ g)\cdot(4.186\ J/g\cdot°C)\cdot(30\ °C - 10\ °C) / (50\ W)$$

$$t = 151\ s$$

4. A is correct. Convert 15 minutes to seconds:

$$t = (15\ min/1)\cdot(60\ s/1\ min)$$

$$t = 900\ s$$

Find total energy generated:

$$Q = P \times t$$

$$Q = (1{,}260\ J/s)\cdot(900\ s)$$

$$Q = 1{,}134\ kJ$$

Find mass of water needed to carry away energy:

$Q = mL_v$

$m = Q / L_v$

$m = (1{,}134 \text{ kJ}) / (22.6 \times 10^2 \text{ kJ/kg})$

$m = 0.5 \text{ kg} = 500 \text{ g}$

5. C is correct. Phase changes occur at a constant temperature. Once the phase change is complete the temperature of the substance then either increases or decreases.

For example, water remains at 0 °C until it has completely changed phase to ice before the temperature decreases further.

6. B is correct.

The amount of energy needed to melt a sample of mass m is:

$Q = m L_f$

Where L_f is the latent heat of fusion.

$Q = (55 \text{ kg}) \cdot (334 \text{ kJ/kg})$

$Q = 1.8 \times 10^4 \text{ kJ}$

7. D is correct. Metals are good heat and electrical conductors because of their bonding structure. In metallic bonding, the outer electrons are held loosely and can travel freely. Electricity and heat require high electron mobility. Thus, the looseness of the outer electrons in the materials allows them to be excellent conductors.

8. A is correct. Find heat of phase change from steam to liquid:

$Q_1 = mL_v$

Find heat of phase change from liquid to solid:

$Q_2 = mL_f$

Find heat of temperature from 100 °C to 0 °C:

$Q_3 = mc\Delta T$

Total heat:

$Q_{net} = Q_1 + Q_2 + Q_3$

$Q_{net} = mL_v + mL_f + mc\Delta T$

To find mass:

$Q_{net} = m(L_v + c\Delta T + L_f)$

$m = Q_{net} / (L_v + c\Delta T + L_f)$

Solve:

$$Q_{net} = 200 \text{ kJ}$$

$$Q_{net} = 2 \times 10^5 \text{ J}$$

$$m = (2 \times 10^5 \text{ J}) / [(22.6 \times 10^5 \text{ J/kg}) + (4{,}186 \text{ J/kg·K}) \cdot (100 \text{ °C} - 0 \text{ °C}) + (33.5 \times 10^4 \text{ J/kg})]$$

$$m = 0.066 \text{ kg}$$

9. C is correct.

Fusion is the process whereby a substance changes from a solid to liquid (i.e., melting).

Condensation is the process whereby a substance changes from a vapor to liquid.

Sublimation is the process whereby a substance changes directly from a solid to the gas phase without passing through the liquid phase.

10. D is correct.

$$Q = mc\Delta T$$

$$Q = (0.2 \text{ kg}) \cdot (14.3 \text{ J/g·K}) \cdot (1{,}000 \text{ g/kg}) \cdot (280 \text{ K} - 250 \text{ K})$$

$$Q = 86{,}000 \text{ J} = 86 \text{ kJ}$$

11. B is correct. Heat needed to raise temperature of aluminum:

$$Q_A = m_A c_A \Delta T$$

Heat needed to raise temperature of water:

$$Q_W = m_W c_W \Delta T$$

Total heat to raise temperature of system:

$$Q_{net} = Q_A + Q_W$$

$$Q_{net} = m_A c_A \Delta T + m_W c_W \Delta T$$

$$Q_{net} = \Delta T (m_A c_A + m_W c_W)$$

$$Q_{net} = (98 \text{ °C} - 18 \text{ °C}) \cdot [(0.5 \text{ kg}) \cdot (900 \text{ J/kg·K}) + (1 \text{ kg}) \cdot (4{,}186 \text{ J/kg·K})]$$

$$Q_{net} = 370{,}880 \text{ J}$$

Time to produce Q_{net} with 500 W:

$$Q_{net} = (500 \text{ W})t$$

$$t = Q_{net} / (500 \text{ W})$$

$$t = (370{,}880 \text{ J}) / 500 \text{ W}$$

$$t = 741.8 \text{ s}$$

Convert to minutes:

$$t = (741.8 \text{ s}/1) \cdot (1 \text{ min}/60 \text{ s})$$

$$t = 12.4 \text{ min} \approx 12 \text{ min}$$

12. A is correct. When a substance goes through a phase change, the temperature doesn't change.

It can be assumed that the lower plateau is L_f and the upper plateau is L_v.

Count the columns: $L_f = 2$, $L_v = 7$

> $L_v / L_f = 7 / 2$
>
> $L_v / L_f = 3.5$

13. B is correct.

Specific heat is the amount of heat (i.e., energy) needed to raise the temperature of the unit mass of a substance by a given amount (usually one degree).

14. D is correct. Find ½ of KE of the BB:

> $KE = \frac{1}{2}mv^2$
>
> $\frac{1}{2}KE = \frac{1}{2}(\frac{1}{2}mv^2)$
>
> $\frac{1}{2}KE_{BB} = \frac{1}{2}(\frac{1}{2}) \cdot (0.0045 \text{ kg}) \cdot (46 \text{ m/s})^2$
>
> $\frac{1}{2}KE_{BB} = 2.38 \text{ J}$

The $\frac{1}{2}KE_{BB}$ is equal to energy taken to change temperature:

> $Q = \frac{1}{2}KE_{BB}$
> $Q = mc\Delta T$
>
> $mc\Delta T = \frac{1}{2}KE_{BB}$
>
> $\Delta T = \frac{1}{2}KE_{BB} / mc$

Calculate to find ΔT:

> $\Delta T = (2.38 \text{ J}) / (0.0045 \text{ kg}) \cdot (128 \text{ J/kg·K})$
>
> $\Delta T = 4.1 \text{ K}$

15. C is correct.

Vaporization is the process whereby a substance changes from a liquid to a gas. The process can be either boiling or evaporation.

Sublimation is the process whereby a substance changes from a solid to a gas.

16. A is correct. Carnot efficiency:

> $\eta = $ work done / total energy
>
> $\eta = W / Q_H$
>
> $\eta = 5 \text{ J} / 18 \text{ J}$
>
> $\eta = 0.28$

The engine's efficiency:

$$\eta = (T_H - T_C) / T_H$$

$$0.28 = (233 \text{ K} - T_C) / 233 \text{ K}$$

$$(0.28) \cdot (233 \text{ K}) = (233 \text{ K} - T_C)$$

$$65.2 \text{ K} = 233 \text{ K} - T_C$$

$$T_C = 168 \text{ K}$$

17. D is correct. Heat needed to change temperature of a mass:

$$Q = mc\Delta T$$

Calculate to find Q:

$$Q = (0.92 \text{ kg}) \cdot (113 \text{ cal/kg} \cdot °C) \cdot (96 °C - 18 °C)$$

$$Q = 8{,}108.9 \text{ cal}$$

Convert to joules:

$$Q = (8{,}108.9 \text{ cal}) \cdot (4.186 \text{ J/cal})$$

$$Q = 33{,}940 \text{ J}$$

18. B is correct.

During a change of state, the addition of heat does not change the temperature (i.e., a measure of the kinetic energy). The heat energy added only adds to the potential energy of the substance until the substance completely changes state.

19. C is correct. The work done for a cyclic process carried out in a gas is equal to the area enclosed by the cyclic process. (Use P for pressure and V for volume on the graph).

20. A is correct.

Specific heat of A is larger than B:

$$c_A > c_B$$

Energy to raise the temperature:

$$Q = mc\Delta T$$

If m and ΔT are equal for A and B:

$$Q_A = m_A c_A \Delta T_A$$

$$Q_B = m_B c_B \Delta T_B$$

$$Q_A > Q_B$$

This is valid because all other factors are equal and the magnitude of Q only depends on c.

21. D is correct. Find kinetic energy of meteor:

$$KE = \tfrac{1}{2}mv^2$$

$$KE = \tfrac{1}{2}(0.0065 \text{ kg}){\cdot}(300 \text{ m/s})^2$$

$$KE = 292.5 \text{ J}$$

Find temperature rise:

$$Q = KE$$

$$Q = mc\Delta T$$

$$mc\Delta T = KE$$

$$\Delta T = KE \, / \, mc$$

Convert KE to calories:

$$KE = (292.5 \text{ J}/1){\cdot}(1 \text{ cal}/4.186 \text{ J}) = 69.9 \text{ cal}$$

Calculate ΔT:

$$\Delta T = (69.9 \text{ cal}) \, / \, [(0.0065 \text{ kg}){\cdot}(120 \text{ cal/kg}{\cdot}°C)] = 89.6 \ °C \approx 90 \ °C$$

22. A is correct. When a liquid freezes it undergoes a phase change from liquid to solid. For this to occur heat energy must be dissipated (removed). During any phase change, the temperature remains constant.

23. B is correct. For an isothermal process:

$$\Delta U = 0$$

$$\Delta U = Q - W$$

$$Q = W$$

Work to expand an ideal gas in an isothermal process:

$$W = nRT \ln(V_f \, / \, V_i)$$

From the ideal gas law, $nRT = P_f V_f$, giving:

$$W = P_f V_f \ln(V_f \, / \, V_i)$$

$$W = (130 \text{ kPa}){\cdot}(0.2 \text{ m}^3) \ln[(0.2 \text{ m}^3) \, / \, (0.05 \text{ m}^3)]$$

$$W = 36 \text{ kJ}$$

$$Q = W$$

$$Q = 36 \text{ kJ}$$

Since the process is isothermal, there is no change in the internal energy. Since the surroundings are doing negative work on the system:

$$\Delta E = 0 = Q + W = Q - 36 \text{ kJ}$$

Therefore:

$$Q = 36 \text{ kJ}$$

24. D is correct.

Find the potential energy of 1 kg of water:

$PE = mgh$

$PE = (1 \text{ kg}) \cdot (9.8 \text{ m/s}^2) \cdot (30 \text{ m})$

$PE = 294 \text{ J}$

Assume all potential energy is converted to heat for maximum temperature increase:

$PE = Q$

$Q = mc\Delta T$

$mc\Delta T = PE$

$\Delta T = PE / mc$

$\Delta T = (294 \text{ J}) / [(1 \text{ kg}) \cdot (4{,}186 \text{ J/kg/K})]$

$\Delta T = 0.07 \text{ °C}$

For temperature differences it is not necessary to convert to Kelvin because a temperature change in Kelvin is equal to a temperature change in Celsius.

25. A is correct.

Find heat from phase change:

$Q = mL_f$

$Q = (0.75 \text{ kg}) \cdot (33{,}400 \text{ J/kg})$

$Q = 25{,}050 \text{ J}$

Because the water is freezing, Q should be negative due to heat being released.

$Q = -25{,}050 \text{ J}$

Find the change in entropy:

$\Delta S = Q / T$

$\Delta S = -25{,}050 \text{ J} / (0 \text{ °C} + 273 \text{ K})$

$\Delta S = -92 \text{ J} / \text{K}$

A negative change in entropy indicates that the disorder of the isolated system has decreased. When water freezes the entropy is negative because water is more disordered than ice. Thus, the disorder has decreased.

26. A is correct.

Copper has a larger coefficient of linear expansion than iron, so it expands more than iron during a given temperature change. The bimetallic bar bends due to the difference in expansion between the copper and iron.

27. D is correct. Calculate heat needed to raise temperature:

$Q = mc\Delta T$

$Q = (0.110 \text{ kg})\cdot(4{,}186 \text{ J/kg}\cdot\text{K})\cdot(30 \text{ °C} - 20 \text{ °C})$

$Q = 4{,}605 \text{ J}$

Calculate time needed to raise temperature with 60 W power source:

$Q = P \times t$

$Q = (60 \text{ W})t$

$t = Q / (60 \text{ W})$

$t = (4{,}605 \text{ J}) / (60 \text{ W})$

$t = 77 \text{ s}$

28. B is correct. During a change of state, the addition of heat does not change the temperature (i.e., a measure of the kinetic energy). The heat energy added only adds to the potential energy of the substance until the substance completely changes state.

29. C is correct.

Convert to Kelvin:

$T = -243 \text{ °C} + 273$

$T = 30 \text{ K}$

Double temperature:

$T_2 = (30 \text{ K})\cdot(2)$

$T_2 = 60 \text{ K}$

Convert back to Celsius:

$T_2 = 60 \text{ K} - 273$

$T_2 = -213 \text{ °C}$

30. D is correct. The specific heat is the quantity that would be most helpful if a researcher is attempting to determine how much the temperature of a particular piece of material would rise when a known amount of heat is added to it.

31. B is correct. Convert units:

$1.7 \times 10^5 \text{ J/kg} = 170 \text{ kJ/kg}$

Change in internal energy = heat added (Q)

$Q = mL_v$

$Q = (1 \text{ kg})\cdot(170 \text{ kJ/kg})$

$Q = 170 \text{ kJ}$

32. D is correct.

$Q = mc\Delta\text{T}$

If m and c are constant, the relationship is directly proportional.

To double Q, T must be doubled:

> 5 C + 273 = 278 K
>
> 278 K × 2 = 556 K
>
> 556 K - 273 = 283 C

33. B is correct.

The mass of each is required to determine which object experiences the greater temperature change during the time the system takes to reach thermal equilibrium.

34. B is correct.

Body heat gives energy to the water molecules in the sweat. This energy is transferred via collisions until some molecules have enough energy to break the hydrogen bonds and escape the liquid (i.e., evaporation). However, if a body stayed dry, the heat would not be given to the water, and the person would stay hot because the heat is not lost due to the evaporation of the water.

35. D is correct.

Calculate heat released when 0 °C water converts to 0 °C ice:

> $Q_1 = mL_f$
>
> $Q_1 = (2{,}200 \text{ kg}) \cdot (334 \times 10^3 \text{ J/kg})$
>
> $Q_1 = 734{,}800 \text{ kJ}$

Calculate heat released for temperature drop ΔT

> $Q_2 = mc\Delta\text{T}$
>
> $Q_2 = (2{,}200 \text{ kg}) \cdot (2{,}050 \text{ J/kg K}) \cdot [(0 \text{ °C} - (-30 \text{ °C})]$

$\Delta\text{K} = \Delta\text{°C}$, so units cancel:

> $Q_2 = 135{,}300 \text{ kJ}$

Add heat released to get Q_{net}:

> $Q_{net} = Q_1 + Q_2$
>
> $Q_{net} = (734{,}800 \text{ kJ}) + (135{,}300 \text{ kJ})$
>
> $Q_{net} = 870{,}100 \text{ kJ}$

36. A is correct.

Object 1 has three times the specific heat capacity and four times the mass of Object 2:

$c_1 = 3c_2$; $m_1 = 4m_2$

A single-phase substance obeys the specific heat equation:

$Q = mc\Delta T$

In this case, the same amount of heat is added to each substance, therefore:

$Q_1 = Q_2$

$m_1 c_1 \Delta T_1 = m_2 c_2 \Delta T_2$

$(4m_2)(3c_2)\Delta T_1 = m_2 \, c_2 \Delta T_2$

$12 m_2 c_2 \Delta T_1 = m_2 c_2 \Delta T_2$

$12 \, \Delta T_1 = \Delta T_2$

37. C is correct.

Conduction is a form of heat transfer in which the collisions of the molecules of the material transfer energy through the material. Higher temperature of the material causes the molecules to collide with more energy which eventually is transferred throughout the material through subsequent collisions.

Radiation is a form of heat transfer in which electromagnetic waves carry energy from the emitting object and deposit the energy to the object that absorbs the radiation.

Convection is a form of heat transfer in which mass motion of a fluid (i.e., liquids and gases) transfers energy from the source of heat.

38. A is correct.

From the ideal gas law:

$p_3 V_3 = nRT_3$

$T_3 = p_3 V_3 \, / \, nR$

$T_3 = 1.5 p_1 V_3 \, / \, nR$

$T_3 = 1.5 V_3 (p_1 \, / \, nR)$

Also from the ideal gas law:

$(p_1 \, / \, nR) = T_1 \, / \, V_1$

$(p_1 \, / \, nR) = (293.2 \text{ K}) \, / \, (100 \text{ cm}^3)$

$(p_1 \, / \, nR) = 2.932 \text{ K/cm}^3$

Calculate T$_3$:

$$T_3 = 1.5V_3 \ (2.932 \ \text{K/cm}^3)$$

$$T_3 = 1.5 \ (50 \ \text{cm}^3) \cdot (2.932 \ \text{K/cm}^3)$$

$$T_3 = 219.9 \ \text{K}$$

$$T_3 = -53.3 \ °\text{C} \approx -53 \ °\text{C}$$

Calculate T$_4$:

$$T_4 = 1.5V_4 \ (2.932 \ \text{K/cm}^3)$$

$$T_4 = 1.5 \ (150 \ \text{cm}^3) \cdot (2.932 \ \text{K/cm}^3)$$

$$T_4 = 659.6 \ \text{K}$$

$$T_4 = 386.5 \ °\text{C} \approx 387 \ °\text{C}$$

39. B is correct.

Steel is a very conductive material that can transfer thermal energy very well. The steel feels colder than the plastic because its higher thermal conductivity allows it to remove more heat and thus makes touching it feel colder.

40. B is correct. An isobaric process involves constant pressure.

An isochoric (also isometric) process involves a closed system at constant volume.

An adiabatic process occurs without transfer of heat or matter between a system and its surroundings.

An isothermal process involves the change of a system in which the temperature remains constant.

41. D is correct.

Carnot coefficient of performance of a refrigeration cycle:

$$C_P = T_C / (T_H - T_C)$$

$$C_P = Q_C / W$$

$$Q_C / W = T_C / (T_H - T_C)$$

$$W = (Q_C / T_C) \cdot (T_H - T_C)$$

$$W = (20 \times 10^3 \ \text{J} / 293 \ \text{K}) \cdot (307 \ \text{K} - 293 \ \text{K})$$

$$W = 955.6 \ \text{J} = 0.956 \ \text{kJ}$$

Power = Work / time

$$P = W / t$$

$$P = 0.956 \ \text{kJ} / 1 \ \text{s}$$

$$P = 0.956 \ \text{kW} \approx 0.96 \ \text{kW}$$

42. C is correct.

Heat energy is measured in units of Joules and calories.

43. B is correct.

Convection is a form of heat transfer in which mass motion of a fluid (i.e., liquids and gases) transfers energy from the source of heat.

44. A is correct.

Radiation is the transmission of energy in the form of particles or waves through space or a material medium. Examples include electromagnetic radiations such as X-rays, alpha particles, beta particles, radio waves and visible light.

45. D is correct. Convert P_3 to Pascals:

$P_3 = (2 \text{ atm} / 1) \cdot (101{,}325 \text{ Pa} / 1 \text{ atm})$

$P_3 = 202{,}650 \text{ Pa}$

Use the ideal gas law to find V_3:

$PV = nRT$

$V = (nRT) / P$

$V_3 = [(0.008 \text{ mol}) \cdot (8.314 \text{ J/mol·K}) \cdot (2{,}438 \text{ K})] / (202{,}650 \text{ Pa})$

$V_3 = 8 \times 10^{-4} \text{ m}^3$

Convert to cm^3:

$V_3 = (8 \times 10^{-4} \text{ m}^3 / 1) \cdot (100^3 \text{ cm}^3 / 1 \text{ m}^3)$

$V_3 = 800 \text{ cm}^3$

46. C is correct.

An adiabatic process involves no heat added or removed from the system.

From the First Law of Thermodynamics:

$\Delta U = Q + W$

If $Q = 0$, then:

$\Delta U = W$

Because work is being done to expand the gas, it is considered negative, and then the change in internal energy is negative (decreases).

$-\Delta U = -W$

47. B is correct.

Standing in a breeze while wet feels colder than when dry because of the evaporation of water off the skin. Water requires heat to evaporate, so this is taken from the body making a person feel colder than if they were dry and the evaporation did not occur.

48. A is correct.

Conduction is a form of heat transfer in which the collisions of the molecules of the material transfer energy through the material. Higher temperature of the material causes the molecules to collide with more energy which eventually is transferred throughout the material through subsequent collisions.

49. D is correct.

An isobaric process is a constant pressure process, so the resulting pressure is always the same.

50. B is correct.

This question is asking which type of surface has a higher emissivity than others and therefore can radiate more energy over a set period. A blackbody is an idealized radiator and has the highest emissivity. As such, a surface most similar to a blackbody (the black surface) is the best radiator of thermal energy.

A black surface is considered to be an ideal blackbody and therefore has an emissivity of 1 (perfect emissivity). The black surface will be the best radiator as compared to another surface which cannot be considered as blackbodies and have an emissivity of <1.

51. C is correct.

Calculate gap between the rods:

The gap in between the rods will be filled by both expanding, so total thermal expansion length is equal to 1.1 cm.

$$\Delta L = L_0 \alpha \Delta T$$

$$\Delta L_{tot} = \Delta L_B + \Delta L_A$$

$$\Delta L_{tot} = (\alpha_B L_B + \alpha_A L_A)\, \Delta T$$

Rearrange the equation for ΔT:

$$\Delta T = \Delta L_{tot} / (\alpha_B L_B + \alpha_A L_A)$$

$$\Delta T = 1.1 \text{ cm} / [(2 \times 10^{-5} \text{ K}^{-1}){\cdot}(59.1 \text{ cm}) + (2.4 \times 10^{-5} \text{ K}^{-1}){\cdot}(39.3 \text{ cm})]$$

$$\Delta T = 517.6 \text{ K} \approx 518 \text{ K}$$

Measuring difference in temperature in K is the same as in °C, so it is not required to convert:

$$\Delta T = 518 \text{ °C}$$

52. A is correct. Find seconds in a day:

$t = (24 \text{ h} / 1 \text{ day}) \cdot (60 \text{ min} / 1 \text{ h}) \cdot (60 \text{ s} / 1 \text{ min})]$

$t = 86,400 \text{ s}$

Find energy lost in a day:

$E = \text{Power} \times \text{time}$

$E = (60 \text{ W})t$

$E = (60 \text{ W}) \cdot (86,400 \text{ s})$

$E = 5,184,000 \text{ J}$

Convert to kcal:

$E = (5,184,000 \text{ J}/1) \cdot (1 \text{ cal}/4.186 \text{ J}) \cdot (1 \text{ kcal}/10^3 \text{ cal})$

$E = 1,240 \text{ kcal}$

53. D is correct.

Conduction is a form of heat transfer in which the collisions of the molecules of the material transfer energy through the material. Higher temperature of the material causes the molecules to collide with more energy which eventually is transferred throughout the material through subsequent collisions.

54. B is correct.

Heat given off by warmer water is equal to that absorbed by the frozen cube. This heat is split into heat needed to melt the cube and bring the temperature to equilibrium.

$Q_{\text{H2O,1}} + Q_{\text{alcohol,Temp1}} + Q_{\text{alcohol,Phase1}} = 0$

$(mc\Delta T)_{\text{H2O,1}} + (mc\Delta T)_{\text{alcohol,Temp1}} + (mL_f)_{\text{alcohol}} = 0$

$Q_{\text{H2O,2}} + Q_{\text{alcohol,Temp2}} + Q_{\text{alcohol,Phase2}} = 0$

$(mc\Delta T)_{\text{H2O,2}} + (mc\Delta T)_{\text{alcohol,Temp2}} + (mL_f)_{\text{alcohol}} = 0$

Set equal to each other to cancel heat from phase change (since they are equal):

$(mc\Delta T)_{\text{H2O,1}} + (mc\Delta T)_{\text{alcohol,Temp1}} = (mc\Delta T)_{\text{H2O,2}} + (mc\Delta T)_{\text{alcohol,Temp2}}$

$(m_{\text{alcohol}})(c_{\text{alcohol}}) \cdot (\Delta T_{\text{alcohol1}} - \Delta T_{\text{alcohol2}}) = c_{\text{H2O}}(m\Delta T_{\text{H2O,2}} - m\Delta T_{\text{H2O,1}})$

$c_{\text{alcohol}} = (c_{\text{H2O}} / m_{\text{alcohol}}) \cdot [(m\Delta T_{\text{H2O,2}} - m\Delta T_{\text{H2O,1}}) / (\Delta T_{\text{alcohol1}} - \Delta T_{\text{alcohol2}})]$

Solving for c_{alcohol}:

$c_{\text{alc}} = [(4,190 \text{ J/kg·K}) / (0.22 \text{ kg})] \cdot [(0.4 \text{ kg}) \cdot (10 - 30 \text{ °C}) - (0.35 \text{ kg}) \cdot (5 - 26 \text{ °C})]$

$\qquad / [(5 \text{ °C} - (-10 \text{ °C}) - (10 \text{ °C} - (-10 \text{ °C})]$

$c_{\text{alc}} = (19,045 \text{ J/kg·K}) \cdot [(-0.65 \text{ °C}) / (-5 \text{ °C})]$

$c_{\text{alc}} = 2,475 \text{ J/kg·K}$

55. D is correct.

Using the calculated value for c_{alc} in the problem above:

$$Q_{H2O,1} + Q_{alcohol,Temp1} + Q_{alcohol,Phase1} = 0$$

$$(mc\Delta T)_{H2O,1} + (mc\Delta T)_{alcohol} + (mL_f)_{alcohol} = 0$$

$$L_{f\,alcohol} = [-(mc\Delta T)_{H2O,1} - (mc\Delta T)_{alcohol}] / m_{alcohol}$$

Solve:

$$L_{f\,alcohol} = -[(0.35 \text{ kg}) \cdot (4,190 \text{ J/kg·K}) \cdot (5 \text{ °C} - 26 \text{ °C})$$

$$- (0.22 \text{ kg}) \cdot (2,475 \text{ J/kg·K}) \cdot (5 \text{ °C} - (-10 \text{ °C})] / (0.22 \text{ kg})$$

$$L_{f\,alcohol} = (30,796.5 \text{ J} - 8,167.5 \text{ J}) / (0.22 \text{ kg})$$

$$L_{f\,alcohol} = 103 \times 10^3 \text{ J/kg} = 10.3 \times 10^4 \text{ J/kg}$$

56. C is correct.

The silver coating reflects thermal radiation into the bottle to reduce heat loss by radiation. Radiation is a form of heat transfer in which electromagnetic waves carry energy from an emitting object and deposit the energy in an object absorbing the radiation.

57. B is correct.

Convert calories to Joules:

$$E = (16 \text{ kcal/1}) \cdot (10^3 \text{ cal/1 kcal}) \cdot (4.186 \text{ J/1 cal})$$

$$E = 66,976 \text{ J}$$

Convert hours to seconds:

$$t = (5 \text{ h}) \cdot (60 \text{ min/h}) \cdot (60 \text{ s/min})$$

$$t = 18,000 \text{ s}$$

Find power expended:

$$P = E / t$$

$$P = (66,976 \text{ J}) / (18,000 \text{ s})$$

$$P = 3.7 \text{ W}$$

58. A is correct.

$$\Delta Q = cm\Delta T$$

$$\Delta T = \Delta Q / cm$$

$$\Delta T = (50 \text{ kcal}) / [(1 \text{ kcal/kg·°C}) \cdot (5 \text{ kg})]$$

$$\Delta T = 10 \text{ °C}$$

59. C is correct.

For melting, use L_f:

$Q = mL_f$

$Q = (30 \text{ kg}) \cdot (334 \text{ kJ/kg})$

$Q = 1 \times 10^4 \text{ kJ}$

60. B is correct. Find temperature change:

$Q = mc\Delta T$

$\Delta T = Q / mc$

$\Delta T = (160 \times 10^3 \text{ J}) / [(6 \text{ kg}) \cdot (910 \text{ J/kg·K})]$

$\Delta T = 29 \text{ °C}$

Find final temperature:

$\Delta T = T_f - T_i$

$T_f = T_i + \Delta T$

$T_f = 12 \text{ °C} + 29 \text{ °C}$

$T_f = 41 \text{ °C}$

61. A is correct. After 5 minutes the sample is at a constant temperature indicating a phase change from solid to liquid (a mixture of solid and liquid).

B: heat capacity of the liquid phase is much greater than that of the solid.

C: the sample begins to boil at the second plateau which represents the liquid to gas phase change.

D: the heat of fusion is less than the heat of vaporization.

62. D is correct. Warm air is less dense than cold air. It follows that a mass of warm air is subject to buoyancy force, which is due to the density gradient in the cold air. The direction of the buoyancy force is toward lower density. Air with lower density also has lower pressure.

63. B is correct. Heat needed to raise temperature of iron:

$Q_I = m_I c_I \Delta T$

Heat needed to raise temperature of copper:

$Q_C = m_C c_C \Delta T$

Total heat needed for system:

$Q_{net} = Q_I + Q_C$

Calculate to find Q_{net}:

$Q_{net} = m_I c_I \Delta T + m_C c_C \Delta T$

$Q_{net} = \Delta T (m_I c_I + m_C c_C)$

$Q_{net} = (58 \,°C - 23 \,°C) \cdot [(0.15 \text{ kg}) \cdot (470 \text{ J/kg·K}) + (0.2 \text{ kg}) \cdot (390 \text{ J/kg·K})]$

$Q_{net} = 5{,}198 \text{ J}$

64. C is correct.

$\Delta Q = cm\Delta T$

$\Delta Q = (0.11 \text{ kcal/kg·°C}) \cdot (0.3 \text{ kg}) \cdot (20 \,°C)$

$\Delta Q = 0.66 \text{ kcal} = 660 \text{ cal}$

65. B is correct. Heat is the total energy of molecular motion in a substance, while the temperature is the average energy of molecular motion.

The amount of heat is dependent on mass. The larger container has more heat than the smaller container since it is larger in mass and therefore has more total thermal energy.

66. D is correct. Find mass of water:

$V = (200 \text{ L}) \cdot (0.001 \text{ m}^3/\text{L})$

$V = 0.2 \text{ m}^3$

density = mass / volume

$m = V\rho$

$m = (0.2 \text{ m}^3) \cdot (1{,}000 \text{ kg/m}^3)$

$m = 200 \text{ kg}$

Find heat added to raise temperature:

$Q = mc\Delta T$

$Q = (200 \text{ kg}) \cdot (4{,}186 \text{ J/kg·K}) \cdot (80 \,°C - 28 \,°C)$

$Q = 43534.4 \text{ kJ}$

Find time needed to raise temperature:

$4 \text{ kW} = Q / t$

$t = Q / (4 \text{ kW})$

$t = 43{,}534.4 \text{ kJ} / 4 \text{ kW}$

$t = 10{,}884 \text{ s}$

Convert to hours:

$t = (10{,}884 \text{ s}) / (60 \text{ s}) / (60 \text{ min})$

$t = 3 \text{ hours}$

67. A is correct. The First Law of Thermodynamics states:

$\Delta U = Q + W$

This is equivalent to the Law of Conservation of Energy because the change in internal energy of a system (ΔU) is equal to the energy added as heat and work ($Q + W$).

68. C is correct. Heat flux lost through conduction is:

$Q / t = kA(T_H - T_C) / d$

where k = thermal conductivity and t = time

$Q / t = [(0.8 \text{ W/m·°C})·(3.1 \text{ m} \times 1.8 \text{ m})·(22 \text{ °C} - 7 \text{ °C})] / (0.009 \text{ m})$

$Q / t = 7{,}440 \text{ J/s}$

To find heat energy lost in an hour multiply by seconds in an hour:

$Q_{total} = (7{,}440 \text{ J/s})·(3{,}600 \text{ s/1h})$

$Q_{total} = 2.7 \times 10^7 \text{ J}$

69. D is correct. A temperature difference is a difference in thermal energy. Heat always flows from warm (high energy) to colder (low energy) regions to balance the differences in thermal energy.

70. A is correct. Find heat liberated from 30 °C to 0 °C:

$Q_1 = mc\Delta T$

$Q_1 = (0.435 \text{ kg})·(4{,}186 \text{ J/kg·K})·(30 \text{ °C} - 0 \text{ °C})$

$Q_1 = 54{,}600 \text{ J} = 54.6 \text{ kJ}$

Find heat liberated by phase change:

$Q_2 = mL_f$

$Q_2 = (0.435 \text{ kg})·(33.5 \times 10^4 \text{ J/kg})$

$Q_2 = 145{,}700 \text{ J} = 145.7 \text{ kJ}$

Find heat liberated by 0 °C to –8 °C:

$Q_3 = mc\Delta T$

$Q_3 = (0.435 \text{ kg})·(2{,}090 \text{ J/kg·K})·[(0 \text{ °C} - (-8 \text{ °C})]$

$Q_3 = 7{,}300 \text{ J} = 7.3 \text{ kJ}$

Find total Q heat liberated:

$Q_{net} = Q_1 + Q_2 + Q_3$

$Q_{net} = (54.6 \text{ kJ} + 145.7 \text{ kJ} + 7.3 \text{ kJ})$

$Q_{net} = 208 \text{ kJ}$

71. A is correct.

$Q = mL_f$

$Q = (0.4 \text{ kg}) \cdot (80 \text{ kcal/kg})$

$Q = 32 \text{ kcal}$

72. D is correct.

Carnot efficiency:

$\eta = (T_H - T_C) / T_H$

$\eta = (420 \text{ K} - 270 \text{ K}) / 420 \text{ K}$

$\eta = 0.357$

$W = Q_H \times \eta$

$W = (3{,}650 \text{ J}) \cdot (0.357)$

$W = 1{,}303 \text{ J}$

73. B is correct.

Find heat needed to raise temperature to boiling point:

$Q = mc\Delta T$

$Q = (0.8 \text{ kg}) \cdot (4{,}186 \text{ J/kg} \cdot \text{K}) \cdot (100 \text{ °C} - 70 \text{ °C})$

$Q = 100{,}464 \text{ J}$

Subtract from 800 kJ:

$Q_{remaining} = (800 \times 10^3 \text{ J}) - 100{,}464 \text{ J}$

$Q_{remaining} = 699{,}536 \text{ J}$

Use $Q_{remaining}$ to find mass of water that has evaporated:

$Q_R = mL_v$

$m = Q_R / L_v$

$m = (699{,}536 \text{ J}) / (22.6 \times 10^5 \text{ J/kg})$

$m = 0.310 \text{ kg}$

Subtract from original mass to find mass remaining:

$m_R = 0.800 \text{ kg} - 0.310 \text{ kg}$

$m_R = 0.490 \text{ kg} = 490 \text{ g}$

74. A is correct.

In any adiabatic process heat is not added to the system thus:

$Q = 0$

75. D is correct.

$C_P = Q_H / W$

$C_P = 50 \text{ kW} / 7.5 \text{ kW}$

$C_P = 6.7$

76. D is correct. Convection is a form of heat transfer in which mass motion of a fluid (i.e., liquids and gases) transfers energy from the source of heat.

77. C is correct. Find heat for temperature change from 300 K to 1,357 K:

$Q_1 = mc\Delta T$

$Q_1 = (740 \text{ kg}){\cdot}(386 \text{ J/kg}{\cdot}\text{K}){\cdot}(1{,}357 \text{ K} - 250 \text{ K})$

$Q_1 = 316.2 \text{ MJ}$

Find heat for phase change:

$Q_2 = mL_f$

$Q_2 = (740 \text{ kg}){\cdot}(205{,}000 \text{ J/kg})$

$Q_2 = 151.7 \text{ MJ}$

Find total heat:

$Q_{net} = Q_1 + Q_2$

$Q_{net} = 316.2 \text{ MJ} + 151.7 \text{ MJ}$

$Q_{net} = 468 \text{ MJ}$

$Q_{net} = 4.70 \times 10^5 \text{ kJ}$

78. B is correct.

Because the block can be thought of as infinitely large, equilibrium temperature = 0.

$\Delta Q = mc\Delta T$

$\Delta Q = (0.008 \text{ kg}){\cdot}(1 \text{ kcal/kg}{\cdot}\text{°C}){\cdot}(100 \text{ °C} - 0 \text{ °C})$

$\Delta Q = 0.8 \text{ kcal}$

This heat is transferred to the ice, which has a latent heat of fusion of 80 kcal/kg.

$Q / L_f = m$

$(0.8 \text{ kcal}) / (80 \text{ kcal/kg}) = 0.01 \text{ kg} = 10 \text{ g of ice is melted}$

79. D is correct.

$\eta = (T_H - T_C) / T_H$

$0.13 T_H = T_H - 1.9 \text{ K}$

$1.9 \text{ K} = T_H - 0.13 T_H$

$1.9 \text{ K} = T_H(1 - 0.13)$

$1.9 \text{ K} = T_H(0.87)$

$T_H = 1.9 \text{ K} / (0.87)$

$T_H = 2.2 \text{ K}$

80. C is correct.

Efficiency of a heat engine is given as:

$\eta = (Q_H - Q_C) / Q_H$

$\eta = (1{,}200 \text{ J} - 800 \text{ J}) / 1{,}200 \text{ J}$

$\eta = 0.33 = 33\%$

81. B is correct.

Thermal conductivity equation:

$Q / t = kA(T_H - T_C) / d$

where k is thermal conductivity constant

$Q / t = (0.105 \text{ W/m·K})\cdot(0.35 \text{ m} \times 0.55 \text{ m})\cdot[30 - (-10 \text{ °C})] / (0.006 \text{ m})$

$Q / t = 135 \text{ W}$

82. A is correct.

Stefan Boltzmann law for objects radiating energy to cooler surroundings:

$Q / t = Ae\sigma(T_H^4 - T_C^4)$

Surface area of a sphere:

$A = 4\pi r^2$

Surface area of hot inner sphere:

$A = 4\pi(0.3 \text{ m})^2$

$A = 1.13 \text{ m}^2$

Power radiated by hot inner sphere:

$P = (1.13 \text{ m}^2)\cdot(0.55)\cdot(5.67 \times 10^{-8} \text{ W/m}^2\text{K}^4)\cdot(500^4 \text{ K} - 400^4 \text{ K})$

$P = 1.3 \text{ kW outwards}$

The direction is out because radiation always radiates from hot to cold.

83. D is correct.

Assuming the system is isolated, no heat can enter or leave the system. Heat can only be exchanged between the lead and the water.

$$0 = Q_L + Q_W$$

$$0 = m_L c_L (T_{Li} - T_f) + m_W c_W (T_f - T_{Wi})$$

Solve for T_f:

$$T_f = (m_L c_L T_{Li} + m_W c_W T_{Wi}) / (m_L c_L + c_W T_{Wi})$$

Note that this is the weighted average of the two initial temperatures.

$$T_f = [(0.050 \text{ kg}) \cdot (0.11 \text{ kcal/kg/°C}) \cdot (100 \text{ °C}) - (0.080 \text{ kg}) \cdot (1 \text{ kcal/kg/°C}) \cdot (0 \text{ °C})] /$$

$$[(0.050 \text{ kg}) \cdot (0.11 \text{ kcal/kg/°C}) + (0.080 \text{ kg}) \cdot (1 \text{ kcal/kg/°C})]$$

$$T_f = 6.4 \text{ °C}$$

84. C is correct.

Work is equal to the area enclosed.

$$\text{Area} = \frac{1}{2}(\text{base} \times \text{height})$$

Area of this triangle:

$$\text{Area} = \frac{1}{2}(\Delta P) \cdot (\Delta V)$$

Convert units:

$$\Delta P = (3 - 1) P_0$$

$$\Delta P = (2) \cdot (4.8 \text{ atm})$$

$$\Delta P = (9.6 \text{ atm}) \cdot [(1 \times 10^5 \text{ N/m}^2) / (1 \text{ atm})]$$

$$\Delta P = 9.6 \times 10^5 \text{ N/m}^2$$

$$\Delta V = 600 \text{ cm}^3 - 200 \text{ cm}^3$$

$$\Delta V = 400 \text{ cm}^3 \times (1 \text{ m}/100 \text{ cm})^3$$

$$\Delta V = 4 \times 10^{-4} \text{ m}^3$$

$$W = \frac{1}{2}(9.6 \times 10^5 \text{ N/m}^2) \cdot (4 \times 10^{-4} \text{ m}^3)$$

$$W = 192 \text{ N·m} = 192 \text{ J}$$

85. D is correct.

$$PE = Q$$

$mgh = mc\Delta T$, cancel m from both sides of the expression

$$gh = c\Delta T$$

$$gh / c = \Delta T$$

$$\Delta T = [(10 \text{ m/s}^2) \cdot (60 \text{ m})] / 4{,}186 \text{ J/kg·K}$$

$$\Delta T = 0.14 \text{ °C}$$

86. B is correct.

Heat Radiation:

$$Q / t = Ae\sigma(T_H^4 - T_C^4)$$

Set constants $Ae\sigma = n$:

$$Q / t = n(T_H^4 - T_C^4)$$

$$80 \text{ J/s} = n[T_H^4 - (25 \text{ °C} + 273 \text{ K})^4]$$

$$0 \text{ J/s} = n[T_H^4 - (298 \text{ K})^4] - 80 \text{ J/s}$$

$$95 \text{ J/s} = n[T_H^4 - (20 \text{ °C} + 273 \text{ K})^4]$$

$$0 \text{ J/s} = n[T_H^4 - (293 \text{ K})^4] - 95 \text{ J/s}$$

Set equal and solve for n:

$$n[(T_H^4 - (298 \text{ K})^4] - 80 \text{ J/s} = n[(T_H^4 - (293 \text{ K})^4] - 95 \text{ J/s}$$

$$15 \text{ J/s} = n[T_H^4 - (293 \text{ K})^4] - n[T_H^4 - (298 \text{ K})^4]$$

$$15 \text{ J/s} = n[T_H^4 - (293 \text{ K})^4 - T_H^4 + (298 \text{ K})^4]$$

$$15 \text{ J/s} = n[(298 \text{ K})^4 - (293 \text{ K})^4]$$

$$15 \text{ J/s} = n(51.6 \times 10^7 \text{ K}^4)$$

$$n = 2.9 \times 10^{-8} \text{ W/K}^4$$

Solve for T_H:

$$0 = (2.9 \times 10^{-8} \text{ W/K}^4) \cdot [T_H^4 - (293 \text{ K})^4] - 95 \text{ J/s}$$

$$T_H^4 = 1.06 \times 10^{10} \text{ K}^4$$

$$T_H = 321 \text{ K}$$

$$T_H = 48 \text{ °C}$$

87. A is correct.

Efficiency of a heat engine:

$$\eta = (Q_H - Q_C) / Q_H$$

$$\eta = (6{,}000 \text{ J} - 4{,}000 \text{ J}) / (6{,}000 \text{ J})$$

$$\eta = 0.33 \times 100\% = 33\%$$

88. C is correct.

$$\Delta L = L_0 \alpha \Delta T$$

$$\Delta L = (40 \text{ m}) \cdot (1.2 \times 10^{-5} \text{ K}^{-1}) \Delta T$$

$$\Delta L = (40 \text{ m}) \cdot (1.2 \times 10^{-5} \text{ K}^{-1}) \cdot (160 \text{ °C} - 15 \text{ °C})$$

$$\Delta L = 0.07 \text{ m} = 70 \text{ mm}$$

89. D is correct.

$\Delta S = -L_{v}m / T$

$\Delta S = -(22.6 \times 10^5 \text{ J/kg}) \cdot (2 \text{ kg}) / (100 \,^{\circ}\text{C} + 273 \text{ K})$

$\Delta S = -12{,}118 \text{ J/K} = -12.1 \times 10^3 \text{ J/K}$

A negative change in entropy indicates that the disorder of the isolated system has decreased. When steam condenses to water the entropy is negative because steam is more disordered than water.

90. A is correct. Change in internal energy is $Q + W$.

91. C is correct. Entropy increase for two temperatures:

$\Delta S = Q(1 / T_2 - 1 / T_1)$

Let R be the rate of change of entropy. Then:

$R = (25 \text{ kW}) \cdot [(1 / -20 \,^{\circ}\text{C} + 273 \text{ K}) - (1 / 20 \,^{\circ}\text{C} + 273 \text{ K})]$

$R = (25 \text{ kW}) \cdot [(1 / 253 \text{ K}) - (1 / 293 \text{ K})]$

$R = 0.013 \text{ kW/K}$

$R = 13 \text{ W/K}$

92. D is correct. $Q = mc\Delta T$

Find heat released for temperature drop from 160 °C to 150 °C:

$Q_1 = (3.4 \text{ kg}) \cdot (400 \text{ J/kg·K}) \cdot (160 \,^{\circ}\text{C} - 150 \,^{\circ}\text{C})$

$Q_1 = 13{,}600 \text{ J}$

Find heat released due to condensation:

$Q_2 = mL_v$

$Q_2 = (3.4 \text{ kg}) \cdot (7.2 \times 10^4 \text{ J/kg})$

$Q_2 = 244{,}800 \text{ J}$

Find heat released for temperature drop from 150 °C to 75 °C:

$Q_3 = mc\Delta T$

$Q_3 = (3.4 \text{ kg}) \cdot (1{,}000 \text{ J/kg·K}) \cdot (150 \,^{\circ}\text{C} - 75 \,^{\circ}\text{C})$

$Q_3 = 255{,}000 \text{ J}$

Sum the heats:

$Q_{net} = Q_1 + Q_2 + Q_3$

$Q_{net} = (13{,}600 \text{ J} + 244{,}800 \text{ J} + 255{,}000 \text{ J})$

$Q_{net} = 513{,}400 \text{ J} = 513 \text{ kJ}$

93. C is correct.

Find heat from phase change:

$$Q = mL_f$$

$$Q = (0.2 \text{ kg}) \cdot (1.04 \times 10^5 \text{ J/kg})$$

$$Q = 20,800 \text{ J}$$

Because the ethanol is freezing, Q should be negative due to heat being released.

$$Q = -20,800 \text{ J}$$

Find change in entropy:

$$\Delta S = Q / T$$

$$\Delta S = -20,800 \text{ J} / (-114.4 \text{ °C} + 273 \text{ K})$$

$$\Delta S = -131 \text{ J} / \text{K}$$

94. B is correct. $W = P\Delta V$

Isobaric means pressure is constant, and volume is changing.

95. C is correct. Adiabatic means that no heat enters or leaves the system.

$$Q = 0 \text{ kJ}$$

96. C is correct. $Q = mc\Delta T$

Find heat added to aluminum calorimeter:

$$Q_A = (0.08 \text{ kg}) \cdot (910 \text{ J/kg·K}) \cdot (35 \text{ °C} - 20 \text{ °C})$$

$$Q_A = 1,092 \text{ J}$$

Find heat added to water:

$$Q_W = (0.36 \text{ kg}) \cdot (4,190 \text{ J/kg·K}) \cdot (35 \text{ °C} - 20 \text{ °C})$$

$$Q_W = 22,626 \text{ J}$$

Find total heat added to the system:

$$Q_{total} = Q_A + Q_W$$

$$Q_{total} = 1,092 \text{ J} + 22,626 \text{ J}$$

$$Q_{total} = 23,718 \text{ J}$$

Find specific heat of the metal:

$$Q = mc\Delta T$$

$$c = Q / m\Delta T$$

$$c = (23,718 \text{ J}) / [(0.18 \text{ kg}) \cdot (305 \text{ °C} - 35 \text{ °C})]$$

$$c = 488 \text{ J/kg·K}$$

97. D is correct.

Watt = 1 J/s

Thermal energy:

Q = Power × time

$Q = mc\Delta T$

$P \times t = mc\Delta T$

$t = (mc\Delta T) / P$

$t = [(120 \text{ g})\cdot(4.186 \text{ J/g}\cdot{}^\circ\text{C})\cdot(50 \text{ }^\circ\text{C} - 20 \text{ }^\circ\text{C})] / (65 \text{ W})$

$t = 232 \text{ s}$

98. C is correct.

The Second Law of Thermodynamics states that entropy is either constant or increasing over time. A constant entropy process is an idealized process and doesn't exist. Thus, entropy is always increasing over time.

99. B is correct.

The Second Law of Thermodynamics states that through thermodynamic processes, there is an increase in the sum of entropies of the system. Thus, no engine process is 100% efficient.

100. D is correct. Find heat from phase change:

$Q = mL_f$

$Q = (0.02 \text{ kg})\cdot(22.6 \times 10^5 \text{ J/kg})$

$Q = 45,200 \text{ J}$

Because the water is vaporizing, Q should be positive due to heat being absorbed.

$Q = 45,200 \text{ J}$

Find the change in entropy:

$\Delta S = Q / T$

$\Delta S = 45,200 \text{ J} / (100 \text{ }^\circ\text{C} + 273 \text{ K})$

$\Delta S = 121 \text{ J / K}$

A positive change in entropy indicates that the disorder of the isolated system has increased. When water evaporates into steam, the entropy is positive because the disorder of steam is higher than water.

101. A is correct.

Coefficient of performance assuming ideal Carnot cycle:

$$C_p = Q_H / W$$

$$C_p = T_H / (T_H - T_C)$$

$$Q_H / W = T_H / (T_H - T_C)$$

$$W = Q_H \cdot (T_H - T_C) / T_H$$

$$W = (32 \times 10^3 \text{ J/s}) \cdot (293 \text{ K} - 237 \text{ K}) / (293 \text{ K})$$

$$W = 6{,}116 \text{ J/s} \approx 6{,}100 \text{ W}$$

102. D is correct.

Carnot efficiency engines can be written as:

$$\eta = 1 - T_C / T_H$$

$$\eta = 1 - | Q_C / Q_H |$$

Thus:

$$Q_C / Q_H = T_C / T_H$$

103. C is correct.

Find heat from phase change:

$$Q = m L_f$$

$$Q = (8 \text{ kg}) \cdot (80 \text{ kcal/kg})$$

$$Q = 640 \text{ kcal/kg}$$

Because the water is freezing, Q should be negative due to heat being released.

$$Q = -640 \text{ kcal/kg}$$

Find the change in entropy:

$$\Delta S = Q / T$$

$$\Delta S = -640 \text{ kcal/kg} / (0 \text{ °C} + 273 \text{ K})$$

$$\Delta S = -2.3 \text{ kcal/K}$$

A negative change in entropy indicates that the disorder of the isolated system has decreased. When water freezes the entropy is negative because water is more disordered than ice. Thus, the disorder has decreased, and entropy is negative.

104. A is correct.

$$Q_H = 515 \text{ J}$$

$$Q_C = 340 \text{ J}$$

Carnot cycle efficiency:

$$\eta = (Q_H - Q_C) / Q_H$$
$$\eta = (515 \text{ J} - 340 \text{ J}) / (515 \text{ J})$$
$$\eta = 0.34 = 34\%$$

105. B is correct.

$$Q = (mc\Delta T)_{water} + (mc\Delta T)_{beaker}$$

Change in temperature is the same for both:

$$Q = \Delta T[(mc)_{water} + (mc)_{beaker}]$$
$$1,800 \text{ cal} = (20 \text{ °C}) \cdot [(65 \text{ g}) \cdot (1 \text{ cal/g·°C}) + (m_{beaker}) \cdot (0.18 \text{ cal/g·°C})]$$
$$90 \text{ cal/°C} = 65 \text{ cal/°C} + (m_{beaker}) \cdot (0.18 \text{ cal/g·°C})$$
$$25 \text{ cal/°C} / (0.18 \text{ cal/g·°C}) = (m_{beaker})$$
$$m_{beaker} = 139 \text{ g}$$

106. C is correct.

Heat to melt ice cube:

$$Q_1 = mL_f$$

Heat to raise the temperature:

$$Q_2 = mc\Delta T$$

Total heat:

$$Q_{total} = Q_1 + Q_2$$
$$Q_{total} = mL_f + mc\Delta T$$
$$Q_{total} = (0.3 \text{ kg}) \cdot (334 \text{ kJ/kg}) + (0.3 \text{ kg}) \cdot (4.186 \text{ kJ/kg·K}) \cdot (60 \text{ °C} - 0 \text{ °C})$$
$$Q_{total} = 176 \text{ kJ}$$

Fluid Statics and Dynamics – Explanations

1. C is correct. Refer to the unknown liquid as "A" and the oil as "O."

$\rho_A h_A g = \rho_O h_O g$, cancel g from both sides of the expression

$\rho_A h_A = \rho_O h_O$

$h_A = 5$ cm

$h_O = 20$ cm

$h_A = \frac{1}{4} h_O$

$\rho_A (\frac{1}{4}) h_O = \rho_O h_O$

$\rho_A = 4\rho_O$

$\rho_A = 4(850 \text{ kg/m}^3)$

$\rho_A = 3{,}400 \text{ kg/m}^3$

2. D is correct.

$P = \rho_{oil} \times V_{oil} \times g / (A_{tube})$

$P = [\rho_o \pi (r_{tube})^2 \times hg] / \pi (r_{tube})^2$

cancel $\pi (r_{tube})^2$ from both the numerator and the denominator.

$P = \rho_o g h$

$P = (850 \text{ kg/m}^3) \cdot (9.8 \text{ m/s}^2) \cdot (0.2 \text{ m})$

$P = 1{,}666 \text{ Pa}$

3. A is correct.

$m_{oil} = \rho_{oil} V_{oil}$

$V = \pi r^2 h$

$m_{oil} = \rho_{oil} \pi r^2 h$

$m_{oil} = \pi (850 \text{ kg/m}^3) \cdot (0.02 \text{ m})^2 \times (0.2 \text{ m})$

$m_{oil} = 0.21 \text{ kg} = 210 \text{ g}$

4. A is correct. Gauge pressure is the pressure experienced by an object referenced at atmospheric pressure. When the block is lowered its gauge pressure increases according to:

$P_G = \rho g h$

At $t = 0$, the block just enters the water and $h = 0$ so $P_G = 0$. As time passes, the height of the block below the water increases linearly, so P_G increases linearly as well.

5. D is correct.

Using Bernoulli's principle and assuming the opening of the tank is so large that the initial velocity is essentially zero:

$\rho gh = \frac{1}{2}\rho v^2$, cancel ρ from both sides of the expression

$gh = \frac{1}{2}v^2$

$v^2 = 2gh$

$v^2 = 2 \cdot (9.8 \text{ m/s}^2) \cdot (0.8 \text{ m})$

$v^2 = 15.68 \text{ m}^2/\text{s}^2$

$v = 3.96 \text{ m/s} \approx 4 \text{ m/s}$

Note: the diameter is not used to solve the problem.

6. C is correct.

The ideal gas law is:

$PV = nR\text{T}$

Keeping $nR\text{T}$ constant:

If $P_{final} = \frac{1}{2}P_{initial}$

$V_{final} = \frac{1}{2}V_{initial}$

However, in an isothermal process there is no change in internal energy.

Therefore, because energy must be conserved:

$\Delta U = 0$

7. B is correct.

For most substances, the solid form is denser than the liquid phase. Therefore, a block of most solids sinks in the liquid. With regards to pure water though, a block of ice (solid phase) floats in liquid water because ice is less dense.

Like other substances, when liquid water is cooled from room temperature, it becomes increasingly dense. However, at approximately 4 °C (39 °F), water reaches its maximum density, and as it's cooled further, it expands and becomes less dense. This phenomenon is known as negative thermal expansion and is attributed to strong intermolecular interactions that are orientation-dependent.

The density of water is about 1 g/cm^3 and depends on the temperature. When frozen, the density of water is decreased by about 9%. This is due to the decrease in intermolecular vibrations, which allows water molecules to form stable hydrogen bonds with other water molecules around. As these hydrogen bonds form, molecules are locking into positions similar to form hexagonal structures. Even though hydrogen bonds are shorter in the crystal than in the liquid, this position locking decreases the average coordination number of water molecules as the liquid reaches the solid phase.

8. C is correct.

The object sinks when the buoyant force is less than the weight of the object.

Since the buoyant force is equal to the weight of the displaced fluid, an object sinks precisely when the weight of the fluid it displaces is less than the weight of the object itself.

9. A is correct.

$P = \rho gh$

$P = (10^3 \text{ kg/m}^3) \cdot (9.8 \text{ m/s}^2) \cdot (100 \text{ m})$

$P = 9.8 \times 10^5 \text{ N/m}^2$

10. C is correct.

Absolute pressure = gauge pressure + atmospheric pressure

$P_{abs} = P_G + P_{atm}$

$P_{abs} = \rho gh + P_{atm}$

Atmospheric pressure is added to the total pressure at the bottom of a volume of liquid.

Therefore, if the atmospheric pressure increases, absolute pressure increases by the same amount.

11. A is correct.

Surface tension increases as temperature decreases. Generally, the cohesive forces maintaining surface tension decrease as molecular thermal activity increases.

12. B is correct.

By Poiseuille's Law, the volumetric flow rate of a fluid is given by:

$V = \Delta P A r^2 / 8\eta L$

Volumetric flow rate is the volume of fluid that passes a point per unit time:

$V = A v$

where v is the speed of the fluid.

Therefore:

$A v = \Delta P A r^2 / 8\eta L$

$v = \Delta P r^2 / 8\eta L$

$v = (225 \times 10^3 \text{ Pa}) \cdot (0.0032 \text{ m})^2 / [8 (0.3 \text{ Ns/m}^2) \cdot (1 \text{ m})]$

$v = 0.96 \text{ m/s}$

13. A is correct.

The buoyant force upward must balance the weight downward.

Buoyant force = weight of the volume of water displaced

$F_B = W_{object}$

$\rho V g = W_{object}$

$W_{object} = 60$ N

$W_{object} = (\rho_{water}) \cdot (V_{water}) \cdot (g)$

60 N $= (1{,}000$ kg/m$^3) \cdot (V_{water}) \cdot (10$ m/s$^2)$

$V_{water} = 60$ N $/ (1{,}000$ kg/m$^3) \cdot (10$ m/s$^2)$

$V_{water} = 0.006$ m^3

14. B is correct. Volume flow rate:

$Q = vA$

$Q = (2.5$ m/s$)\pi r^2$

$Q = (2.5$ m/s$) \cdot (0.015$ m$)^2 \pi$

$Q = 1.8 \times 10^{-3}$ m^3/s

15. C is correct. Force equation for the cork that is not accelerating:

$F_B - mg = 0$

Let *m* be the mass and V be the volume of the cork.

Replace:

$m = \rho V$

$F_B = (\rho_{water}) \cdot (V_{disp}) \cdot (g)$

$(\rho_{water}) \cdot (V_{disp}) \cdot (g) = (\rho_{cork}) \cdot (V) \cdot (g)$

$V_{disp} = \tfrac{3}{4} V$

$\rho_{water} (\tfrac{3}{4} V g) = (\rho_{cork}) \cdot (V) \cdot (g)$, cancel *g* and V from both sides of the expression

$\tfrac{3}{4}\rho_{water} = \rho_{cork}$

$\rho_{cork} / \rho_{water} = \tfrac{3}{4} = 0.75$

16. D is correct.

volume = mass / density

$V = (600$ g$) / (0.93$ g/cm$^3)$

$V = 645$ cm^3

17. C is correct.

For monatomic gases:

$$U = 3/2k_BT$$

where U is average KE per molecule and k_B is the Boltzmann constant

18. B is correct.

The object weighs 150 N less while immersed because the buoyant force is supporting 150 N of the total weight of the object.

Since the object is totally submerged, the volume of water displaced equals the volume of the object.

$$F_B = 150 \text{ N}$$

$$F_B = \rho_{water} \times V_{water} \times g$$

$$V = F_B / \rho g$$

$$V = (150 \text{ N}) / (1{,}000 \text{ kg/m}^3) \cdot (10 \text{ m/s}^2)$$

$$V = 0.015 \text{ m}^3$$

19. C is correct.

$$F_B / \rho_w = (m_c g) / \rho_c$$

$$F_B = (\rho_w m_c g) / \rho_c$$

$$F_B = [(1 \text{ g/cm}^3) \cdot (0.03 \text{ kg}) \cdot (9.8 \text{ m/s}^2)] / (8.9 \text{ g/cm}^3)$$

$$F_B = 0.033 \text{ N}$$

$$m_{total} = m_w + (F_B / g)$$

$$m_{total} = (0.14 \text{ kg}) + [(0.033 \text{ N}) / (9.8 \text{ m/s}^2)]$$

$$m_{total} = 0.143 \text{ kg} = 143 \text{ g}$$

20. D is correct.

$$v_1 A_1 = v_2 A_2$$

$$v_2 = v_1 A_1 / A_2$$

$$v_2 = [v_1(\pi/4)d_1^2] / (\pi/4)d_2^2$$

cancel $(\pi/4)$ from both the numerator and denominator

$$v_2 = v_1(d_1^2 / d_2^2)$$

$$v_2 = (1 \text{ m/s}) \cdot [(6 \text{ cm})^2 / (3 \text{ cm})^2]$$

$$v_2 = 4 \text{ m/s}$$

21. A is correct.

Static fluid pressure:

$$P = \rho g h$$

Pressure is only dependent on gravity (g), the height (h) of the fluid above the object and density (ρ) of the fluid. It does depend on the depth of the object but does not depend on the surface area of the object.

Both objects are submerged to the same depth, so the fluid pressure is equal. Note that the buoyant force on the blocks is NOT equal, but pressure (force / area) is equal.

22. C is correct. Surface tension force acts as the product of surface tension and the total length of contact.

$$F = AL$$

For a piece of thread, the length of contact is *l* as shown:

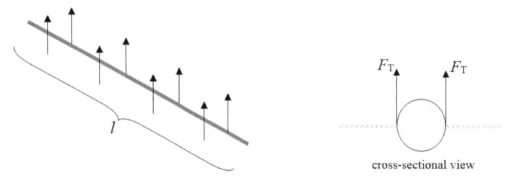

cross-sectional view

$F = 2L$ because the force acts on both sides of the thread.

Thus, for a thread rectangle, the total contact length is the total length times two.

$$L = 2(l + w + l + w)$$
$$F_{max} = 2A(l + w + l + w)$$
$$F_{max} = 2A(2l + 2w)$$
$$F_{max} = 4A(l + w)$$

23. D is correct.

Gauge pressure is the measure of pressure with respect to the atmospheric pressure. So, if the pressure inside the tire is equal to the air pressure outside, the gauge reads zero.

24. B is correct.

Pressure is measured in force per unit area, which is the force divided by the area.

25. D is correct.

The shear stress is the force per unit area and has units of N/m^2.

26. B is correct. Because the area of the reservoir is assumed to be essentially infinite, the velocity of the flow at the top of the tank is assumed to be zero.

Using Bernoulli's equation, find the speed through the 3 cm pipe:

$(\frac{1}{2}\rho v^2 + \rho gh)_{out} = (\frac{1}{2}\rho v^2 + \rho gh)_{in}$

$\frac{1}{2}\rho v^2 = \rho gh$, cancel ρ from both sides of the expression

$\frac{1}{2}v^2 = gh$

$v^2 = 2gh$

$v = \sqrt{(2gh)}$

$v = \sqrt{[2(9.8 \text{ m/s}^2) \cdot (4 \text{ m})]}$

$v_{3cm} = 8.9 \text{ m/s}$

To find the speed through the 5 cm pipe use the continuity equation:

$A_{3cm}v_{3cm} = A_{5cm}v_{5cm}$

$(\pi / 4) \cdot (3 \text{ cm})^2 \cdot (8.9 \text{ m/s}) = (\pi / 4) \cdot (5 \text{ cm})^2 \cdot (v_{5cm})$

$v_{5cm} = 3.2 \text{ m/s}$

27. C is correct. The ideal gas law is:

$PV = n\text{RT}$ where n, R and T are constants.

P is pressure, V is volume, n is the number of particles, R is the ideal gas law constant, and T is temperature. If $P \rightarrow 3P$, then $V \rightarrow (1/3)V$ to maintain a constant temperature.

28. D is correct. $F = PA + F_{cover}$

$P = \rho gh$

$F = \rho ghA + F_{cover}$

$F = [(1,000 \text{ kg/m}^3) \cdot (10 \text{ m/s}^2) \cdot (1 \text{ m}) \cdot (1 \text{ m}^2)] + 1,500 \text{ N}$

$F = 11,500 \text{ N}$

29. B is correct. The buoyant force on a totally submerged object is independent of its depth below the surface (since any increase in the water's density is ignored).

The buoyant force on the ball at a depth of 4 m is 20 N, the same as the buoyant force at 1 m.

When it sits at the bottom of the pool, the two upward forces (i.e., the buoyant force F_B and the normal force F_N), must balance the downward force of gravity.

$F_B + F_N = F_g$

$(20 \text{ N}) + F_N = 80 \text{ N}$

$F_N = 80 \text{ N} - 20 \text{ N}$

$F_N = 60 \text{ N}$

30. B is correct. $V_{\text{Fluid Displaced}} = \frac{1}{2}V_{\text{block}}$

Buoyant force:

$$F_B = \rho g V$$

$$\rho_F g V_F = \rho_B g V_B, \text{ cancel } g \text{ from both sides of the expression}$$

$$\rho_F V_F = \rho_B V_B$$

$$\rho_F(\frac{1}{2}V_B) = \rho_B V_B, \text{ cancel } V_B \text{ from both sides of the expression}$$

$$\frac{1}{2}\rho_F = \rho_B$$

$$\rho_F = (1.6)\rho_{\text{water}}$$

$$\rho_B = (1.6)\cdot(10^3 \text{ kg/m}^3)\cdot(\frac{1}{2})$$

$$\rho_B = 800 \text{ kg/m}^3$$

31. C is correct.

$$F_{\text{net}} = F_{\text{object}} - F_B$$

$$F_{\text{net}} = mg - \rho_{\text{fluid}}Vg$$

$$\rho_{\text{fluid}} = -(F_{\text{net}} - mg) / V_{\text{sphere}}g$$

$$\rho_{\text{fluid}} = -[42 \text{ N} - (9.2 \text{ kg})\cdot(9.8 \text{ m/s}^2)] / [(9.2 \text{ kg} / 3{,}650 \text{ kg/m3})\cdot(9.8 \text{ m/s}^2)]$$

$$\rho_{\text{fluid}} = 1{,}950 \text{ kg/m}^3$$

32. A is correct. The pressure due to the density of a fluid surrounding an object submerged at depth *d* below the surface is given by:

$$P = \rho g d$$

Since the distance that the objects are below the surface is not specified, the only conclusion that can be drawn is that object B experiences less fluid pressure than object A. This difference is because object B is higher off the floor of the container and thus its depth is less than object A.

33. B is correct.

$$A_1 v_1 = A_2 v_2$$

$$A = \pi r^2$$

$$A_2 = \pi(2r)^2$$

$$A_2 = 4\pi r^2$$

$$A_2 = 4A_1$$

If r is doubled, then area is increased by 4 times.

$$A_1(14 \text{ m/s}) = (4A_1)v_2$$

$$v_2 = (A_1 \times 14 \text{ m/s}) / (4 \times A_1)$$

$$v_2 = (14 \text{ m/s}) / (4)$$

$$v_2 = 3.5 \text{ m/s}$$

Use Bernoulli's equation to find resulting pressure:

$$P_1 + \tfrac{1}{2}\rho v_1{}^2 = P_2 + \tfrac{1}{2}\rho v_2{}^2$$

$$(3.5 \times 10^4 \text{ Pa}) + \tfrac{1}{2}(1{,}000 \text{ kg/m}^3)\cdot(14 \text{ m/s})^2 = P_2 + \tfrac{1}{2}(1{,}000 \text{ kg/m}^3)\cdot(3.5 \text{ m/s})^2$$

$$P_2 = (13.3 \times 10^4 \text{ Pa}) - (6.1 \times 10^3 \text{ Pa})$$

$$P_2 = 12.7 \times 10^4 \text{ Pa}$$

34. D is correct. The pressure due to the atmosphere is equal to its weight per unit area. At an altitude of 2 km, there is less atmosphere pushing down than at the Earth's surface.

Therefore, atmospheric pressure decreases with increasing altitude.

35. C is correct. The buoyant force:

$F_B = \rho_{air}V_{disp}g$, and V_{disp} is the volume of the man m / ρ_{man}

$$F_B = (\rho_{air} / \rho_{man})mg$$

$$F_B = [(1.2 \times 10^{-3} \text{ g/cm}^3) / (1 \text{ g/cm}^3)]\cdot(80 \text{ kg})\cdot(9.8 \text{ m/s}^2)$$

$$F_B = 0.94 \text{ N}$$

36. D is correct. Graham's law states that the rate at which gas diffuses is inversely proportional to the square root of the density of the gas.

37. D is correct.

$$F_B = \rho V g$$

$$F_{net} = F_{object} - F_B$$

$$F_{net} = (41{,}800 \text{ N}) - (1{,}000 \text{ kg/m}^3)(4.2 \text{ m}^3)(9.8 \text{ m/s}^2)$$

$$F_{net} = (41{,}800 \text{ N}) - (41{,}160 \text{ N})$$

$$F_{net} = 640 \text{ N}$$

38. D is correct.

$$A = \pi r^2$$

$$A_T v_T = A_P v_P$$

$$v_T = v_P A_P / A_T$$

The ratio of the square of the diameter is equal to the ratio of area:

$$v_T = v_P(d_1 / d_2)^2$$

$$v_T = (0.03 \text{ m/s})\cdot[(0.12 \text{ m}) / (0.002 \text{ m})]^2$$

$$v_T = 108 \text{ m/s}$$

39. B is correct.

Specific gravity:

$\rho_{object} / \rho_{water}$

Archimedes' principle:

$F = \rho g V$

$\rho_{water} = F / g(0.9V)$

$\rho_{object} = F / gV$

$\rho_{object} / \rho_{water} = (F / gV) / [F / g(0.9V)]$

$\rho_{object} / \rho_{water} = 0.9$

V_{water} is 0.9V because only 90% of the object is in the water, so 90% of the object's volume equals water displaced.

40. C is correct.

The factors considered are length, density, radius, pressure difference, and viscosity.

The continuity equation does not apply here because it can only relate velocity and radius to the flow rate.

Bernoulli's equation does not apply because it only relates density and velocity.

The Hagen-Poiseuille equation is needed because it includes all the terms except for density and therefore is the most applicable to this question.

Volumetric flow rate (Q) is:

$Q = \Delta P \pi r^4 / 8\eta L$

The radius is raised to the fourth power.

A 15% change to *r* results in the greatest change.

41. A is correct.

A force meter provides a force, and the reading indicates what the force is.

Since the hammer is not accelerating, the force equation is:

$F_{meter} + F_B - m_h g = 0$

$m_h g = (0.68 \text{ kg}) \cdot (10 \text{ m/s}^2)$

$m_h g = 6.8 \text{ N}$

The displaced volume is the volume of the hammer:

$V_{disp} = m_h / \rho_{steel}$

$V_{disp} = (680 \text{ g}) / (7.9 \text{ g/cm}^3)$

$V_{disp} = 86 \text{ cm}^3$

$$F_B = \rho_{water} \times V_{disp} \times g$$

$$F_B = (1 \times 10^{-3} \text{ kg/cm}^3) \cdot (86 \text{ cm}^3) \cdot (10 \text{ m/s}^2)$$

$$F_B = 0.86 \text{ N}$$

$$F_{meter} = m_h g - F_B$$

$$F_{meter} = 6.8 \text{ N} - 0.86 \text{ N}$$

$$F_{meter} = 5.9 \text{ N}$$

42. D is correct. Pascal's Principle states that pressure is transmitted undiminished in an enclosed static fluid.

43. B is correct. The normal force exerted by the sea floor is the net force between the weight of the submarine and the buoyant force:

$$F_N = F_{net}$$

$$F_{net} = mg - F_B$$

$$F_{net} = mg - \rho g V$$

$$F_{net} = mg - W_{water}$$

$$F_N = mg - W_{water}$$

44. D is correct. $P = \rho g h$

Because the bottom of the brick is at a lower depth than the rest of the brick, it will experience the highest pressure.

45. A is correct. Mass flow rate:

$$\dot{m} = \text{cross-sectional area} \times \text{density} \times \text{velocity}$$

$$\dot{m} = A_C \rho v$$

$$\dot{m} = (7 \text{ m}) \cdot (14 \text{ m}) \cdot (10^3 \text{ kg/m}^3) \cdot (3 \text{ m/s})$$

$$\dot{m} = 2.9 \times 10^5 \text{ kg/s}$$

46. C is correct. Since the object is motionless:

$$a = 0$$

$$F_{net} = 0$$

The magnitude of the buoyant force upward = weight downward:

$$F = W$$

$$F = mg$$

$$F = (3 \text{ kg}) \cdot (10 \text{ m/s}^2) = 30 \text{ N}$$

47. A is correct. $P = P_{atm} + \rho g h$

$$P = (1.01 \times 10^5 \text{ Pa}) + (10^3 \text{ kg/m}^3) \cdot (10 \text{ m/s}^2) \cdot (6 \text{ m})$$

$$P = (1.01 \times 10^5 \text{ Pa}) + (0.6 \times 10^5 \text{ Pa})$$

$$P = 1.6 \times 10^5 \text{ Pa}$$

48. B is correct.   density = mass / volume

49. C is correct. The bulk modulus is defined as how much a material is compressed under a given external pressure:

$$B = \Delta P / (\Delta V / V)$$

Most solids and liquids compress slightly under external pressure. However, gases have the highest change in volume and thus the lowest value of B.

50. C is correct. $P_1 = P_2 + \rho g h$

$$F_1 / A_1 = F_2 / A_2 + \rho g h$$

$$F_1 = A_1(F_2 / A_2 + \rho g h)$$

$$F_1 = \pi(0.06 \text{ m})^2 \cdot [(14{,}000 \text{ N}) / \pi(0.16 \text{ m})^2 + (750 \text{ kg/m}^3) \cdot (9.8 \text{ m/s}^2) \cdot (1.5 \text{ m})]$$

$$F_1 = \pi(0.0036 \text{ m}^2) \cdot [(14{,}000 \text{ N}) / \pi(0.0256 \text{ m}^2) + (750 \text{ kg/m}^3) \cdot (9.8 \text{ m/s}^2) \cdot (1.5 \text{ m})]$$

$$F_1 = (0.0036 \text{ m}^2) \cdot [(14{,}000 \text{ N}) / (0.0256 \text{ m}^2) + (11{,}025 \text{ N})\pi]$$

$$F_1 = 1{,}969 \text{ N} + 125 \text{ N}$$

$$F_1 = 2{,}094 \text{ N}$$

51. C is correct. Solve for density of ice and saltwater:

$$SG = \rho_{substance} / \rho_{water}$$

$$SG_{ice} = 0.98 = \rho_{ice} / 10^3 \text{ kg/m}^3$$

$$\rho_{ice} = 980 \text{ kg/m}^3$$

$$SG_{saltwater} = 1.03 = \rho_{saltwater} / 10^3 \text{ kg/m}^3$$

$$\rho_{saltwater} = 1{,}030 \text{ kg/m}^3$$

Solve for volume of ice:

$$F_B = F_{bear} + F_{ice}$$

$$\rho_{saltwater} V_{ice} g = m_{bear} g + \rho_{ice} V_{ice} g, \text{ cancel } g \text{ from all terms}$$

$$V_{ice} = m_{bear} / (\rho_{saltwater} - \rho_{ice})$$

$$V_{ice} = (240 \text{ kg}) / (1{,}030 \text{ kg/m}^3 - 980 \text{ kg/m}^3)$$

$$V_{ice} = 4.8 \text{ m}^3$$

Solve for area of ice:

$A = V / h$

$A = (4.8 \text{ m}^3) / (1 \text{ m})$

$A = 4.8 \text{ m}^2$

52. B is correct. Absolute pressure is measured relative to absolute zero pressure (perfect vacuum), and gauge pressure is measured relative to atmospheric pressure. If the atmospheric pressure increases by ΔP, then the absolute pressure increases by ΔP, but the gauge pressure does not change.

Absolute pressure at an arbitrary depth h in the lake:

$P_{abs} = P_{atm} + \rho_{water}gh$

Gauge pressure at an arbitrary depth h in the lake:

$P_{gauge} = \rho_{water}gh$

53. C is correct.

$P_{top} = \rho gh$

$P_{top} = 108 \times 10^3 \text{ Pa}$

$h = (1 / \rho) \cdot (108 \times 10^3 \text{ Pa} / 9.8 \text{ m/s}^2)$

$h = (1 / \rho) \cdot (11,020 \text{ kg/m}^2)$

$P_{bottom} = \rho g(h + 25 \text{ cm})$

$\rho g(h + 25 \text{ cm}) = 114 \times 10^3 \text{ Pa}$

$h = (1 / \rho) \cdot (114 \times 10^3 \text{ Pa} / 9.8 \text{ m/s}^2) - 0.25 \text{ m}$

$h = (1 / \rho) \cdot (11,633) - 0.25 \text{ m}$

Set equal and solve for ρ:

$(1 / \rho) \cdot (11,020 \text{ kg/m}^2) = (1 / \rho) \cdot (11,633 \text{ kg/m}^2) - 0.25 \text{ m}$

$(11,020 \text{ kg/m}^2) = (11,633 \text{ kg/m}^2) - 0.25 \text{ m}(\rho)$

$0.25 \text{ m}(\rho) = 613 \text{ kg/m}^2$

$\rho = (613 \text{ kg/m}^2) / (0.25 \text{ m})$

$\rho = 2,452 \text{ kg/m}^3$

54. D is correct. By Poiseuille's Law:

$v = \Delta Pr^2 / 8\eta L$

$\eta = \Delta Pr^2 / 8Lv_{effective}$

$\eta = (970 \text{ Pa}) \cdot (0.0021 \text{ m})^2 / 8 \cdot (1.8 \text{ m/s}) \cdot (0.19 \text{ m})$

$\eta = 0.0016 \text{ N·s/m}^2$

55. C is correct. Bernoulli's equation:

$$P_1 + \tfrac{1}{2}\rho_1 v_1^2 + \rho_1 g h_1 = P_2 + \tfrac{1}{2}\rho_2 v_2^2 + \rho_2 g h_2$$

There is no height difference, so the equation reduces to:

$$P_1 + \tfrac{1}{2}\rho_1 v_1^2 = P_2 + \tfrac{1}{2}\rho_2 v_2^2$$

If the flow of air across the wing tip is v_1 then:

$$v_1 > v_2$$

Since the air that flows across the top has a higher velocity, as it travels a larger distance (curved surface of the top) over the same period of time, then:

$$\tfrac{1}{2}\rho_1 v_1^2 > \tfrac{1}{2}\rho_2 v_2^2$$

In order to keep both sides equal:

$$P_1 < P_2$$

$$\Delta P = (P_2 - P_1)$$

Thus, the lower portion of the wing experiences greater pressure and therefore lifts the wing.

56. A is correct. As the air bubble rises toward surface, volume of the bubble increases.

57. B is correct. The Bulk Modulus is expressed as:

$$B = \Delta P / (\Delta V / V)$$

$$B = (\Delta P V) / \Delta V$$

Solve for ΔV:

$$\Delta V = (\Delta P V) / B$$

$$\Delta V = (10^7 \text{ N/m}^2) \cdot (1 \text{ m}^3) / (2.3 \times 10^9 \text{ N/m}^2)$$

$$\Delta V = 0.0043 \text{ m}^3$$

58. B is correct. Pascal's Principle states that pressure is transmitted undiminished in an enclosed static fluid. This principle makes hydraulic lift possible because, for equal pressure across a fluid, force can be multiplied through an area difference:

$$P_1 = P_2$$

$$F_1 / A_1 = F_2 / A_2$$

$$F_1 = (A_1 / A_2) F_2$$

59. A is correct. Gauge pressure is referenced relative to atmospheric pressure and is calculated by:

$$P_{gauge} = \rho g h$$

$$P_{gauge} = (1{,}025 \text{ kg/m}^3) \cdot (9.8 \text{ m/s}^2) \cdot (11{,}030 \text{ m})$$

$$P_{gauge} = 1.1 \times 10^8 \text{ Pa}$$

60. D is correct. $P = \rho g h$

$P = (10^3 \text{ kg/m}^3) \cdot (9.8 \text{ m/s}^2) \cdot (1 \text{ m})$

$P = 9,800 \text{ Pa} \approx 1 \times 10^4 \text{ Pa}$

61. C is correct.

Assuming there is a vacuum on the inside of the sphere, and using Archimedes' principle:

$(\rho g V)_{\text{sphere}} = (\rho g V)_{\text{disp-water}}$

$(\rho V)_{\text{sphere}} = (\rho V)_{\text{disp-water}}$

$V_{\text{sphere}} = 4/3 \pi r^3$

Define r_o as outer radius and r_i as inner radius:

$\rho_{\text{steel}}(4/3\pi) \cdot (r_o^3 - r_i^3) = \rho_{\text{water}}(4/3\pi r_o^3)$

$\rho_{\text{steel}}(r_o^3 - r_i^3) = \rho_{\text{water}} r_o^3$

$r_i^3 = [(-\rho_{\text{water}} r_o^3) / (\rho_{\text{steel}})] + r_o^3$

$r_i^3 = -[(10^3 \text{ kg/m}^3) \cdot (1.5 \text{ m})^3 / (7,870 \text{ kg/m}^3)] + (1.5 \text{ m})^3$

$r_i^3 = 2.95 \text{ m}^3$

$r_i = 1.43 \text{ m}$

Thickness $= r_o - r_i$

Thickness $= 1.5 \text{ m} - 1.43 \text{ m}$

Thickness $= 0.07 \text{ m} = 7 \text{ cm}$

62. A is correct. According to the Bernoulli effect air moving with a higher velocity exerts less pressure against a surface then air with a lower velocity. Thus, to produce lift, the pressure on the underside of a wing should be higher, and thus the air should be slower on the bottom surface of the wing compared to air on the top surface.

63. D is correct.

Poiseuille's law:

$Q = \pi \Delta P r^4 / 8\eta L$

$D_B = 2D_A$

$r_B = 2r_A$

$Q_A = \pi \Delta P r_A^4 / 8\eta L$

$Q_B = \pi \Delta P (2r_A)^4 / 8\eta L$

$Q_B = 16(\pi \Delta P r_A^4 / 8\eta L)$

$Q_B = 16 Q_A$

64. B is correct. Mass flow rate $\dot{m}$ is:

$\dot{m} = \rho v A_C$

where ρ = density of the fluid, v = velocity of flow, A_C = cross-sectional area

The dimensions of the tank are irrelevant to this answer, so $\dot{m}$ is calculated as:

$\dot{m} = (1,000 \text{ kg/m}^3) \cdot (13 \text{ m/s}) \cdot (0.04 \text{ m}^2)$

$\dot{m} = 520 \text{ kg/s}$

65. C is correct. Relationship between area and velocity of both exists:

$A_1 v_1 = A_2 v_2$

$v_1 = A_2 v_2 / A_1$

$v_1 = [(0.04 \text{ m}^2) \cdot (13 \text{ m/s})] / [(\pi / 4) \cdot (5 \text{ m/s})]$

$v_1 = 0.26 \text{ m/s} = 26 \text{ mm/s}$

66. D is correct. Gauge pressure is the pressure reference against the surrounding air pressure. Therefore, it is valid to ignore both the pressure in the tank and atmospheric pressure.

$P = \rho g h$

$P = (10^3 \text{ kg/m}) \cdot (9.8 \text{ m/s}^2) \cdot (10 \text{ m})$

$P = 98,000 \text{ Pa} = 98 \text{ kPa}$

67. B is correct. According to Pascal's Law, the pressure is transmitted undiminished in an enclosed static fluid. Thus, the pressure increases by ΔP everywhere in the oil.

If the chamber is cubic, the top and bottom sides have the same area and experience the same increase in force:

$A_{top} = A_{bottom}$

$\Delta P_{top} = \Delta P_{bottom}$

$P = F / A$

Thus, force is directly proportional to pressure, and if the area of the top is equal to the area of the bottom:

$\Delta F_{top} = \Delta F_{bottom}$

Geometric and Physical Optics – Explanations

1. A is correct.

Soap film that reflects a given wavelength of light exhibits constructive interference.

The expression for constructive interference of a thin film:

$2t = (m + \frac{1}{2})\lambda$

where t = thickness, m = 0, 1, 2, 3… and λ = wavelength

To find the minimum thickness set m = 0:

$2t = (0 + \frac{1}{2})\lambda = \frac{1}{2}\lambda$

$t = \frac{1}{4}\lambda$

2. A is correct.

By the law of reflection, the angle of incidence is equal to the angle of reflection.

Thus, as the angle of incidence increases, the angle of reflection increases as well to be equal to the angle of incidence.

3. B is correct.

If image is twice her height and upright, then:

$2h_o = h_i$

$m = h_i / h_o$

$m = -d_i / d_o$

$m = 2h_o / h_o$

$m = 2$

$2 = -d_i / d_o$

$-2d_o = d_i$

Use lens equation to solve:

$1 / f = 1 / d_o + 1 / d_i$

$1 / 100 \text{ cm} = 1 / d_o + (-1 / 2 d_o)$

$1 / 100 \text{ cm} = 1 / 2 d_o$

$2d_o = 100 \text{ cm}$

$d_o = 50 \text{ cm}$

4. D is correct.

If a person's eye is too long, the light entering the eye is focused in front of the retina causing myopia. This condition is also referred to as nearsightedness.

Hyperopia is also referred to as farsightedness.

5. C is correct.

Visible light:

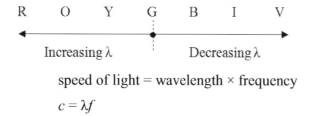

speed of light = wavelength × frequency

$c = \lambda f$

Wavelength to frequency:

$f = c / \lambda$

Frequency and wavelength are inversely proportional:

As λ increases, f decreases.

As λ decreases, f increases.

Thus, because $E = hf$:

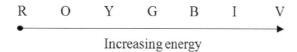

6. B is correct.

The lens equation:

$1 / f = 1 / d_o + 1 / d_i$

$1 / d_i = 1 / f - 1 / d_o$

$1 / d_i = -1 / 3 \text{ m} - 1 / 4 \text{ m}$

$1 / d_i = (-3 \text{ m} - 4 \text{ m}) / 12 \text{ m}$

$1 / d_i = -7 \text{ m} / 12 \text{ m}$

$d_i = -12 / 7 \text{ m}$

Magnification:

$m = -d_i / d_o$

$m = -(-12 / 7 \text{ m}) / 4 \text{ m}$

$m = 3 / 7$

Height of the candle image:

$$h_i = mh_o$$

$$h_i = (3/7) \cdot (18 \text{ cm})$$

$$h_i = 54 / 7 \text{ cm}$$

$$h_i = 7.7 \text{ cm}$$

7. C is correct.

$$\theta_{\text{syrup}} = \tan^{-1} (0.9 \text{ m} / 0.66 \text{ m})$$

$$\theta_s = \tan^{-1} (1.36)$$

$$\theta_s = 53.7°$$

$$\theta_{\text{oil}} = \tan^{-1} [(2 \text{ m} - 0.9 \text{ m}) / 1.58 \text{ m}]$$

$$\theta_o = \tan^{-1} (0.7)$$

$$\theta_o = 34.8°$$

$$n_o \sin \theta_o = n_{\text{air}} \sin \theta_{\text{air}}$$

$$n_o \sin 34.8° = (1) \sin 90°$$

$$n_o = 1 / (\sin 34.8°)$$

$$n_o = 1.75$$

8. D is correct.

$$\theta_{\text{syrup}} = \tan^{-1} (0.9 \text{ m} / 0.66 \text{ m})$$

$$\theta_s = \tan^{-1} (1.36)$$

$$\theta_s = 53.7°$$

$$\theta_{\text{oil}} = \tan^{-1} [(2 \text{ m} - 0.9 \text{ m}) / 1.58 \text{ m}]$$

$$\theta_o = \tan^{-1} (0.7)$$

$$\theta_o = 34.8°$$

$$n_o \sin \theta_o = n_{\text{air}} \sin \theta_{\text{air}}$$

$$n_o \sin 34.8° = (1) \sin 90°$$

$$n_o = 1 / (\sin 34.8°)$$

$$n_o = 1.75$$

$$n_s \sin \theta_s = n_o \sin \theta_o$$

$$n_s = n_o \sin \theta_o / \sin \theta_s$$

$$n_s = (1.75) \cdot (\sin 34.8°) / (\sin 53.7°)$$

$$n_s = 1.24$$

9. A is correct. The photoelectric effect cannot be explained with the wave theory of light.

10. D is correct.

Geometrical optics, or ray optics, describes light propagation in terms of rays and fronts to approximate the path along which light propagates in certain circumstances.

11. D is correct.

First find the critical angle:

$$n_{fiber} \sin \theta_c = n_{air} \sin \theta_{air}$$

$$(1.26) \sin \theta_c = (1) \sin 90°$$

$$\sin \theta_c = 1 / 1.26$$

$$\theta_c = \sin^{-1} (1 / 1.26)$$

$$\theta_c = 52.5°$$

Find θ_2:

$$\theta_2 + \theta_c + 90° = 180°$$

$$(\theta_2 + 52.5° + 90°) = 180°$$

$$\theta_2 = 37.5°$$

Find θ_1:

$$n_{air} \sin \theta_1 = n_{fiber} \sin \theta_2$$

$$(1) \sin \theta_1 = (1.26) \sin 37.5°$$

$$\sin \theta_1 = 0.77$$

$$\theta_1 = \sin^{-1} (0.77)$$

$$\theta_1 = 50°$$

12. A is correct. If the power of the lens is 10 diopters,

$$1 / f = 10 \text{ D}$$

where f is the focal length in m

Thin Lens Equation:

$$1 / f = 1 / d_o + 1 / d_i$$

$$10 \text{ m}^{-1} = 1 / 0.5 \text{ m} + 1 / d_i$$

$$1 / d_i = 10 \text{ m}^{-1} - 1 / 0.5 \text{ m}$$

$$1 / d_i = 8 \text{ m}^{-1}$$

$$d_i = 1 / 8 \text{ m}$$

$$d_i = 0.13 \text{ m}$$

13. D is correct. Most objects observed by humans are virtual images, or objects which reflect incoming light to project an image.

14. D is correct. An image from a convex mirror will always have the following characteristics, regardless of object distance:

- located behind the convex mirror
- virtual
- upright
- reduced in size from the object (image < object)

15. A is correct. The mirror has a positive focal length which indicates that the mirror is concave.

The object is at a distance greater than the focal length. Therefore, it is inverted.

Use lens equation to solve image distance:

$$1 / f = 1 / d_o + 1 / d_i$$

$$1 / 10 \text{ m} = 1 / 20 \text{ m} + 1 / d_i$$

$$d_i = 20 \text{ cm}$$

The image distance is positive so the image is real.

Use the magnification equation to determine if it is upright or inverted.

$$m = -d_i / d_o$$

$$m = h_i / h_o$$

$$-(20 \text{ m} / 20 \text{ m}) = h_i / h_o$$

$$-1 = h_i / h_o$$

The object height h_o is always positive so the image height h_i must be negative to satisfy the equation.

A negative image height indicates an inverted image.

16. B is correct.

For a converging lens, if an object is placed beyond $2f$ from the lens, the image is real, inverted and reduced.

Use the lens equation to determine if the image is real (or vitual):

$$\text{Assume } f = 1 \text{ m and } d_o = 3f \text{ (because } d_o > 2f)$$

$$1 / f = 1 / d_o + 1 / d_i$$

$$1 / f = 1 / 3f + 1 / d_i$$

$$d_i = 1.5$$

A positive d_i indicates a real image.

Use the magnification equation to determine if the image is inverted and reduced.

$$m = -d_i / d_o$$

$$m = -(1.5 \text{ m} / 3 \text{ m})$$

$$m = -\tfrac{1}{2}$$

$$|m| = \tfrac{1}{2}$$

$$|m| < 1$$

A negative magnification factor with an absolute value less than 1 a reduced and inverted image.

17. C is correct.

Radio waves range from 3 kHz to 300 GHz, which is lower than all forms of radiation listed.

Since the energy of radiation is proportional to frequency ($E = hf$), radio waves have the lowest energy.

18. B is correct.

A medium's index of refraction is the ratio of the speed of refracted light in a vacuum to its speed in the reference medium.

$$n = c / v$$

$$n = 2.43$$

$$2.43 = c / v_{\text{diamond}}$$

$$c = 2.43(v_{\text{diamond}})$$

19. D is correct.

$$1 / f = 1 / d_o + 1 / d_i$$

$$1 / 20 \text{ cm} = 1 / 15 \text{ cm} + 1 / d_i$$

$$3 / 60 \text{ cm} - 4 / 60 \text{ cm} = 1 / d_i$$

$$-1 / 60 \text{ cm} = 1 / d_i$$

$$d_i = -60 \text{ cm}$$

The negative sign indicates that the image is projected back the way it came.

20. B is correct.

Red paper absorbs all colors but reflects only red light giving it the appearance of being red. Cyan is the complementary color to red, so when the cyan light shines upon the red paper, no light is reflected, and the paper appears black.

21. B is correct. $1/f = 1/d_o + 1/d_i$

If $d_i = f$,

$$1/d_o = 0$$

Thus, d_o must be large.

22. A is correct. Since the index of refraction depends on the frequency, and the focal length depends on the refraction of the beam in the lens, dispersion causes the focal length to depend on frequency.

23. C is correct. Use the equation for magnification:

$$m = -d_i/d_o$$

$$d_i = d_o$$

$$m = 1$$

Thus, there is no magnification, so the image is the same size as the object.

24. D is correct. When viewed straight down (90° to the surface), an incident light ray moving from water to air is refracted 0°.

25. C is correct. He observes complete darkness, since no light would be transmitted.

26. C is correct. First, find the angle that the ray makes with the normal of the glass:

$$180° = x + 90° + 54°$$

$$x = 36°$$

Find θ_1:

$$\theta_1 = 90° - 36°$$

$$\theta_1 = 54°$$

Referring to the diagram, $\theta_1 = 54°$

Snell's Law:

$$n_1 \sin \theta_1 = n_2 \sin \theta_2$$

$$\sin^{-1}[(n_1/n_2)\sin \theta_1] = \theta_2$$

$$\theta_2 = \sin^{-1}[(1.45/1.35)\sin 54°]$$

$$\theta_2 = 60°$$

Solve for the angle with the horizontal:

$$\theta_H = 60° - 54°$$

$$\theta_H = 6°$$

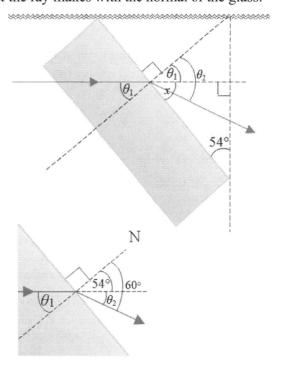

27. A is correct.

The angle at which the ray is turned is the sum of the angles if reflected off each mirror once:

$$\theta_{turned} = \theta_1 + \theta_2 + \theta_3 + \theta_4$$

By law of reflection:

$$\theta_1 = \theta_2$$

$$\theta_3 = \theta_4$$

Note the triangle formed (sum of interior angles is 180°):

$$30° + (90° - \theta_2) + (90° - \theta_3) = 180°$$

$$\theta_2 + \theta_3 = 30°$$

Given:

$$\theta_2 + \theta_3 = \theta_1 + \theta_4$$

Thus:

$$\theta_{turned} = 30° + 30°$$

$$\theta_{turned} = 60°$$

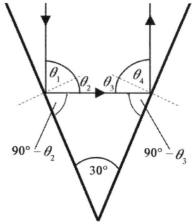

Note: figure is not to scale

In general: for two plane mirrors that meet at an angle of $\theta \leq 90°$ the ray that is deflected off both mirrors is deflected through an angle of 2θ.

28. D is correct. All of the following statements about light is true: a packet of light energy is known as a photon; color can be used to determine the approximate energy of visible light and light travels through space at a speed of 3.0×10^8 m/s

29. A is correct.

The angle of incidence is < the angle of refraction if the light travels into a less dense medium.

The angle of incidence is > the angle of refraction if the light travels into a denser medium.

The angle of incidence is = the angle of refraction if the densities of the mediums are equal.

30. B is correct.

Plane mirrors do not distort the size or the shape of an object since light is reflected at the same angle it was received by the mirror.

Magnification equation:

$$m = h_i / h_o$$

For a plane mirror m = 1:

$$1 = h_i / h_o$$

$$h_i = h_o$$

The image size is the same as object size, and the image is virtual (i.e., behind mirror).

31. C is correct.

A spherical concave mirror has a focal length of:

$$f = R / 2$$

32. B is correct.

Refracted rays bend further from the normal than the original incident angle when the refracting medium is optically less dense than the incident medium. Therefore, $n_1 > n_2$.

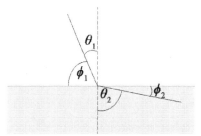

The index of refraction for a medium can never be less than 1.

33. B is correct.
If a person's eye is too short, then the light entering the eye is focused behind the retina causing farsightedness (hyperopia).

34. A is correct.
Hot air is less dense than cold air. Light traveling through both types of air experiences refractions, which appear as shimmering or "wavy" air.

35. C is correct.

Chromatic aberration occurs when a lens focuses different wavelengths of color at different positions in the focal plane.

It always occurs in the following pattern for converging lens:

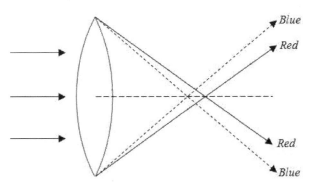

36. B is correct.

$$1 / f_{\text{total}} = 1 / f_1 + 1 / f_2$$
$$1 / f_{\text{total}} = 1 / 2 \text{ m} + 1 / 4 \text{ m}$$
$$1 / f_{\text{total}} = 3 / 4 \text{ m}$$
$$f_{\text{total}} = 4 / 3 \text{ m}$$

37. C is correct. The angle in the water respective to the normal:

$\theta = \tan^{-1}(37.5 \text{ ft.} / 50 \text{ ft.})$

$\theta = \tan^{-1}(0.75)$

$\theta = 36.9°$

$n_{air} \sin(90 - \theta) = n_{water} \sin\theta$

$(1) \sin(90 - \theta) = (1.33) \sin 36.9°$

$\sin(90 - \theta) = 0.8$

$(90 - \theta) = \sin^{-1}(0.8)$

$(90 - \theta) = 52.9$

$\theta = 37.1° \approx 37°$

38. A is correct. Violet light has the highest energy and frequency, and therefore has the shortest wavelength.

39. D is correct. Objects directly in front of plane mirrors are reflected in their likeness since plane mirrors are not curved and therefore reflect light perpendicularly to their surface.

40. B is correct. A virtual image is always upright and can be formed by both a diverging lens and a converging lens.

Diverging lens → reduced and virtual image

Converging lens → enlarged and virtual image

41. B is correct.

Neon light is the light emitted from neon atoms as their energized electrons cascade back down to ground level. When this occurs, energy is released in the form of light at very specific wavelengths known as the emission spectrum.

When this light is passed through a prism, a series of bright discontinuous spots or lines will be seen due to the specific wavelengths of the emission spectrum of neon.

42. D is correct.

The law of reflection states that the angle of incidence is equal to the angle of reflection (with respect to the normal) and is true for all mirrors.

$\theta_i = \theta_r$

43. C is correct.

A concave lens always forms an image that is virtual, upright and reduced in size.

44. B is correct.

Virtual images are always upright.

There is no correlation between the size and nature – virtual or real – of an image.

Images may be larger, smaller, or the same size as the object.

45. A is correct.

Red is the light with the lowest frequency (longest wavelength) detected by humans.

46. D is correct.

$$1 / f = 1 / d_o + 1 / d_i$$
$$1 / 6 \text{ m} = 1 / 3 \text{ m} + 1 / d_i$$
$$1 / d_i = 1 / 6 \text{ m} - 1 / 3 \text{ m}$$
$$1 / d_i = -1 / 6 \text{ m}$$
$$d_i = -6 \text{ m}$$

where the negative sign indicates the image is on the same side as the object.

The image is upright and virtual since the rays must be extended to intersect.

47. A is correct. A diverging lens (concave) always produces an image that is virtual, upright and reduced in size.

48. C is correct.

Thin lens formula:

$$1 / f = 1 / d_o + 1 / d_i$$

d_i is negative because the image is virtual

$$1 / f = 1 / 14 \text{ cm} + 1 / -5 \text{ cm}$$
$$f = -7.8 \text{ cm}$$

The focus is negative because the lens is diverging.

Lens maker formula:

$$1 / f = (n - 1) \cdot (1 / R_1 - 1 / R_2)$$

R_1 is negative by convention because the light ray passes its center of curvature before the curved surface.

$$1 / (-7.8 \text{ cm}) = (n - 1) \cdot (1 / -15 \text{ cm} - 1 / 15 \text{ cm})$$
$$(1 / -7.8 \text{ cm}) \cdot (15 \text{ cm} / -2) + 1 = n$$
$$n = 2$$

49. B is correct.

The magnification equation relates the image and object distance:

$$m = -d_i / d_o$$

or

The magnification equation relates the image and object height:

$$m = h_i / h_o$$

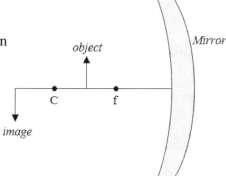

50. D is correct.

For a concave mirror, if an object is located between the focal point and center of curvature, the image is formed beyond the center of curvature.

In this problem, Mike does not see his image because he is in front of where it forms.

51. D is correct.

For a concave spherical mirror, the produced image characteristics depend upon the placement of the object in relation to the focal point and center of curvature. The image can be smaller, larger or the same size as the object.

52. A is correct. Lens power is the reciprocal of the focal length in meters:

$$P = 1 / f$$

If the effective focal length of the lens combination is less than the focal length of either individual lens, then the power of the combination must be greater than the power of either individual lens.

53. B is correct. A medium's index of refraction is the ratio of the speed of refracted light in a vacuum to its speed in the reference medium.

$$n = c / v$$

54. D is correct. As it is a plane mirror, the image is not distorted.

Only some of the light rays are reflected, the others create an image behind the mirror's surface.

For a plane mirror:

$$m = 1$$
$$m = -d_i / d_o$$
$$1 = -d_i / d_o$$
$$d_o = -d_i$$

The negative indicates the image is virtual and behind the mirror.

55. C is correct. The radius length is the center of curvature, $r = 50$ cm

Find the focal length:

$f = r / 2$

$f = 50$ cm $/ 2$

$f = 25$ cm

For a concave mirror with an object between the center of curvature and the focal length, the resulting image is real and inverted.

56. B is correct.

Find index of refraction of glass:

Snell's Law:

$n_1 \sin \theta_1 = n_2 \sin \theta_2$

$n_g \sin 48° = (1.33) \sin 68°$

$n_g = (1.33) \sin 68° / \sin 48°$

$n_g = 1.66$

Find refracted angle of ray:

$(1.66) \sin 29° = (1.33) \sin \theta$

$\sin \theta = (1.66) \sin 29° / (1.33)$

$\sin \theta = 0.605$

$\theta = \sin^{-1} (0.605)$

$\theta = 37°$

57. A is correct.

In a compound microscope, the image of the objective serves as the object for the eyepiece.

58. D is correct.

The refractive index is given by:

$n = c / v$

Because $v \approx c$ in air,

$n_{air} \approx n_{vacuum}$

$n_{air} = 1$

$n_{vacuum} = 1$

All other transparent materials slow the speed of light.

Thus, n is greater than 1 because $v_{other\ materials} < c$.

---

59. D is correct.

Lens maker formula:

$$1 / f = (n - 1) \cdot (1 / R_1 - 1 / R_2)$$

For a flat surface:

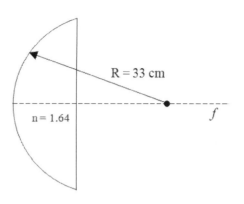

$$R_2 = \infty$$

$$1 / f = (1.64 - 1) \cdot [(1 / 33 \text{ cm}) - (1 / \infty)]$$

$$1 / f = (0.64) \cdot (1 / 33 \text{ cm})$$

$$f = 51.6 \text{ cm} \approx 52 \text{ cm}$$

60. C is correct.

Water doesn't absorb visible light very easily ($\lambda = 400$ to 700 nm) but absorbs infrared light ($\lambda = 700$ nm to 1 mm) from vibrational motion of the molecule. It also absorbs microwaves through rotational motion.

61. A is correct.

Any ray parallel to the principal axis of a concave spherical mirror is reflected through the focal point.

62. B is correct.

Real images are inverted, while virtual images are upright.

Mirror equation:

$$1 / f = 1 / d_o + 1 / d_i$$

If d_o (object) is positive (always for a real object), then a negative f (focal length) must form a negative d_i (image).

Therefore, since convex mirrors have negative focal lengths, only virtual, upright images form.

A negative $d_i \rightarrow$ virtual

$$m = -d_i / d_o$$

In this case, d_i is negative, so:

$$m = -(-d_i) / d_o = \text{positive m, and thus image is upright}$$

63. A is correct.

Both the photoelectric effect and quantization of energy rely upon the particle/wave nature of light to be explained. Polarization, however, is only a property of waves and cannot be explained through particle theory.

64. C is correct.

For a concave spherical mirror, no image is formed when the object is placed at the focal point. The reflected rays neither converge nor diverge, and thus formation of an image is impossible.

65. B is correct.

$$1 / f = 1 / d_o + 1 / d_i$$
$$1 / 16 \text{ m} = 1 / \infty + 1 / d_i$$
$$1 / d_i = 1 / 16 \text{ m}$$
$$d_i = 16 \text{ m}$$

If the object is an infinite distance away, then the focus is on the focal plane, 16 m in front of the mirror.

66. D is correct.

$$1 / f = 1 / d_o + 1 / d_i$$
$$1 / f = 1 / 2f + 1 / d_i$$
$$1 / f - 1 / 2f = 1 / d_i$$
$$1 / 2f = 1 / d_i$$
$$d_i = 2f$$

67. A is correct.

Violet light has the highest frequency of the visible light colors with a range of 668 to 789 THz. Because frequency is related to photon energy by:

$$E = hf$$

Violet light is also the most energetic of the visible light spectrum.

68. D is correct.

The index of refraction for a given material is expressed as the speed of light in a vacuum divided by the speed of light in that material:

$$n = c / v$$

If the index of refraction is less than one, it implies that the speed of light in the material is greater than the speed of light in vacuum. However, this is never the case because the speed of light in a vacuum can never be exceeded.

69. D is correct. The colors observed on an oil slick pool are caused by reflection and thin film interference. This is the process by which the incoming light is reflected off the top and bottom layer of the oil slick and producing reflected waves in and out of phase with each other. This phase change determines the type of interference (constructive or destructive) and colors form as a result.

70. B is correct.

$f = \frac{1}{2}R$

where R is the radius of curvature

71. D is correct.

The first lens has a power:

$P_1 = 1 / f$

$P_1 = \frac{1}{2}$ D

For a combination of total power:

$P_{tot} = 1 / f_{tot}$

$P_{tot} = 1/3$ D

Thus,

$P_2 = P_{tot} - P_1$

$P_2 = 1/3$ D $- 1/2$ D

$P_2 = -1/6$ D

72. A is correct.

$n_1 \sin \theta_1 = n_1 \sin \theta_2$

$(1) \sin (90° - 30°) = (1.73) \sin \theta_2$

$\sin (60°) = 1.73 \sin \theta_2$

$\sin \theta_2 = \sin (60°) / 1.73$

$\sin \theta_2 = 0.5$

$\theta_2 = \sin^{-1} (0.5)$

$\theta_2 = 30°$

73. D is correct. A mirage is produced due to the higher index of refraction of cold air compared to warm air. As light from the sky goes through denser cold air and approaches the warm air (which is less dense and therefore has a lower refraction index) near the ground (generated by a hot surface of asphalt or sand), the light bends away from the warm air and the reflection of the sky can be observed on the ground.

74. A is correct.

Mirror equation:

$$1/f = 1/d_o + 1/d_i$$

If the object is placed at the focus:

$$d_o = f$$
$$1/f = 1/f + 1/d_i$$
$$1/f - 1/f = 1/d_i$$
$$0 = 1/d_i$$

Only if $d_i = \infty$ this is true.

This implies that no image is formed; thus the light rays neither converge nor diverge and travel parallel to each other to infinity.

75. B is correct.

An optically active material can rotate plane-polarized light.

76. D is correct.

When light enters a material of a higher index of refraction, its speed decreases.

77. C is correct.

The correct order of the electromagnetic spectrum from shortest to longest wavelength is:

Gamma rays → X-rays → Ultraviolet radiation → Visible light → Infrared radiation → Microwaves → Radio waves

78. C is correct.

Angle of incidence ranges from 0° to 90°.

Convert degrees to radians:

$$0° = 0 \text{ radians}$$
$$(90° / 1) \cdot (\pi / 180°) = \pi/2 \text{ radians}$$

79. A is correct.

Double convex lens:

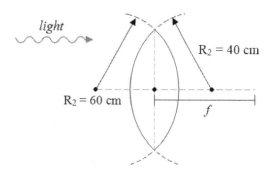

Lens maker formula:

$$1 / f = (n - 1) \cdot (1 / R_1 - 1 / R_2)$$

$$1 / f = (1.54 - 1) \cdot (1 / 40 \text{ cm} - (1 / -60 \text{ cm}))$$

$$1 / f = -0.0225 \text{ cm}^{-1}$$

$$f = 44 \text{ cm}$$

If light passes through the center of the radii of curvature (as it does to R_2) before the curve itself in the lens, then that R is negative by convention.

80. D is correct.

Light does not experience a change in frequency, wavelength or speed when it reflects from a stationary surface.

81. A is correct.

The Doppler effect is qualitatively similar for both light and sound waves.

If the source and the observer move towards each other, the f_{det} is higher than the f_{source}.

If the source and the observer move away from each other, the f_{det} is lower than the f_{source}.

Since the galaxy is moving away from the Earth, the f_{det} is lower.

The speed of light through space is constant ($c = \lambda f$).

A lower f_{det} means a longer λ_{det}, so the λ_{det} is longer than the λ_{source}.

The λ has been shifted towards the red end of the visible spectrum because red light is the visible light with the longest λ.

Atomic and Nuclear Physics – Explanations

1. A is correct. Though alpha particles have low penetrating power and high ionizing power, they are not harmless. All forms of radiation present risks and cannot be thought of as completely harmless.

2. C is correct. A beta particle (β) is a high-energy, high-speed electron (β^-) or positron (β^+) emitted in the radioactive decay of an atomic nucleus.

Electron emission (β^- decay) occurs in an unstable atomic nucleus with an excess of neutrons, whereby a neutron is converted into a proton, an electron, and an electron antineutrino.

Positron emission (β^+ decay) occurs in an unstable atomic nucleus with an excess of protons, whereby a proton is converted into a neutron, a positron and an electron neutrino.

3. D is correct. The de Broglie wavelength is given as:

$\lambda = h / p$

where h is Planck's constant and p is momentum

$p = mv$

$\lambda_1 = h / mv$

$\lambda_2 = h / m(2v)$

$\lambda_2 = \frac{1}{2}h / mv$

$\lambda_2 = \frac{1}{2} \lambda_1$

λ decreases by factor of 2

4. B is correct. The Bohr model places electrons around the nucleus of the atom at discrete energy levels. The Balmer series line spectra agreed with the Bohr model because the energy of the observed photons in each spectrum matched the transition energy of electrons within these discrete predicted states.

5. C is correct. A radioactive element is an element that spontaneously emits radiation in the form of one or a combination of the following: alpha radiation, beta radiation, gamma radiation.

6. D is correct. This is an example of an electron capture nuclear reaction.

When this happens, the atomic number decreases by one, but the mass number stays the same.

$$^{100}_{44}\text{Ru} + \,^{0}_{-1}\text{e}^- \rightarrow \,^{100}_{43}\text{Tc}$$

Ru: 100 = mass number (# protons + # neutrons)

Ru: 44 = atomic number (# protons)

From the periodic table, Tc is the element with 1 less proton than Ru.

7. B is correct.

A nucleon is a particle that makes up the nucleus of an atom. The two known nucleons are protons and neutrons.

8. D is correct.

An alpha particle is composed of two neutrons and two protons and is identical to the nucleus of a ^{4}He atom.

Total mass of two alpha particles:

$2 \times (2$ neutrons $+ 2$ protons$) = 8$

Mass of a ^{9}Be atom:

5 neutrons $+ 4$ protons $= 9$

Mass of a ^{9}Be atom > total mass of two alpha particles

The mass of a ^{9}Be atom is greater than the mass of two alpha particles, so its mass is also greater than twice the mass of a ^{4}He atom.

9. C is correct.

The superscript is the mass number (atomic weight), which is both neutrons and protons.

The subscript is the atomic number, which is the number of protons.

Therefore, the number of neutrons is equal to the superscript minus the subscript.

$181 - 86 = 95$, which is the greatest number of neutrons among the choices.

10. A is correct. The number of neutrons and protons must be equal after the reaction.

Thus, the sum of the atomic number before and mass number before should be equal to after the reaction.

Mass number (superscript):

$(1 + 235) - (131 + 3) = 102$

Atomic number (subscript):

$92 - (53) = 39$

$^{102}_{39}$Y properly balances the reaction.

11. B is correct.

Balmer equation is given by:

$\lambda = B[(n^2) / (n^2 - 2^2)]$

$\lambda = (3.6 \times 10^{-7}) \cdot [(12^2) / (12^2 - 2^2)]$

$\lambda = 3.7 \times 10^{-7}$ m

Where c is the speed of light:

$$c = \lambda f$$

Convert wavelength to frequency:

$$f = c / \lambda$$

$$f = (3 \times 10^8 \text{ m/s}) / (3.7 \times 10^{-7} \text{ m})$$

$$f = 8.1 \times 10^{14} \text{ s}^{-1} = 8.1 \times 10^{14} \text{ Hz}$$

12. D is correct.

Gamma rays are the most penetrating form of radiation because they are the highest energy and least ionizing. A gamma ray passes through a given amount of material without imparting as much of its energy into removing electrons from atoms and ionizing them like other forms of radiation do.

Gamma rays retain more of their energy passing through matter and can penetrate further.

13. A is correct.

Use the Rydberg Formula:

$$E = hf$$

$$f = c / \lambda$$

$$E = (hc) \cdot (1 / \lambda)$$

$$1 / \lambda = R(1 / n_1^2 - 1 / n_2^2), \text{ where } n_1 = 1 \text{ and } n_2 = 2$$

$$E = hcR[(1 / n_1^2) - (1 / n_2^2)]$$

$$E = (4.14 \times 10^{-15} \text{ eV·s}) \cdot (3 \times 10^8 \text{ m/s}) \cdot (1.097 \times 10^7 \text{ m}^{-1}) \cdot [(1 / 1^2) - (1 / 2^2)]$$

$$E = 13.6[1 - (1 / 4)]$$

$$E = 10.2 \text{ eV}$$

The positive energy indicates that a photon was absorbed and not emitted.

14. C is correct.
In β^- (beta minus) decay, the atomic number (subscript) increases by 1, but the atomic mass stays constant.

$$^{87}_{37}\text{Rb} \rightarrow {}^{87}_{38}\text{Sr} + {}^{0}_{-1}\text{e} + {}^{0}_{0}v$$

Sr is the element with 1 more proton (subscript) than Rb.

${}^{0}_{0}v$ represents an electron antineutrino.

15. C is correct.

The nucleus of an atom is bound together by the strong nuclear force from the nucleons within it. The strong nuclear force must overcome the Coulomb repulsion of the protons (due to their like charges).

Neutrons help stabilize and bind the nucleus together by contributing to the strong nuclear force so that it is greater than the Coulomb repulsion experienced by the protons.

16. A is correct.

Geiger-Muller counters operate using a Geiger-Muller tube, which consists of a high voltage shell and small rod in the center, filled with a low pressure inert gas (e.g., argon). When exposed to radiation (specifically particle radiation), the radiation particles ionize atoms of the argon allowing for a brief charge to be conducted between the high voltage rod and outer shell. The electric pulse is then displayed visually or via audio to indicate radioactivity.

17. B is correct.

The half-life calculation:

$A = A_0(\tfrac{1}{2})^{t/h}$

where A_0 = original amount, t = time elapse and h = half-life

If three half-life pass, $t = 3h$

$A = (1) \cdot (\tfrac{1}{2})^{3h/h}$

$A = (1) \cdot (\tfrac{1}{2})^3$

$A = 0.125 = 12.5\%$

18. D is correct.

In the Lyman series, electron transitions always go from $n \geq 2$ to $n = 1$.

19. B is correct.

Most of the volume of an atom is occupied by empty space.

20. A is correct.

Alpha particles are positively charged due to their protons, while beta minus particles are negatively charged (i.e., electrons). When exposed to a magnetic field, alpha particles and electrons deflect in opposite directions due to their opposite charges and thus experience opposite forces due to the magnetic field.

21. D is correct.

Chemical reactions store and release energy in their chemical bonds, but do not convert mass into energy. However, nuclear reactions convert a small amount of mass into energy, which can be measured and calculated via the equation:

$$E = \Delta mc^2$$

22. C is correct.

The Curie is a non-SI unit of radioactivity equivalent to 3.7×10^{10} decays (disintegrations) per second. It is named after the early radioactivity researchers Marie and Pierre Curie.

23. B is correct.

The atomic numbers: $^{235}_{92}\text{U} \rightarrow\ ^{141}_{56}\text{Ba} +\ ^{92}_{36}\text{Kr}$

The subscripts on each side of the expression sum to 92, so adding a proton ($^{1}_{1}\text{H}$) to the right side would not balance.

The superscripts sum to 235 on the left and sum to 233 on the right.

Add two neutrons ($^{1}_{0}\text{n} +\ ^{1}_{0}\text{n}$) to the right side to balance both sides of the equation.

24. D is correct.

The atomic number is the subscript and represents the number of protons. The superscript is the mass number and is the sum of protons and neutrons. The number of neutrons can be found by taking the difference between the mass number and atomic number. In this example, there are 16 protons and 18 neutrons.

25. A is correct.

$A = A_0(\tfrac{1}{2})^{t/h}$

where A_0 = original amount, t = time elapse and h = half-life

Consider: (2 days)·(24 hours / 1 day) = 48 hours

$A = (1)\cdot(\tfrac{1}{2})^{(48/12)}$

$A = 0.5^4$

$A = 0.0625 = 1/16$

26. C is correct. An alpha particle consists of two protons and two neutrons and is identical to a helium nucleus so that it can be written as $^{4}_{2}\text{He}$

For a nuclear reaction to be written correctly, it must be balanced, and the sum of superscripts and subscripts must be equal on both sides of the reaction. The superscripts add to 238, and the subscripts add to 92 on both sides. Therefore, it is the only balanced answer.

27. D is correct.

The question is asking for the λ of the emitted photon so use the Rydberg Formula:

$$1 / \lambda = R(1 / n_1^2 - 1 / n_2^2)$$

$$\lambda = 1 / [R(1 / n_1^2 - 1 / n_2^2)]$$

Use $n_1 = 5$ and $n_2 = 20$ because we are solving for λ of an emitted (not absorbed) photon.

$$\lambda = 1 / [(1.097 \times 10^7 \, m^{-1}) \cdot (1 / 5^2 - 1 / 20^2)]$$

$$\lambda = 2.43 \, \mu m$$

28. D is correct.

When writing a nuclear reaction, the superscript represents the mass number, while the subscript represents the atomic number. A correct nuclear reaction is balanced when the sum of superscripts (mass number) and subscripts (atomic number) is equal on both sides of the reaction.

29. C is correct.

A blackbody is an ideal system that absorbs 100% of all light incident upon it and reflects none. It also emits 100% of the radiation it generates. Therefore, it has perfect absorption and emissivity.

30. D is correct.

Carbon dating relies upon a steady creation of ^{14}C and knowledge of the rate of creation at various points in time to determine the approximate age of objects.

If a future archeologist is unaware of nuclear bomb testing and the higher levels of ^{14}C created, then the dates they calculate for an object would be too young. This is because a higher amount of ^{14}C would be present in samples and make them seem as if they had not had time to decay and thus appear to be younger.

31. A is correct.

Gamma radiation is an electromagnetic wave and is not a particle. Thus, when gamma radiation is emitted, the atomic number and mass number remain the same.

32. C is correct.

In β^- decay a neutron is converted to a proton and an electron and electron antineutrino are emitted. In β^+ decay a proton is converted to a neutron, and a positron and an electron neutrino are emitted.

$$^{14}_{6}C \rightarrow \, ^{14}_{7}N + e^+ + v_e$$

33. D is correct.

In a balanced nuclear equation, the number of nucleons must be conserved.

The sum of mass numbers and atomic numbers must be equal on both sides of the equation.

The product (i.e., daughter nuclei) should be on the right side of the equation.

34. B is correct.

The atomic number is the number of protons within the nucleus which characterizes the element's nuclear and chemical properties.

35. C is correct.

The Balmer series is the name of the emission spectrum of hydrogen when electrons transition from a higher state to the $n = 2$ state.

Within the Balmer series, there are four visible spectral lines with colors ranging from red to violet (i.e., ROY G BIV)

36. D is correct.

Electrons were discovered through early experiments with electricity, specifically in high voltage vacuum tubes (cathode ray tubes). Beams of electrons were observed traveling through these tubes when high voltage was applied between the anode and cathode, and the electrons struck fluorescent material at the back of the tube.

37. B is correct.

Beams a and c both deflect when an electric field is applied, indicating they have a net charge and therefore must be particles.

Beam b is undisturbed by the applied electric field, indicating it has no net charge and must be a high energy electromagnetic wave since all other forms of radioactivity (alpha and beta radiation) are charged particles.

38. C is correct.

Beam a is composed of negatively charged particles, while beam c is composed of positively charged particles; therefore, both beams are deflected by the electric field.

Beam b is also composed of particles; however, these particles are neutral because the electric field does not deflect them. An example of this kind of radiation would be a gamma ray, which consists of neutral photons.

39. C is correct.

A helium nucleus is positively charged, so it is deflected away from the top plate and attracted toward the negative plate.

40. B is correct.

5.37 eV is the amount of energy required to excite the electron from the ground state to the zero energy state.

Calculate the wavelength of a photon with this energy:

$E = hf$

$f = c / \lambda$

$E = hc / \lambda$

$\lambda = hc / E$

$\lambda = (4.14 \times 10^{-15} \text{ eV·s})·(3 \times 10^8 \text{ m/s}) / (5.37 \text{ eV})$

$\lambda = 2.3 \times 10^{-7} \text{ m}$

41. D is correct.

Elements with atomic numbers of 84 and higher are radioactive because the strong nuclear force binding the nucleus together cannot overcome the Coulomb repulsion from the high number of protons within the atom. Thus, these nuclei are unstable and emit alpha radiation to decrease the number of protons within the nucleus.

42. D is correct.

Beta particles, like all forms of ionizing radiation, cannot be considered harmless.

43. C is correct.

Gamma rays are the highest-energy electromagnetic radiation and require extremely dense materials to shield effectively. Several centimeters of lead are required to reduce gamma rays considerably.

44. B is correct. Planck's constant quantizes the amount of energy that can be absorbed or emitted. Therefore, it sets a discrete lowest amount of energy for energy transfer.

45. D is correct. The decay rate of any radioactive isotope or element is constant and independent of temperature, pressure, or surface area.

46. B is correct. Larger nuclei (atomic number above 83) tend to decay because the attractive force of the nucleons (strong nuclear force) has a limited range and the nucleus is larger than this range. Therefore, these nuclei tend to emit alpha particles to decrease the size of the nucleus.

Smaller nuclei are not large enough to encounter this problem, but some isotopes have an irregular ratio of neutrons to protons and become unstable. ^{14}Carbon has 8 neutrons and 6 protons, and its neutron to proton ratio is too large. Therefore, it is unstable and radioactive.

47. C is correct.

Positron emission occurs during β^+ decay. In β^+ decay a proton converts to a neutron and emits a positron and electron neutrino.

The decay can be expressed as:

$$^{44}_{21}\text{Sc} \rightarrow {}^{44}_{20}\text{Ca} + e^+ + v_e$$

48. C is correct.

A scintillation counter operates by detecting light flashes from the scintillator material. When radiation strikes the scintillator crystal (often NaI), a light flash is emitted and detected by a photomultiplier tube, which then passes an electronic signal to audio or visual identification equipment.

49. B is correct.

When a Geiger counter clicks, it indicates that it has detected the radiation from one nucleus decaying. The click could be from an alpha, beta, or even gamma-ray source, but cannot be determined without other information.

50. A is correct.

The Pauli Exclusion Principle states that in an atom no two electrons can have the same set of quantum numbers. Thus, every electron in an atom has a unique set of quantum numbers, and a particular set belongs to only one electron.

51. D is correct.

The atomic number indicates the number of protons within the nucleus of an atom.

52. C is correct.

Gamma rays are high-energy electromagnetic radiation rays and have no charge or mass.

Due to their high energy and speed, they have high penetrating power.

53. B is correct. Calculate mass defect:

m_1 = (2 protons)·(1.0072764669 amu) + (2 neutrons)·(1.0086649156 amu)

m_1 = 4.031882765 amu

Δm = 4.031882765 amu – 4.002602 amu

Δm = 0.029280765 amu

Convert to kg:

$$\Delta m = (0.029280765 \text{ amu} / 1) \cdot (1.6606 \times 10^{-27} \text{ kg} / 1 \text{ amu})$$

$$\Delta m = 4.86236 \times 10^{-29} \text{ kg}$$

Find binding energy:

$$E = \Delta m c^2$$

$$E = (4.86236 \times 10^{-29} \text{ kg}) \cdot (3 \times 10^8 \text{ m/s})^2$$

$$E = 4.38 \times 10^{-12} \text{ J} \approx 4.4 \times 10^{-12} \text{ J}$$

54. D is correct.

Boron has an atomic number of five and thus has five protons and five electrons.

The $1s$ orbital is filled by two electrons; then the $2s$ orbital is filled with two electrons.

Only one electron remains, and it is in the $2p$ orbital, leaving it partially filled.

The electron configuration of boron: $1s^2 2s^2 2p$

55. C is correct.

$$E = mc^2$$

$$m = E / c^2$$

$$m = (3.85 \times 10^{26} \text{ J}) / (3 \times 10^8 \text{ m/s})^2$$

$$m = 4.3 \times 10^9 \text{ kg}$$

56. D is correct.

When any form of ionizing radiation interacts with the body, the high energy particles or electromagnetic waves cause atoms within the tissue to ionize.

This process creates unstable ions and free radicals that are damaging and pose serious health risks.

57. B is correct.

When a gamma ray is emitted the atom must lose energy due to the conservation of energy.

Thus, the atom will have less energy than before.

58. A is correct.

The lower case symbol "n" signifies a neutron.

An atomic number of zero indicates that there are no protons.

A mass number of one indicates that it contains a neutron.

59. C is correct.

The uncertainty principle states that the position and momentum of a particle cannot be simultaneously measured over a set precision.

Additionally, the energy and time cannot be simultaneously known over a set precision.

Mathematically this is stated as:

$\Delta x \Delta p > \hbar / 2$

$\Delta E \Delta t > \hbar / 2$

where x = position, p = momentum, $\hbar$ = reduced Planck's constant, E = energy, t = time

60. D is correct.

$A = A_0 (\frac{1}{2})^{t/h}$

where A_0 = original amount, t = time elapse and h = half-life

$0.03 = (1)\cdot(\frac{1}{2})^{(t / 20,000 \text{ years})}$

$\ln (0.03) = (t / 20,000 \text{ years})\cdot\ln (\frac{1}{2})$

$t = 101,179$ years

61. B is correct.

A positron is the antiparticle of an electron; the same mass, but an opposite charge of +1.

62. C is correct.

Beta radiation is characterized as β^- or β^+. In β^- decay an electron is released, while in β^+ decay a positron is released. Beta radiation is the only type of radiation that emits a negatively charged particle (electron) that would deflect towards the positive electrode.

63. D is correct.

The principal quantum number "n" describes the size of the orbital and large values of n indicate a larger orbital shell size. Consequently, the radial distance between the nucleus and the outer bounds of the orbital shell will increase with increasing values of n.

64. A is correct.

The electron was discovered in 1897 by J. J. Thompson.

The proton was discovered c. 1920 by Ernest Rutherford.

The neutron was discovered in 1932 by James Chadwick.

65. C is correct.

Alpha particles consist of 2 protons and 2 neutrons, hence the +2 charge and mass of 4 amu.

They have a high mass; thus they have a low speed and a low penetrating power.

66. A is correct.

^{56}Fe has the highest binding energy because its nucleus is "in the middle" in terms of nuclear size.

Thus, the strong nuclear force and the electromagnetic repulsion are most balanced, and the nucleus is at the lowest energy configuration.

Note: all nuclei are most stable at the lowest energy configuration.

67. B is correct.

Nuclear fusion is the process whereby lighter nuclei fuse to form a heavier element with a greater atomic number, equal to the sum of the atomic numbers of the combining nuclei.

68. D is correct.

The reactants are $^{15}_{7}N + ^{1}_{1}p$

The superscripts sum to 16 while the subscripts sum to 8.

$^{12}C + ^{4}He$ is the only possible set of products because both the superscript and subscript add to 16 and 8, respectively.

$$^{15}_{7}N + ^{1}_{1}p \rightarrow ^{12}_{6}C + ^{4}_{2}He$$

The products $^{14}B + ^{2}Li$ sum to the correct superscript and subscript, but lithium has three protons, so the representation ^{2}Li is not possible.

69. B is correct. Smoke detectors use a small amount of ^{241}americium to detect the smoke.

70. C is correct.

During β⁻ decay, a neutron is converted into a proton which increases the atomic number (# protons) by 1, while the atomic mass (sum of protons and neutrons) remains constant.

71. D is correct.

Because nuclide I has a half-life of about a day, after a few days, only a small fraction of nuclide I will be present and its emitted radioactivity will be greatly reduced.

Nuclide II has a half-life of about a week. After a few days, some of it will have decayed, but a larger fraction (greater than 50%) will be present, so its radioactivity is not considerably reduced. Thus, nuclide II contributes most to the radioactivity of the sample after a few days.

72. A is correct.

Photoelectric effect is when increasing the intensity of light upon a metal increases the electron ejection rate, but does not increase their kinetic energy.

73. D is correct.

The d shell has 5 orbitals with two electrons per orbital for a total of 10 electrons.

74. B is correct.

All elements with atomic numbers greater than 83 will be radioactive. Bismuth has an atomic number of 83, so all successive elements after bismuth are radioactive.

75. A is correct.

A γ ray has 0 protons and 0 neutrons. It is an electromagnetic wave.

76. D is correct.

Balmer equation:

$$\lambda = B(n^2 / n^2 - 2^2)$$

The wavelength is shorter when n becomes larger, such that the term in parentheses approaches 1. Thus, when n = ∞ (the term in parentheses) is minimized (goes to 1) the shortest λ is produced.

$$\lambda = (3.645 \times 10^{-7} \text{ m}) \cdot [\infty^2 / (\infty^2 - 2^2)]$$
$$\lambda = 3.645 \times 10^{-7} \text{ m}$$

77. C is correct.

The sum of protons and neutrons in the nucleus is known as the mass number.

78. B is correct.

Beta decay is more powerful then alpha decay, but less powerful than gamma rays.

Alpha decay is the weakest form of radiation and can be blocked by a sheet of paper.

Beta decay is more powerful and can penetrate the skin, paper, or even a light layer of clothing, such as a T-shirt. Thicker materials, such as leather, are needed to provide beta radiation shielding.

Gamma radiation is the most powerful and requires thick lead barriers or immersion in water to shield effectively.

79. D is correct.

Alpha particles are composed of two protons and two neutrons, which is identical to a helium nucleus ($^4_2$He).

The mass number is the combined amount of protons and neutrons; thus the mass number of an alpha particle is 4 (2 protons + 2 neutrons = 4 mass number).

80. C is correct.

$^0_{-1}$e$^-$ is the notation for an electron which is identical to a beta particle from β$^-$ decay.

81. C is correct.

The reactants are $^3_2$He + $^3_2$He, so the superscripts must sum to 6 while the subscripts must sum to 4.

82. D is correct.

The Sievert is the SI unit for a dose of ionizing radiation and is equal to 100 rems.

83. A is correct.

Positron emission only occurs in β$^+$ decay and does not occur in α decay.

84. D is correct.

Heavier elements contain more neutrons than protons to increase the strength of the nuclear strong force binding the nucleus together.

The increase in nuclear strong force magnitude is necessary because heavier elements contain more protons and the Coulomb repulsion force within the nucleus is higher within these elements.

85. A is correct.

In classical wave theory, the three main predictions for the photoelectric effect are:

1) Intensity of light should be proportional to KE of the photoelectrons (i.e., the photocurrent).

2) Photoelectric effect should occur for any light, regardless of frequency.

3) There should be a delay between radiation contact and the initial release of electrons.

86. B is correct.

Half-life formula:

$$A = A_0(\tfrac{1}{2})^{t/h}$$

where A_0 = original amount, t = time elapse, h = half-life

$A = (10 \text{ g}) \cdot (\frac{1}{2})^{(6 \text{ days} / 2 \text{ days})}$

$A = 1.25$ grams

87. D is correct. Nuclear fusion is the process whereby two lighter elements fuse to form a heavier element. It produces non-radioactive elements, releases a larger amount of energy (as heat), and is the energy source of stars (including the Sun).

88. C is correct.

Alpha radiation consists of alpha particles which have two neutrons and two protons.

Alpha particles are the most massive form of radiation and also have the highest charge of +2 thus they possess the least penetrating ability.

89. A is correct. The Bohr model separates electrons into discrete energy levels with the levels (shells) increasing in the distance away from the nucleus, but the energy difference between the adjacent shells decreases as they get further away from the nucleus.

90. C is correct. The rem is the notation for the Roentgen equivalent in humans and measures the biological damage of ionizing radiation. One rem = .01 Sieverts.

91. B is correct.

An X-ray tube produces X-rays by accelerating electrons through a vacuum tube using a potential difference. If the voltage (potential difference) is doubled, the electric potential energy is doubled:

$\text{PE}_{\text{electric}} = q\text{V}$

$2\text{PE}_{\text{electric}} = q(2\text{V})$

The electric potential energy is equal to the kinetic energy given to the electrons, which is equal to the energy of the X-rays produced:

$\text{PE}_{\text{electric}} = \text{KE}_{\text{electrons}} = \text{E}_{\text{X-ray}}$

$2\text{PE}_{\text{electric}} = 2\text{KE}_{\text{electrons}} = 2\text{E}_{\text{X-ray}}$

$E = hf$

$f = c / \lambda$

$E = h(c / \lambda)$

The energy of an electromagnetic wave is inversely proportional to the wavelength, so by doubling the energy, the X-ray wavelength will be reduced by half.

92. C is correct.

Gamma rays are electromagnetic radiation; thus they are not composed of particles.

Alpha and beta decay both change the atomic number through particle ejection or neutron/proton conversion.

93. A is correct.

In alpha decay, the nucleus loses 2 protons and 2 neutrons in the form of an alpha particle, which is identical to a helium nucleus ($_2^4$He):

$$_{92}^{235}\text{U} \rightarrow {_2^4}\text{He} + {_{90}^{231}}\text{Th}$$

94. B is correct.

$_{17}^{36}$Cl has 19 neutrons and 17 protons; thus it has an excess of neutrons. It will probably not undergo β^+ decay because this would convert a proton to a neutron and increase the neutron-to-proton ratio.

Because it is a smaller nucleus (an atomic number less than 83), it will probably not undergo alpha decay because this form of decay is most often found in larger nuclei that exceed the bounds of the strong nuclear force. Most likely it will undergo β^- decay because this converts an excess neutron to a proton and decreases the neutron-to-proton ratio.

95. D is correct.

A positron is the antiparticle of an electron and has the same mass, but a charge of +1e.

96. D is correct.

All radioactive elements or isotopes decay at a constant rate known as the half-life, which is the time needed for half the original sample to decay. All decay is spontaneous and is towards the formation of a stable element or isotope.

Bismuth has atomic number 83. All elements or isotopes with an atomic number higher than 83 are radioactive. Thus, all elements heavier than bismuth are radioactive.

Radioactivity is part of the natural environment in the form of cosmic rays and trace quantities of radioactive elements or isotopes.

97. D is correct.

Atomic mass is specified by the sum of the protons and neutrons within the nucleus of an atom. Isotopes have more or fewer neutrons than the characteristic element; thus they have different masses.

98. D is correct.

All statements are correct. Nucleons are protons and neutrons, and their mass is different outside the nucleus versus within it. Nucleons in the nucleus change mass slightly due to some mass being converted to bond energy. When nuclei are broken apart, the energy released is from the mass of the nucleons and is converted into the bond energy.

99. C is correct.

$$E = mc^2$$

Calculate the mass needed to produce 10^{12} J of energy:

$$10^{12} \text{ J} = m(3 \times 10^8 \text{ m/s})^2$$

$$m = 10^{-5} \text{ kg}$$

$$m = 10^{-2} \text{ g}$$

100. D is correct. In the photoelectric effect, the frequency of the incident photon must be greater than a certain minimum value to eject an electron. Frequency is directly proportional to photon energy:

$$E = hf$$

Thus, a minimum frequency corresponds to minimum energy needed for the metal to eject an electron. Wavelength is inversely proportional to photon energy:

$$E = hc / \lambda$$

The photon wavelength must be less than a minimum value for the minimum energy to be attained.

101. A is correct. A beta particle is an electron ejected from the nucleus with a charge of $-1e$ and an atomic mass of 0 amu. Beta particles have medium penetrating power. They are more penetrating than alpha particles but less penetrating than gamma rays.

102. B is correct. Control rods in a nuclear reactor are composed of neutron-absorbing material and serve to regulate the flux of neutrons within the reactor, therefore regulating the fission chain reaction.

103. D is correct.

Alpha particles consist of 2 neutrons and 2 protons and are identical to a ^{4}He nucleus.

104. A is correct. The spin quantum number $-\frac{1}{2}$ or $+\frac{1}{2}$ describes the angular momentum of an electron.

Each orbital of an atom can hold two electrons with an opposite spin of $+/-\frac{1}{2}$.

105. C is correct. The nucleus was discovered by Ernest Rutherford when he was using a radioactive alpha emitter to shoot alpha particles at gold foil to measure the angle of deflection.

106. B is correct. The number of nucleons in a nuclear reaction is always conserved, so II must be incorrect.

107. D is correct. Beta decay occurs as either β^+ (positron emission) or β^- (electron emission).

β^+ decay: $\qquad\qquad\qquad {}^A_Z X \rightarrow {}^{\ A}_{Z-1} Y + {}^{\ 0}_{+1} e + {}^0_0 v_e$

β^- decay: $\qquad\qquad\qquad {}^A_Z X \rightarrow {}^{\ A}_{Z+1} Y + {}^{\ 0}_{-1} e + {}^0_0 v_e$

Thus, in beta decay, the nucleus gains or loses a proton.

108. B is correct.

Positrons are the antiparticles to electrons with a positive electric charge of $+e$.

Positron Symbol: ${}^0_{+1} e$ or e^+

Electron Symbol: ${}^0_{-1} e$ or e^-

109. D is correct.

An alpha particle consists of two protons and two neutrons. Missing an alpha particle results in the atomic number decreasing by 2 and the mass number decreases by 4.

110. C is correct. The half-life equation can be used to determine radioactivity after a set amount of time has elapsed.

$A = A_0(\frac{1}{2})^{t/h}$

where A_o = original amount, t = time elapse and h = half-life

$25 \text{ mCi} = (400 \text{ mCi}) \cdot (\frac{1}{2})^{(t\ /\ 14.3\text{ days})}$

$\ln(0.0625) = (t\ /\ 14.3\text{ days}) \cdot \ln(\frac{1}{2})$

$t = 57.2\text{ days}$

111. B is correct.

Beta particles are high-energy, high-speed electrons or positrons.

They can be written as:

β^- decay (electron emission): ${}^0_{-1} e$ or e^-

β^+ decay (positron emission): ${}^0_{+1} e$ or e^+

112. A is correct.

A neon discharge works by applying a voltage to a tube of neon gas such that the electrons gain energy and are promoted from their ground state to an excited state (higher energy orbital). As an electron goes back to its ground state, it releases the energy it gained in the form of a photon. This photon has a characteristic wavelength corresponding to the elemental gas within the tube; for neon, this wavelength corresponds to a red color.

113. C is correct.

Increasing the brightness (intensity) increases the number of photons emitted by the light source, but does not change the energy or speed of the emitted photons. Photon energy is dependent upon frequency, and photon speed is always constant within a specific medium.

114. B is correct.

Electron capture occurs when the nucleus absorbs an electron and emits a neutrino. Additionally, in this process, a proton is converted to a neutron.

115. D is correct. The mass number of an atom is the sum of protons and neutrons within the nucleus and is, therefore, the sum of the nucleons within the atom.

116. C is correct.

Similar chemical properties are due to similar valence electron configurations. Elements are grouped in vertical columns to display these similarities; thus the element below neon has similar chemical properties with the next larger atomic number. Argon has an atomic number of 18 corresponding to 18 protons and 18 electrons.

117. A is correct. Isotopes of iron and nickel ("the iron group") have the maximum binding energy per nucleon of the nucleus. This group has the maximum binding energy per nucleon because the number of nucleons within these elements maximizes the strong nuclear force without maximizing Coulomb repulsion within the nucleus.

Lighter elements do not have as many nucleons and therefore have less energy from the strong nuclear force, while heavier elements have enough protons that Coulomb repulsion lowers their binding energy.

118. A is correct.

$$E = hf$$

If a photon has energy greater than 5.37 eV, this additional amount imparts KE to the electron, which is not necessary to ionize it.

$$f = E_{transition} / h$$

$$f = (5.37 \text{ eV}) / (4.14 \times 10^{-15} \text{ eV·s})$$

$$f = 1.3 \times 10^{15} \text{ Hz}$$

119. C is correct.

Half-life formula:

$$A = A_0(½)^{t\,/\,h}$$

where A_0 = original amount, t = time elapse and h = half-life

$$A = (1)\cdot(½)^{(60\ hours\ /\ 15\ hours)}$$

$$A = 0.5^4$$

$$A = 0.0625 = 6.25\%$$

120. C is correct. The energy of transition is the same as the energy of the photon.

$$f = c\,/\,\lambda$$

$$E_{ph} = hf$$

$$E_{ph} = h(c\,/\,\lambda)$$

$$E_{ph} = (6.63 \times 10^{-34}\ J\cdot s)\cdot[(3 \times 10^8\ m/s)\,/\,(1.25 \times 10^{-7}\ m)]$$

$$E_{ph} = 1.6 \times 10^{-18}\ J$$

The new energy level differs from the 0 J ground state by 1.6×10^{-18} J.

The ground state represents the lowest energy; the excited state must be positive.

121. D is correct. Positron emission occurs during β^+ decay. In β^+ decay:

β^+ decay:

$$^A_Z X \rightarrow\ ^A_{Z-1} Y +\ ^0_{+1}e +\ ^0_0 v_e$$

The mass number remains the same because a proton is converted to a neutron, but the atomic number decreases by one. As such, the nuclear mass does not change, because there is an equal number of nucleons within the nucleus before and after the decay.

122. A is correct. Find energy needed to ionize the electron:

$$E_n = -13.6\ eV\ (1\,/\,n^2 - 1\,/\,\infty)$$

$$E_n = -13.6\ eV\,/\,n^2$$

$$E_2 = (-13.6\ eV)\,/\,2^2$$

$$E_2 = -3.4\ eV$$

The electron must absorb a photon of 3.4 eV to ionize it:

$$E = hc\,/\,\lambda$$

$$\lambda = hc\,/\,E$$

$$\lambda = (4.135 \times 10^{-15}\ eV\cdot s)\cdot(3 \times 10^8\ m/s)\,/\,(3.4\ eV)$$

$$\lambda = 365\ nm$$

123. B is correct.

By the Born Rule, the probability of obtaining any possible measurement outcome is equal to the square of the wave function.

124. A is correct.

In alpha decay, two protons and two neutrons are released as an alpha particle. Thus, the new atomic number is Z–2.

Then when the beta minus decay occurs, a neutron is converted to a proton, giving the atomic number Z–1.

125. C is correct.

Alpha radiation is the emission of a particle with two neutrons and two protons which is identical to a helium nucleus. The alpha particles have a +2 charge due to the two protons and thus are deflected towards the negative electrode of two electrically charged plates.

126. D is correct.

In nuclear fusion, lighter elements fuse to form heavier elements.

During this process, some of the mass of the three helium nuclei is converted to energy by:

$$E = mc^2$$

Thus, the net mass of the three helium nuclei is slightly greater than that of the carbon nucleus due to mass conversion into energy.

127. B is correct.

One of the obvious errors of the planetary model is that electrons cannot orbit the nucleus without experiencing acceleration (due to change in direction). As such, the electron would lose its energy as photons (accelerating charges produce electromagnetic radiation) and eventually collapse into the nucleus.

128. C is correct.

Gamma radiation would be best type of radiation for medical imaging because it penetrates the furthest.

129. D is correct.

Alpha particles have the greatest charge of +2 and consist of two protons and two neutrons. Beta particles (electrons or positrons) have charges of +/–1, and gamma radiation has no charge as it is an electromagnetic wave.

130. B is correct.

Catalysts are substances that lower the activation energy of chemical reactions and bond formation without being consumed within the reaction themselves. Nuclear reactions cannot have their rate increased by a catalyst because the reaction takes place at a nuclear scale and does not involve the formations of bonds.

131. D is correct.

Mass is conserved in a chemical reaction; no particles are created or destroyed. The atoms are rearranged to form products from reactants.

In nuclear reactions, the mass difference is due to mass converting into energy.

132. C is correct. Positron emission occurs during β^+.

The decay equation:

$$^{13}_{7}\text{N} \rightarrow \, ^{13}_{6}\text{C} + \text{e}^+ + \nu_e$$

A proton converts into a neutron, and a positron is ejected with an electron neutrino. The daughter nuclide is ^{13}C.

133. D is correct.

Radon gas is a natural decay product of uranium that accounts for the greatest source of yearly radiation exposure in humans. Radon is more hazardous to smokers due to the combined carcinogenic effects of smoking and radiation exposure.

134. D is correct.

The strong nuclear force is the strongest of the four fundamental forces. However, it only acts within a small range of distance (about the diameter of the nucleus).

135. D is correct.

Natural line broadening is the extension of a spectral line over a range of frequencies. This occurs due in part to the uncertainty principle, which relates the time in which an atom is excited to the energy of its emitted photon.

$\Delta E \Delta t > \hbar / 2$

where $\hbar$ is reduced Planck's constant

Because energy is related to frequency by:

$E = hf$

where h is Planck's constant

The range of frequencies observed (broadening) is due to the uncertainty in energy outlined by the uncertainty principle.

136. B is correct.

Speed is constant for all electromagnetic waves and only changes due to the transmission medium, not the frequency or wavelength of the wave.

Blue photons have higher energy and thus higher frequencies than red light due to:

$E = hf$

However, the frequency is inversely proportional to wavelength:

$\lambda = c / f$

Thus, blue photons have shorter wavelengths than red photons due to their higher frequencies.

137. A is correct.

Gamma radiation is a high energy electromagnetic wave, and as such it has no charge and will not deflect within an electric field.

138. C is correct.

Nuclei with atomic numbers over 83 are inherently unstable and thus radioactive. This limit in size is because the strong nuclear force has a very short range and as the nucleus gets larger, the strong nuclear force cannot overcome the Coulomb repulsion from the protons within the nucleus.

139. D is correct.

A mass of an element or compound can be measured by its molar mass. The molar mass relates the mass of the element or compound to a discrete number of subunits (atoms for elements, molecules for compounds).

140. B is correct.

The rem is short for the Roentgen equivalent in man and is designed to measure the biological damage of ionizing radiation. It does not measure the number of particles absorbed or emitted, nor is it the maximum occupational safety exposure limit for radiation.

141. A is correct.

The intensity of electromagnetic radiation with respect to distance from the point source:

$I = S / 4\pi r^2$

where I = intensity, S = point source strength, and r = radial distance from the point source.

The intensity of the radiation from the point source is inversely proportional to the square of the distance away from the point source.

142. B is correct.

Ionizing radiation can be high energy charged particles (alpha, beta) or high energy electromagnetic waves (X-rays, gamma rays).

All are termed ionizing because they possess enough energy to remove electrons from atoms or molecules and ionize them.

143. C is correct.

Nuclear reaction:

$$^{55}_{28}Ni \rightarrow \, ^{55}_{27}Co + e^+ + v_e$$

where Co = product, e^+ = positron and v_e = electron neutrino

In positron emission (β^+ decay), a proton in the nucleus converts to a neutron while releasing a positron and an electron neutrino.

The atomic number decreases by one, but the mass number stays constant.

144. A is correct.

Gamma rays are high energy electromagnetic waves. They have the highest energy of all radiation (e.g., alpha, beta, and electromagnetic spectrum).

145. D is correct.

Use Wien's displacement law:

$$\lambda_{max} = b \, / \, T$$

$$T = (2.9 \times 10^{-3} \, K{\cdot}m) \, / \, (580 \times 10^{-9} \, m)$$

$$T = 5,000 \, K$$

Particle Physics – Explanations

1. C is correct.

Leptons do not interact via the strong force, so they cannot comprise the hadrons.

Quarks do interact via the strong force, and are the building blocks of hadrons.

Electrons are leptons, while protons and neutrons are hadrons (since they are both made up of quarks).

2. D is correct.

One defining characteristic of hadrons is that they interact by the strong nuclear force. Electrons are leptons, not hadrons (because electrons do not interact by the strong force since they have no quarks), although neutrons and protons are hadrons. Quarks, which are neither leptons nor hadrons, are the building blocks of all hadrons.

3. B is correct.

Leptons interact by all forces except the strong nuclear force.

4. B is correct.

The positron (antielectron) is a lepton and is not made of quarks. The neutron is a hadron. The alpha particle is composed of two protons and two neutrons, both of which are hadrons made of quarks.

5. B is correct.

Hadrons have charge +1e, 0e, or −1e. They are combinations of two (mesons) or three (baryons) quarks. The only possible ways of combining two or three fractionally charged objects so that the net charge is +1e, 0e or −1e is if the charges of the objects are taken from sets (1/3 e, −2/3 e) or (−1/3 e, +2/3 e).

The former set represents the quarks, and the latter the antiquarks.

Note that it is not possible to ever see a quark by itself (i.e., not bound to other quarks/antiquarks).

Thus, any actual particle that can be observed will have integer charge; the fractional charge for any particle that can exist by itself is never measured.

6. D is correct.

The deuteron is composed of two baryons, one proton, and one neutron. The baryons each have three quarks, so the total number of quarks in the deuteron is six.

7. D is correct.

The tritium nucleus, the triton, is composed of three baryons, one proton, and two neutrons.

The baryons each have three quarks, so the total number of quarks in the triton is nine.

8. B is correct.

The more massive the particle, the more decay channels are available, resulting in a shorter lifetime and reducing the range of the exchange mediated force. One can also think of this using the uncertainty principle. The exchange particle is a "virtual particle," meaning it appears temporarily and disappears once the exchange is complete.

The uncertainty principle sets a limit on how long such a particle can exist: $\Delta E \, \Delta t > \hbar/2$. Since the exchange particle's energy increases with greater mass, a heavier particle can only survive for a shorter time Δt.

A shorter lifetime means it cannot cover as much distance as a lighter particle, so the range for a heavier particle will be less.

9. A is correct.

The total mass-energy of the system is the rest mass of the electron and positron combined.

Since two photons are emitted, each photon will have the energy equal to the mass-energy of one electron.

The energy of each photon is, therefore:

$$E = mc^2$$

where m is the mass of an electron.

The relationship between the energy of a photon and frequency and wavelength is:

$$E = hf = hc/\lambda$$

Combining these formulas:

$$\lambda = (hc) / (mc^2) = h / mc$$

Entering the values given:

$$\lambda = 2.42 \times 10^{-12} \, \text{m}$$

$$\lambda = 2.42 \text{ pm}$$

10. A is correct.

The proton has a charge of $+1e$. Answer A is the only answer in which the sum of the quark charges is $+1e$.

A proton is made of two up quarks and one down quark.

11. C is correct.

The positron is quickly annihilated by an electron in the sample, producing two gamma rays each having energy equal to the mass-energy of an electron or positron (the mass of a positron is the same as the mass of an electron).

The mass-energy of an electron (and thus a positron) is 0.511 MeV.

Note that *two* photons must be emitted because a final state with only one photon would violate conservation of linear momentum.

To see this, imagine a reference frame where the center-of-mass of the electron-positron pair is stationary.

Thus, before the annihilation, the total momentum is zero (since the center-of-mass is not moving in this reference frame).

It is impossible for a final state of just one photon to have zero momentum.

12. C is correct.

To produce a proton-antiproton pair, an amount of energy is necessarily equal at least to the combined mass of the proton and antiproton.

The proton and antiproton both have mass energy of 938 MeV, so the minimum energy to produce a pair is twice this, 1876 MeV.

13. C is correct.

Each gamma ray will have energy equal to half the mass of η. The energy of each gamma is therefore:

$$E = mc^2 / 2$$

where m is the mass of an η meson.

The relationship between the energy of a photon and frequency and wavelength is:

$$E = hf = hc/\lambda$$

Combining these:

$$\lambda = (2hc) / (mc^2)$$

Entering the values given for hc and rest energy mc^2 and converting units:

$$\lambda = (2 \times 1240 \text{ eV nm} \times 10^{-9} \text{ m/nm}) / (548 \times 10^6 \text{ eV})$$

$$\lambda = 4.5 \times 10^{-15} \text{ m}$$

14. D is correct.

The kinetic energy of a relativistic particle is the total energy less the rest energy.

$$K = E - mc^2 = \gamma mc^2 - mc^2 = (\gamma - 1)mc^2$$

where

$$\gamma = 1 / \sqrt{(1 - \beta^2)} \text{ and } \beta = v / c$$

Rearranging:

$$\gamma - 1 = K / mc^2$$

$$\gamma = 1 + K / mc^2$$

$$1 / \sqrt{(1 - \beta^2)} = 1 + K / mc^2$$

Square both sides and invert:

$$1 - \beta^2 = 1 / (1 + K / mc^2)^2$$

$$\beta^2 = 1 - [1 / (1 + K / mc^2)^2]$$

$$\beta = \sqrt{\{1 - [1 / (1 + K / mc^2)^2]\}}$$

The mass of a proton is $mc^2 = 0.938$ GeV.

Using this and the given value of kinetic energy, $K = 2$ GeV:

$$\beta = 0.948$$

so,

$$v = 0.948c \approx 0.95c$$

15. D is correct.

The energy of a relativistic particle is:

$$E = \gamma mc^2 = (mc^2) / \sqrt{(1 - \beta^2)}$$

where $\beta = v / c$. Divide by mc^2 and square:

$$(E / mc^2)^2 = 1 / (1 - \beta^2)$$

Solve for β:

$$\beta = \sqrt{[1 - (mc^2 / E)^2]}$$

For an electron, $mc^2 = 0.511$ MeV.

Using this and the given value $E = 2$ MeV, gives:

$$\beta = 0.967$$

or

$$v = 0.97\, c$$

16. B is correct.

Using the definition of Boltzmann's constant, the relationship between temperature and energy is:

$$kT = E$$

$$T = E / k$$

where k is Boltzmann's constant, $k = 8.617 \times 10^{-5}$ eV/K.

With an energy of 50 GeV = 50×10^9 eV:

$$T = (50 \times 10^9 \text{ eV}) / (8.617 \times 10^{-5} \text{ eV/K})$$

$$T = 5.8 \times 10^{14} \text{ K}$$

The commonly quoted conversion factor is 1eV = 11600K.

17. D is correct.

Hubble's law relates the speed of a receding galaxy to its distance from Earth.

$$d = v / H$$

$$d = 0.5 \ (3.0 \times 10^8 \text{ m/s}) / (0.022 \text{ m/s/lightyear})$$

$$d = 6.8 \times 10^9 \text{ lightyears}$$

18. A is correct.

Hubble's law relates the speed of a receding galaxy to its distance from Earth.

$$v = dH$$

$$v = (2.7 \times 10^9 \text{ lightyears}) \cdot (0.022 \text{ m/s/lightyear})$$

$$v = 5.94 \times 10^7 \text{ m/s}$$

In terms of the speed of light $c = 3.00 \times 10^8$ m/s:

$$v = 0.2 \ c$$

19. B is correct.

The minimum energy state of an electron and a positron is one in which neither has any kinetic energy.

The total energy of the system is then the rest mass-energy of the electron and positron.

Each has a rest energy of 0.511 MeV, so the total minimum energy is 1.022 MeV.

20. C is correct.

The creation of the meson would violate the principle of conservation of energy unless its lifetime was short enough that its mass-energy fell within the limit set by Heisenberg's uncertainty principle.

$$\Delta E \Delta t \geq h / 2\pi$$

Take the minimum uncertainty to be the rest mass of the meson, as the uncertainty has to be at least sufficient to create the meson.

$$\Delta t \geq h / 2\pi mc^2$$

The meson must decay before this amount of time has elapsed.

Since no particle can travel faster than the speed of light, the maximum range the meson can have is:

$$r = c\Delta t = hc / 2\pi mc^2$$

$$r = (1.24 \text{ eV } \mu m) / [2\pi (140 \text{ MeV})]$$

$$r = 1.4 \times 10^{-15} \text{ m}$$

21. C is correct.

The creation of the boson would violate the principle of conservation of energy unless its lifetime was short enough that its mass-energy fell within the limit set by Heisenberg's uncertainty principle.

$$\Delta E \Delta t \geq h / 2\pi$$

Take the minimum uncertainty to be the rest mass of the boson, as the uncertainty has to be at least sufficient to create the boson.

$$\Delta t \geq h / 2\pi mc^2$$

In order for conservation of energy not to be violated, the boson must decay before this time interval has elapsed. So, the interaction time is:

$$t = h / 2\pi mc^2$$

The rest energy of the meson in SI units is:

$$mc^2 = 91 \times 10^9 \text{ eV } (1.6 \times 10^{-19} \text{ J/eV}) = 1.456 \times 10^{-8} \text{ J}$$

Therefore:

$$t = (6.63 \times 10^{-34} \text{J s}) / [2\pi (1.456 \times 10^{-8} \text{J})]$$

$$t = 7.2 \times 10^{-27} \text{s}$$

22. A is correct.

Since the muons are at rest (no kinetic energy), the total energy of the system is the sum of the rest mass energies of the muons, that is, twice the mass of a single muon.

The annihilation produces two photons of equal energy, so the energy of each is equal to the mass-energy of one muon.

The wavelength of the photon of energy E is:

$\lambda = hc / E$

$\lambda = (1.24 \text{ eV } \mu\text{m}) / (106 \text{ MeV})$

$\lambda = 1.17 \times 10^{-14} \text{ m}$

23. B is correct.

The creation of the boson would violate the principle of conservation of energy unless its lifetime was short enough that its mass-energy fell within the limit set by Heisenberg's uncertainty principle.

$\Delta E \Delta t \geq h / 2\pi$

Take the minimum uncertainty to be the rest mass of the boson, as the uncertainty has to be at least sufficient to create the boson.

$\Delta t \geq h / 2\pi mc^2$

The meson must decay before this amount of time has elapsed.

The maximum range the boson can have is:

$r = c\Delta t = hc / 2\pi mc^2$

$r = (1.24 \text{ eV } \mu\text{m}) / [2\pi \cdot (80 \text{ GeV})]$

$r = 2.5 \times 10^{-18} \text{ m}$

Electrostatics and Magnetism – Explanations

1. D is correct. In Gaus's Law, the area is a vector perpendicular to the plane. Only the component of the electric field strength parallel is used.

Gaus's Law:

$$\Phi = EA \cos \theta$$

where Φ is electric flux (scalar), E is electric field strength, and A is area vector.

Solve:

$$\Phi = EA \cos (\pi / 6)$$

$$A = \pi r^2 = \pi D^2 / 4$$

$$\Phi = (740 \text{ N/C}) \cdot (\pi / 4) \cdot (1 \text{ m})^2 \cos (\pi / 6)$$

$$\Phi = 160\pi \text{ N·m}^2/\text{C}$$

For calculation, use radians mode, not degree mode.

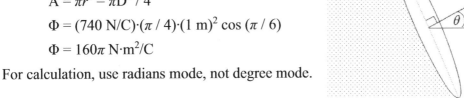

2. A is correct.

The magnitude of the negative charge's electric field:

$$|E_2| = kQ_2 / d_2{}^2$$

$$|E_2| = (9 \times 10^9 \text{ N·m}^2/\text{C}^2) \cdot [(-1.3 \times 10^{-9} \text{ C}) / (+10^{-3} \text{ m})^2]$$

$$|E_2| = 1.17 \times 10^7 \text{ N/C to the left}$$

The magnitude of the positive charge's electric field:

$$|E_1| = kQ_1 / d_1{}^2$$

$$|E_1| = (9 \times 10^9 \text{ N·m}^2/\text{C}^2) \cdot [(1.3 \times 10^{-9} \text{ C}) / (2 \times 10^{-3} \text{ m})^2]$$

$$|E_1| = 2.9 \times 10^6 \text{ N/C to the right}$$

$$\Delta E = E_2 - E_1$$

$$\Delta E = (1.17 \times 10^7 \text{ N/C}) - (2.9 \times 10^6 \text{ N/C})$$

$$\Delta E = 8.8 \times 10^6 \text{ N/C, to the left}$$

3. D is correct.

Calculate the distance between the two charges using the Pythagorean Theorem:

$$r^2 = (1 \text{ nm})^2 + (4 \text{ nm})^2$$

$$r^2 = 17 \text{ nm}^2$$

$$r = 4.1 \text{ nm}$$

$$F = kQ_1Q_2 / r^2$$

$$F = [(9 \times 10^9 \text{ N·m}^2/\text{C}^2) \cdot (1.6 \times 10^{-19} \text{ C}) \cdot (1.6 \times 10^{-19} \text{ C})] / (4.1 \times 10^{-9} \text{ m})^2$$

$$F = 1.4 \times 10^{-11} \text{ N}$$

4. A is correct. Gamma rays are the electromagnetic radiation with photons of the highest energy.

5. D is correct. Forces balance to yield:

$F_{\text{electric}} = F_{\text{gravitation}}$

$F_{\text{electric}} = mg$

The values for an electric field are provided.

$F_{\text{electric}} = QE$

$F_{\text{electric}} - F_{\text{gravitation}} = 0$

$QE - mg = 0$, where Q is the charge on the ball

$QE = mg$

$Q = mg / E$

$Q = (0.008 \text{ kg}) \cdot (9.8 \text{ m/s}^2) / (3.5 \times 10^4 \text{ N/C})$

$Q = -2.2 \times 10^{-6} \text{ C}$

If the electric field points down, then a positive charge experiences a downward force. The charge must be negative, so the electric force balances gravity.

6. A is correct. $a = qE / m$

The electron moves against the electric field, in the upward direction, so its acceleration:

$a_e = qE / m_e$

The proton moves with the electric field, which is down, so:

$a_p = qE / m_p$

However, the masses considered are small to where the gravity component is negligible.

$m_p / m_e = (1.67 \times 10^{-27} \text{ kg}) / (9.11 \times 10^{-31} \text{ kg})$

$m_p / m_e = 1,830$

The mass of an electron is about 1,830 times smaller than the mass of a proton.

$(1,830)m_e = m_p$

$a_p = qE / (1,830)m_e$

$a_p = a_e / (1,830)$

$a_e = 1,830a_p$

7. D is correct. Calculate the strength of the field at point P due to only one charge:

$E = kQ / r^2$

$E_1 = (9 \times 10^9 \text{ N} \cdot \text{m}^2/\text{C}^2) \cdot [(2.3 \times 10^{-11} \text{ C}) / (5 \times 10^{-3} \text{ m})^2]$

$E_1 = 8.3 \times 10^3 \text{ N/C}$

Both electric field vectors point toward the negative charge, so the magnitude of each field at point P is doubled:

$E_T = 2E_1$

$E_T = 2(8.3 \times 10^3 \text{ N/C})$

$E_T = 1.7 \times 10^4 \text{ N/C}$

8. D is correct. Like charges repel each other.

From Newton's Third Law, the magnitude of the force experienced by each charge is equal.

9. B is correct.

Currents occur in a conducting circuit element when there is a potential difference between the two ends of the element, and hence an established electric field.

10. D is correct.

Voltage is related to the number of coils in a wire. More coils yield a higher voltage.

Turns ratio:

$V_s / V_p = n_s / n_p$

In this case:

$n_s < n_p$

Therefore,

$V_s < V_p$

Because the secondary voltage (V_s) is lower than the primary voltage (V_p) the transformer is a step-down transformer.

11. A is correct.

According to Lenz's Law, inserting a magnet into the coil causes the magnetic flux through the coil to change. This produces an emf in the coil which drives a current through the coil:

Lenz's Law:

$\text{emf} = -N\Delta BA / \Delta t$

The brightness of the bulb changes with a change in the current, but it cannot be known if the bulb gets brighter or dimmer without knowing the orientation of the coil with respect to the incoming magnetic pole of the magnet.

12. A is correct.

Initially, the current will flow clockwise, but after 180° of rotation, the current will reverse itself. After 360° of rotation, the current will reverse itself again. Thus, there are 2 current reverses in 1 revolution.

13. D is correct.

The electric field is oriented in a way that a positively-charged particle would be forced to move to the top because negatively-charged particles move to the bottom of the cube to be closer to the source of the electric field.

Therefore, all the positively charged particles are forced upward and the negatively-charged ones downward, leaving the top surface positively charged.

14. C is correct.

The magnitude of the force between the center charge and each charge at a vertex is 5 N. The net force of these two forces is directed toward the third vertex.

To determine the magnitude of the net force, calculate the magnitude of the component of each force acting in that direction:

$$F_{net} = F_1 \sin(½\,\theta) + F_2 \sin(½\,\theta) \qquad \text{(see diagram)}$$

Since it is an equilateral triangle $\theta = 60°$,

$$F_{net} = (5\text{ N} \sin 30°) + (5\text{ N} \sin 30°)$$

$$F_{net} = (5\text{ N}) \cdot (½) + (5\text{ N}) \cdot (½)$$

$$F_{net} = 5\text{ N}$$

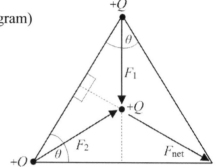

15. A is correct.

Gamma rays have the highest frequency on the electromagnetic spectrum, with frequencies greater than 3×10^{19} Hz.

16. A is correct.

The strength of the electrostatic field due to a single point charge is given by:

$E = kQ / r^2$, assumes that the source charge is in vacuum

E depends on both the magnitude of the source charge Q and the distance r from Q.

The sign of the source charge affects only the direction of the electrostatic field vectors.

The sign of the source charge does not affect the strength of the field.

17. B is correct.

$$F = qvB$$

$$F = mv^2 / r$$

$mv^2 / r = qvB$, cancel v from both sides of the expression

$$mv / r = qB$$

$$r = (mv) / (qB)$$

If the velocity doubles, the radius also doubles.

18. D is correct. Cyclotron frequency is given as:

$$f = qB \, / \, 2\pi m$$

This expression does not consider speed.

19. A is correct.

The given unit can be written $[kg \cdot m^2/s^2] \, / \, C = J \, / \, C$, which is the definition of the Volt, the unit of electric potential difference.

20. A is correct.

Faraday's law states that electromotive force (emf) is equal to the rate of change of magnetic flux. Magnetic flux is the product of the magnetic field and projected area:

$$\Phi = BA_\perp,$$

where $A_\perp$ is the area of the loop projected on a plane perpendicular to the magnetic field.

In this problem, B is vertical (and constant), so the projection plane is horizontal.

Therefore, find the orientation of the axis of rotation that guarantees that as the loop rotates, the projection of its area on a horizontal plane does not change with time.

Notice that if the orientation of the axis is at an arbitrary angle to the field, the emf can be made to be zero by aligning the axis of rotation with the axis of the loop (i.e., perpendicular to the loop). With this orientation, the projection of the area never changes, which is not true of other alignments to the loop.

Although the emf can be made to be zero, it is not *guaranteed* to be zero.

The only orientation of the axis that *guarantees* that the projected area is constant is the vertical orientation. One way to see this is to notice that because of the high symmetry of the vertical-axis orientation, rotating the loop about a vertical axis is equivalent to changing the perspective of the viewer from one angle to another.

The answer cannot depend on the perspective of the viewer.

Therefore, the projected area cannot change as the loop is rotated about the vertical axis; the emf is guaranteed to be zero.

21. B is correct.

The time taken for one revolution around the circular path is $T = 2\pi R/v$, where R is the radius of the circle and v is the speed of the proton. If the speed is increased, the radius also increases. The relationship between speed and radius follows from the fact that the magnetic interaction provides the centripetal force:

$$mv^2 / \, R = qvB$$

Thus:

$$R = mv \, / \, qB$$

If the speed is tripled, the radius triples, all other thigs being equal. The final period for a revolution is:

$$T_f = 2\pi R_f \, / \, v_f = 2\pi(3R) \, / \, 3v = 2\pi R \, / \, v = T$$

22. C is correct. An electrostatic field shows the path that would be taken by a positively-charged particle.

As this positive particle moves closer to the negatively-charged one, the force between them increases.

Coulomb's law:

$$F = kQ_1Q_2 \, / \, r^2$$

By convention, electric field vectors always point towards negative source charges.

Since electrical field strength is inversely proportional to the square of the distance from the source charge, the magnitude of the electric field progressively increases as an object moves towards the source charge.

23. D is correct.

Protons are charges, so they have an electric field.

Protons have mass, so they have a gravitational field.

Protons have an intrinsic magnetic moment, so they have a magnetic field.

24. C is correct. The analog to N/kg would be N/C, the unit for the electric field.

25. D is correct.

All the electromagnetic waves travel through space (vacuum) at the same speed:

$$c = 3 \times 10^8 \text{ m/s}$$

26. A is correct.

As the proton of charge q moves in the direction of the electric field lines, it moves away from a positive charge (because field lines emanate from positive charge).

Electric Potential Energy:

$$U = kQq \, / \, r$$

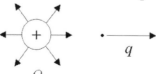

As distance increases, the potential energy decreases because they are inversely proportional.

Electrical potential:

$$V = kQ / r$$

Electrical potential is inversely proportional to distance and decreases as distance increases.

27. B is correct. 1 watt = 1 J/s

28. A is correct. Because point P is symmetric about Q_1 and Q_2 and both charges have the same positive magnitude, the electric field cancels midway between the charges.

$$E = kQ / r^2$$
$$E_1 = -E_2$$
$$E_{tot} = E_1 + E_2$$
$$E_{tot} = (-E_2 + E_2)$$
$$E_{tot} = 0 \text{ N/C}$$

29. D is correct. A sphere or any conduction object that acquires a net charge has the charge collect on the surface. This is due to excess charge repelling itself and moving to the surface to increase the distance between themselves.

30. A is correct. A charged particle only experiences a magnetic force if it moves with a perpendicular velocity component to the field. Thus, there must not be a magnetic field, or the particle moves parallel to the field.

31. D is correct.

$$E = kQ / r^2$$

The magnitude of each electron's electric field will be the same because they have equal charge and the point of measurement is equidistant.

However, the electric field is a vector, and since both charges are the same, the vectors point opposite to each other and cancel to be zero at exactly the midpoint of the charge.

32. B is correct.

Gaus's Law:

$$\Phi = EA \cos \theta$$

where Φ is electric flux (scalar), E is electric field strength, and A is area vector.

33. D is correct. None of the following statements is correct: the north pole of a magnet points towards Earth's geographic North Pole; the north pole of a magnet points towards Earth's geographic South Pole; the Earth's geographic North Pole is the north pole of Earth's magnetic field

34. C is correct.

When the positively charged sphere C is near sphere B, it polarizes the sphere causing its negative charge to migrate towards C and a positive charge to build on the other side of sphere B.

The wire between sphere A and sphere B allows the negative charge to flow to B and create a net positive charge on sphere A. Once the wire is removed and sphere C is removed, sphere A will have a net positive charge and B has a net negative charge.

35. B is correct.

The balloon sticks to the wall because the rubbing on the wool has transferred charges to the balloon, leading to an electrostatic force.

36. A is correct.

If the charge Q is of a greater magnitude than charge q then the electric field points toward Q (because its negative) in section W to Z.

In section VW the electric field is the difference in magnitude between q and Q. If Q has a large enough charge then the difference could equal zero, and there is no electric field.

37. D is correct.

A volt is defined as the potential difference that causes 1 C of charge to increase potential energy by 1 J. Therefore, moving 1 C through 6 V causes the potential energy of the battery to increase by 6 J.

38. C is correct.

A current is caused by a voltage (potential difference) across a conductor.

Whenever a voltage exists an electric field exists, and this travels at near the speed of light. Electrons do not travel quickly when a current is established and only travel at their drift speed which is proportional to voltage.

39. D is correct.

A proton moving perpendicular to electric field lines does not get close to the charges creating the electric field. Thus, its electric potential and potential energy remain constant because these values are related to distance from other charges.

Electric Potential Energy:

$$U = kQq \, / \, r$$

Electric Potential:

$$V = kQ \, / \, r$$

40. C is correct.

In a solid, the locations of the nuclei are fixed; only the electrons move.

41. C is correct.

There is a force on the proton up the page. The electric field points in the direction of the force on positive particles, therefore it is pointed upwards.

The direction of the magnetic field is determined by the right-hand rule.

$F = qvB$, where q is a charge, v is velocity and B is a magnetic field

When F is oriented upwards, curling your fingers from the direction of velocity gives B into the page.

42. A is correct.

Convert all units to their correct form:

$$F = ma$$
$$F = (2 \times 10^{-6}\ \text{kg}) \cdot (0.006\ \text{m/s}^2)$$
$$F = 1.2 \times 10^{-8}\ \text{N}$$

Substituting into the equation for electric field:

$$E = F / q$$
$$E = (1.2 \times 10^{-8}\ \text{N}) / (6 \times 10^{-6}\ \text{C})$$
$$E = 0.002\ \text{N/C}$$

Note: $1\ \text{N} = 1\ \text{kg} \cdot \text{m/s}^2$, not $1\ \text{g} \cdot \text{m/s}^2$

43. B is correct.

$$\Phi = Q / E_0$$

For an enclosed charge, the area of the surface does not affect the flux.

44. A is correct.

γ rays are the electromagnetic waves with the shortest wavelength?

45. B is correct.

Faraday's Law states that the electromotive force (emf) in a coil is:

$$\text{emf} = N\Delta BA \cos\theta / \Delta t$$

where N = number of loops of wire.

If N doubles, the emf also doubles.

46. D is correct.

$$V = kQ / r$$

$$V_B = kQ / r_B$$

$$V_B = (9 \times 10^9 \, \text{N·m}^2/\text{C}^2) \cdot (1 \times 10^{-6} \, \text{C}) / 3.5 \, \text{m}$$

$$V_B = 2{,}571 \, \text{V}$$

$$V_A = kQ / r_A$$

$$V_A = (9 \times 10^9 \, \text{N·m}^2/\text{C}^2) \cdot (1 \times 10^{-6} \, \text{C}) / 8 \, \text{m}$$

$$V_A = 1{,}125 \, \text{V}$$

Potential difference:

$$\Delta V = V_B - V_A$$

$$\Delta V = 2{,}571 \, \text{V} - 1{,}125 \, \text{V}$$

$$\Delta V = 1{,}446 \, \text{V}$$

47. A is correct.

$$E = qV$$

$$E = \tfrac{1}{2}m(\Delta v)^2$$

$$qV = \tfrac{1}{2}m(v_f^2 - v_i^2)$$

$$v_f^2 = (2qV / m) + v_i^2$$

$$v_f^2 = [2(1.6 \times 10^{-19} \, \text{C}) \cdot (100 \, \text{V}) / (1.67 \times 10^{-27} \, \text{kg})] + (1.5 \times 10^5 \, \text{m/s})^2$$

$$v_f^2 = (1.9 \times 10^{10} \, \text{m}^2/\text{s}^2) + (2.3 \times 10^{10} \, \text{m}^2/\text{s}^2)$$

$$v_f^2 = 4.2 \times 10^{10} \, \text{m}^2/\text{s}^2$$

$$v_f = 2.04 \times 10^5 \, \text{m/s} \approx 2 \times 10^5 \, \text{m/s}$$

48. D is correct.

A magnetic field is created only by electric charges in motion.

A stationary charged particle does not generate a magnetic field.

49. D is correct.

$$E = qV$$

$$E = \tfrac{1}{2}mv^2$$

$$qV = \tfrac{1}{2}mv^2$$

$$v^2 = 2qV / m$$

$$v^2 = [2(1.6 \times 10^{-19} \, \text{C}) \cdot (990 \, \text{V})] / (9.11 \times 10^{-31} \, \text{kg})$$

$$v^2 = 3.5 \times 10^{14} \, \text{m}^2/\text{s}^2$$

$$v = 1.9 \times 10^7 \, \text{m/s}$$

50. C is correct.

Electromagnetic induction is the production of an electromotive force across a conductor.

When a changing magnetic field is brought near a coil, a voltage is generated in the coil thus inducing a current.

The voltage generated can be calculated by Faraday's Law:

$\text{emf} = -N\Delta\phi / \Delta t$

where N = number of turns and $\Delta\phi$ = change in magnetic flux

51. D is correct.

$PE_e = PE_1 + PE_2 + PE_3$

$PE_e = (kQ_1Q_2) / r_1 + (kQ_2Q_3) / r_2 + (kQ_1Q_3) / r_3$

$PE_e = kQ^2 [(1 / r_1) + (1 / r_2) + (1 / r_3)]$

$r_1 = 4$ cm and $r_2 = 3$ cm are known, use Pythagorean Theorem to find r_3:

$r_3^2 = r_1^2 + r_2^2$

$r_3^2 = (4 \text{ cm})^2 + (3 \text{ cm})^2$

$r_3^2 = 16 \text{ cm}^2 + 9 \text{ cm}^2$

$r_3^2 = 25 \text{ cm}^2$

$r_3 = 5$ cm

$PE_e = (9.0 \times 10^9 \text{ N·m}^2/\text{C}^2)\cdot(3.8 \times 10^{-9} \text{ C})^2 \times [(1 / 0.04 \text{ m}) + (1 / 0.03 \text{ m}) + (1 / 0.05 \text{ m})]$

$PE_e = (1.2 \times 10^{-7} \text{ N·m}^2)\cdot(25 \text{ m}^{-1} + 33 \text{ m}^{-1} + 20 \text{ m}^{-1})$

$PE_e = (1.2 \times 10^{-7} \text{ N·m}^2)\cdot(78 \text{ m}^{-1})$

$PE_e = 1.0 \times 10^{-5} \text{ J}$

52. A is correct. The magnetic force acting on a charge q moving at velocity v in a magnetic field B is given by:

$F = qv \times B$

If q, v, and the angle between v and B are the same for both charges, then the magnitude of the force F is the same on both charges.

However, if the charges carry opposite signs, each experiences oppositely-directed forces.

53. C is correct. By convention, the direction of electric current is the direction that a positive charge migrates.

Electrons flow from regions of low potential to regions of high potential.

Electric Potential Energy:

$U = (kQq) / r$

Electric Potential:

$$V = (kQ) / r$$

Because the charge of an electron (q) is negative, as the electron moves opposite to the electric field, it must be getting closer to the positive charge Q. As this occurs, an increasingly negative potential energy U is produced; thus, potential energy is decreasing.

Conversely, as the electron approaches Q, the electric potential V increases with less distance. This is because the product is positive and reducing r increases V.

54. B is correct.

The potential energy of a system containing two point charges is:

$$U = kq_1q_2 / r$$

In this problem, one of the charges is positive, and the other is negative. To account for this, write:

$$q_1 = +|q_1| \text{ and } q_2 = -|q_2|$$

The potential energy can be written as:

$$U = -k|q_1||q_2| / r$$

Moreover, the absolute value of the potential energy is:

$$|U| = k|q_1||q_2| / r$$

All quantities are positive. The absolute value of the potential energy is inversely proportional to the orbital radius; therefore, the absolute value of the potential energy decreases as the orbital radius increases.

55. A is correct.

Since force is the cross-product of velocity and magnetic field strength:

$$F = qv \times B$$

The force is at a maximum when v and B are perpendicular:

$$F = qvB \sin 90°$$
$$\sin 90° = 1$$
$$F = qvB$$

56. C is correct.

$$\Delta V = \Delta E / q$$
$$\Delta V = (1 / q)·(\tfrac{1}{2}mv_f^2 - \tfrac{1}{2}mv_i^2)$$
$$\Delta V = (m / 2q)·(v_f^2 - v_i^2)$$
$$\Delta V = [(1.67 \times 10^{-27} \text{ kg}) / (2)·(1.6 \times 10^{-19} \text{ C})] \times [(3.2 \times 10^5 \text{ m/s})^2 - (1.7 \times 10^5 \text{ m/s})^2]$$
$$\Delta V = 384 \text{ V}$$

57. A is correct.

Calculate capacitance:

$$C = k\mathcal{E}_o A / d$$

$$C = [(1)\cdot(8.854 \times 10^{-12} \text{ F/m})\cdot(0.6 \text{ m}^2)] / (0.06 \text{ m})$$

$$C = 8.854 \times 10^{-11} \text{ F}$$

Find potential difference:

$$C = Q / V$$

$$V = Q / C$$

$$V = (7.08 \times 10^{-10} \text{ C}) / (8.854 \times 10^{-11} \text{ F})$$

$$V = 8 \text{ V}$$

58. C is correct.

Faraday's Law: a changing magnetic environment causes a voltage to be induced in a conductor. Metal detectors send quick magnetic pulses that cause a voltage (by Faraday's Law) and subsequent current to be induced in the conductor.

By Lenz's Law, an opposing magnetic field will then arise to counter the changing magnetic field. The detector picks up the magnetic field and notifies the operator.

Thus, metal detectors use Faraday's Law and Lenz's Law to detect metal objects.

59. D is correct.

$$E = qV$$

$$E = (7 \times 10^{-6} \text{ C})\cdot(3.5 \times 10^{-3} \text{ V})$$

$$E = 24.5 \times 10^{-9} \text{ J}$$

$$E = 24.5 \text{ nJ}$$

60. D is correct.

Electric Potential:

$$V = kQ / r$$

All other positions on the square (1, 2 or 3) are equidistant from point p, as is charge $+Q$.

Thus, a negative charge placed at any of these locations would have equal magnitude potential but an opposite sign because the new charge is negative.

Thus: $|V| = |-V|$

$$V + (-V) = 0$$

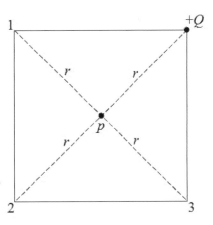

61. B is correct. Electric field energy density:

$u_E = \frac{1}{2}E^2\varepsilon_0$

$u_E = \frac{1}{2}(6 \text{ N/C})^2 \cdot (8.854 \times 10^{-12} \text{ F/m})$

$u_E = 1.6 \times 10^{-10} \text{ J/m}^3$

62. D is correct.

$PE = qU$

$PE = (2.4 \times 10^{-6} \text{ C}) \cdot (320 \text{ V})$

$PE = 7.7 \times 10^{-4} \text{ J}$

63. C is correct. By conservation of energy, the final kinetic energy is equal to the initial kinetic energy plus the energy added by the potential:

$E_{final} = E_{initial} + \Delta E_{potential}$

$\frac{1}{2}mv_f^2 = \frac{1}{2}mv_i^2 + qV$

Solving for v_f

$v_f = \sqrt{v_i^2 + (2qV / m)}$

$v_f = \sqrt{[(1.8 \times 10^5 \text{ m/s})^2 + 2(1.6 \times 10^{-19} \text{ C}) \cdot (100 \text{ V}) / (1.67 \times 10^{-27})]}$

$v_f = 2.27 \times 10^5 \text{ m/s} \approx 2.3 \times 10^5 \text{ m/s}$

64. B is correct.

1 amp = 1 C/s

# of electrons = $(5 \text{ C/s}) \cdot (12 \text{ s} / 1) \cdot (1 \text{ electron} / 1.6 \times 10^{-19} \text{ C})$

# of electrons = 3.8×10^{20} electrons

65. D is correct. Find forces acting on particle:

$F_{centripetal} = F_{magnetic}$

$ma_{centripetal} = qvB$

$mv^2 / r = qvB$

$q = mv / Br$

$q = (0.006 \text{ kg}) \cdot (3 \text{ m/s}) / (6 \text{ T}) \cdot (0.1 \text{ m})$

$q = 0.03 \text{ C}$

DC and RC Circuits – Explanations

1. C is correct.

An ohm Ω is defined as the resistance between two points of a conductor when a constant potential difference of 1 V, applied to these points, produces in the conductor a current of 1 A.

A series circuit experiences the same current through all resistors regardless of their resistance.

However, the voltage across each resistor can be different.

Since the light bulbs are in series, the current through them is the same.

2. D is correct.

The capacitance of a parallel place capacitor demonstrates the influence of material, separation distance and geometry in determining the overall capacitance.

$C = k\mathcal{E}_0 A / d$

where k = dielectric constant or permittivity of material between the plates,

A = surface area of the conductor and d = distance of plate separation

3. B is correct.

Combining the power equation with Ohm's law:

$P = (\Delta V)^2 / R$, where $\Delta V = 120$ V is a constant

To increase power, decrease the resistance.

A longer wire increases resistance, while a thicker wire decreases it:

$A = \pi r^2$

$R = \rho L / A$

Larger radius of the cross-sectional area means A is larger (denominator) which lowers R.

4. B is correct.

Calculate magnetic field perpendicular to loop:

$B_{Perp2} = (12$ T$) \cos 30°$

$B_{Perp2} = 10.4$ T

$B_{Perp1} = (1$ T$) \cos 30°$

$B_{Perp1} = 0.87$ T

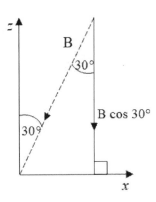

Use Faraday's Law to calculate generated voltage:

$V = N\Delta BA / \Delta t$

$V = N\Delta B(\pi r^2) / \Delta t$

$V = [(1)\cdot(10.4 \text{ T} - 0.87 \text{ T})\cdot(\pi(0.5 \text{ m})^2)] / (5 \text{ s} - 0 \text{ s})$

$V = [(1)\cdot(10.4 \text{ T} - 0.87 \text{ T})\cdot(0.785 \text{ m}^2)] / (5 \text{ s})$

$V = 1.5 \text{ V}$

Use Ohm's Law to calculate current:

$V = IR$

$I = V / R$

$I = (1.5 \text{ V}) / (12 \text{ } \Omega)$

$I = 0.13 \text{ A}$

5. A is correct.

The magnitude of the acceleration is given by:

$F = ma$

$a = F / m$

$F = qE_0$

$a = qE_0 / m$

Bare nuclei = no electrons

^{1}H has 1 proton, and ^{4}He has 2 protons and 2 neutrons

Thus, ^{1}H has ½ the charge and ¼ the mass of ^{4}He.

$a_H = q_H E_0 / m_H$

$a_{He} = q_{He} E_0 / m_{He}$

$a_H = (½q_{He})E_0 / (¼m_{He})$

$a_H = 2(q_{He}E_0 / m_{He})$

$a_H = 2a_{He}$

6. B is correct.

The current will change as the choice of lamp arrangement changes.

Since $P = V^2/R$, power increases as resistance decreases.

To rank the power in increasing order, the equivalent resistance must be ranked in decreasing order.

For arrangement B, the resistors are in series, so:

$R_{eq} = R + R = 2R$

For arrangement C, the resistors are in parallel, so:

$$1/R_{eq} = 1/R + 1/R$$

$$R_{eq} = R/2$$

The ranking of resistance in decreasing order is B to A to C, which is, therefore, the ranking of power in increasing order.

7. D is correct.

$$C = k\mathcal{E}_0 A / d$$

where k = dielectric constant or permittivity of material between the plates, A = area and d = distance of plate separation

$$C = (2.1) \cdot (8.854 \times 10^{-12} \text{ F/m}) \cdot (0.01 \text{ m} \times 0.01 \text{ m}) / (0.001 \text{ m})$$

$$C = (1.9 \times 10^{-15} \text{ F/m}) / (0.001 \text{ m})$$

$$C = 1.9 \times 10^{-12} \text{ F} = 1.9 \text{ pF}$$

8. D is correct.

Root mean square (RMS) voltage equation:

$$V_{rms} = V_{max} / \sqrt{2}$$

$$V_{rms} = 12 / \sqrt{2}$$

$$V_{rms} = (12 / \sqrt{2}) \cdot (\sqrt{2} / \sqrt{2})$$

$$V_{rms} = (12\sqrt{2}) / 2$$

$$V_{rms} = 6\sqrt{2} \text{ V}$$

9. C is correct.

By definition:

$$V_{rms} = V_{max} / \sqrt{2}$$

Therefore:

$$V_{max} = V_{rms}\sqrt{2}$$

$$V_{max} = (150 \text{ V})\sqrt{2}$$

$$V_{max} = 212 \text{ V}$$

10. A is correct.

The capacitance of capacitors connected in parallel is the sum of the individual capacitances:

$$C_{eq} = C_1 + C_2 + C_3 + C_4 = 4C$$

The relationship between the total charge delivered by the battery and the voltage of the battery is:

$V = Q / C_{eq} = Q / 4C$

The charge on one capacitor is:

$Q_1 = CV$

$Q_1 = C(Q / 4C)$

$Q_1 = Q / 4$

11. B is correct. If two conductors are connected by copper wire, each conductor will be at the same potential because current can flow through the wire and equalize the difference in potential.

12. C is correct. $R = (\rho L) / (\pi r^2)$

$R_A = (\rho L) / (\pi r^2)$

$R_B = [\rho(2L)] / [\pi(2r)^2]$

$R_B = (2/4) \cdot [(\rho L) / (\pi r^2)]$

$R_B = \frac{1}{2}[(\rho L) / (\pi r^2)]$

$R_B = \frac{1}{2}R_A$

14. B is correct.

$C = (k\varepsilon_0 A) / d$

$k = (Cd) / A\varepsilon_0$

If capacitance increases by a factor of 4:

$k_2 = (4C)d / A\varepsilon_0$

$k_2 = 4(Cd / A\varepsilon_0)$

$k_2 = 4k$

15. D is correct.

$C = (k\varepsilon_0 A) / d$

$C = [(1) \cdot (8.854 \times 10^{-12} \text{ F/m}) \cdot (0.4 \text{ m}^2)] / (0.04 \text{ m})$

$C = 8.854 \times 10^{-11} \text{ F}$

$V = Q / C$

$V = (6.8 \times 10^{-10} \text{ C}) / (8.854 \times 10^{-11} \text{ F})$

$V = 7.7 \text{ V}$

16. D is correct.

$$Q = VC$$

Even though the capacitors have different capacitances, the voltage across each capacitor is inversely proportional to the capacitance of that capacitor.

Like current, the charge is conserved across capacitors in series.

17. C is correct.

Energy stored in capacitor:

$$U = \frac{1}{2}(Q^2 / C)$$

Capacitance:

$$C = k\varepsilon_0 A / d$$

$$U = \frac{1}{2}(Q^2 d) / (k\varepsilon_0 A)$$

$$Q = \sqrt{[(2U \times k\varepsilon_0 A) / d]}$$

$$Q = \sqrt{\{[(2) \cdot (10 \times 10^3 \text{ J}) \cdot (1) \cdot (8.854 \times 10^{-12} \text{ F/m}) \cdot (2.4 \times 10^{-5} \text{ m}^2)] / 0.0016 \text{ m}\}}$$

$$Q = 52 \text{ } \mu\text{C}$$

18. B is correct.

Potential energy:

$$U = (kQq) / r$$

Electric Potential:

$$V = (kQ) / r$$

As r increases, the potential energy U decreases as does the electric potential V.

Movement in the direction of the electric field is a movement away from a positive charge.

19. D is correct.

Electric field energy density:

$$\eta_E = \frac{1}{2}E^2 \times \varepsilon_0$$

$$\eta_E = \frac{1}{2}(8.6 \times 10^6 \text{ V/m})^2 \cdot (8.854 \times 10^{-12} \text{ F/m})$$

$$\eta_E = 330 \text{ J/m}^3$$

20. D is correct.

$$C_{Eq1} = C_2 + C_3$$

$$C_{Eq1} = 18 \text{ pF} + 24 \text{ pF}$$

$$C_{Eq1} = 42 \text{ pF}$$

Voltage drops is equal in capacitors in parallel, so:

$C_{Eq1} = Q_1 / V_1$

$Q_1 = C_{Eq1} \times V_1$

$Q_1 = (42 \times 10^{-12}\,\text{F}) \cdot (240\,\text{V})$

$Q_1 = 1 \times 10^{-8}\,\text{C}$

Charge is equal in capacitors in series, so:

$1 / C_{Eq2} = 1 / C_{Eq1} + 1 / C_1$

$1 / C_{Eq2} = 1 / 42\,\text{pF} + 1 / 9\,\text{pF}$

$1 / C_{Eq2} = 7.4\,\text{pF}$

$1 / C_{Eq2} = V_{system} / Q_1$

$V_{system} = Q_1 / C_{Eq2}$

$V_{system} = (1 \times 10^{-8}\,\text{C}) / (7.4 \times 10^{-12}\,\text{F})$

$V_{system} = 1{,}350\,\text{V}$

21. A is correct. Energy stored in a capacitor:

$U = \tfrac{1}{2}Q^2 / C$

$U_2 = Q^2 / 2(2C)$

$U_2 = \tfrac{1}{2}Q^2 / 2C$

$U_2 = \tfrac{1}{2}U$

Decreases by half.

22. B is correct. The force on the proton is given by:

$F = qE$

$a = F / m,\ v_1 = 0\,\text{m/s}$

The final velocity is given by:

$v_2 = v_1 + a\Delta t$

$v_2 = (qE / m)\Delta t$

$v_2 = (1.6 \times 10^{-19}\,\text{C}) \cdot (140\,\text{N/C}) \cdot (1.8 \times 10^{-4}\,\text{s}) / (1.67 \times 10^{-27}\,\text{kg})$

$v_2 = 2.4 \times 10^{6}\,\text{m/s}$

23. D is correct.

Potential Energy:

$U = kQq / r$

Electric Potential:

$$V = kQ / r$$

Electric potential decreases when moving away from positive charges toward negative charges. Therefore, as the electron moves from left to right, the potential decreases.

Since the force on the electron points to the left, while its displacement is opposite of that (i.e., to the right), the work done by the field is negative. The change of potential energy is equal to the negative of the work done by the field, thus the potential energy increases.

24. A is correct. Batteries in series add voltage, and like resistors in series, the same current will flow through each.

25. A is correct. In a capacitor, charge is related to capacitance by:

$$Q = CV$$

For a parallel plate capacitor:

$$C = \varepsilon_0 A / d$$

Therefore:

$$Q = \varepsilon_0 A V / d$$

Doubling d:

$$Q_2 = \varepsilon_0 A V / (2d)$$

$$Q_2 = \tfrac{1}{2}\varepsilon_0 A V / d = \tfrac{1}{2}Q$$

The charge will be halved.

26. D is correct. Find area:

$$A = \pi r^2$$

$$A = \pi (7 \times 10^{-3}\ \text{m})^2$$

$$A = 1.54 \times 10^{-4}\ \text{m}^2$$

Find capacitance:

$$C = A\varepsilon_0 k / d$$

$$C = [(1.54 \times 10^{-4}\ \text{m}^2) \cdot (8.854 \times 10^{-12}\ \text{F/m}) \cdot (1)] / (1 \times 10^{-3}\ \text{m})$$

$$C = 1.36 \times 10^{-12}\ \text{F}$$

Find charge:

$$\sigma = 3 \times 10^{-6}\ \text{C/m}^2$$

$$\sigma = Q / A$$

$$Q = \sigma A$$

$$Q = (3 \times 10^{-6}\ \text{C/m}^2) \cdot (1.54 \times 10^{-4}\ \text{m}^2)$$

$$Q = 4.6 \times 10^{-10}\ \text{C}$$

Find potential energy:

$$U = \frac{1}{2}Q^2 / C$$

$$U = \frac{1}{2}(4.6 \times 10^{-10}\,\text{C})^2 / (1.36 \times 10^{-12}\,\text{F})$$

$$U = 78 \times 10^{-9}\,\text{J}$$

27. D is correct.

Use the relationship:

$$Q = CV$$

$$C = Q / V$$

$$C = (3.5 \times 10^{-6}\,\text{C}) / (75\,\text{V})$$

$$C = 4.7 \times 10^{-8}\,\text{F}$$

28. C is correct.

$$Q = A\mathcal{E}_0 V / d$$

$$Q / A = \mathcal{E}_0 V / d$$

$$Q / A = (8.854 \times 10^{-12}\,\text{F/m}) \cdot (3\,\text{V}) / (1 \times 10^3\,\text{m})$$

$$Q / A = 27 \times 10^{-9}\,\text{C/m}^2$$

29. C is correct.

Parallel-plate capacitor voltage:

$$V = Ed$$

$$V = (5.6 \times 10^6\,\text{V/m}) \cdot (0.08 \times 10^{-3}\,\text{m})$$

$$V = 448\,\text{V}$$

30. B is correct.

Capacitive Reactance formula:

$$X_c = 1 / 2\pi Cf$$

If f is doubled:

$$X_{c2} = 1 / [2\pi C(2f)]$$

$$X_{c2} = \frac{1}{2}[1 / 2\pi Cf)]$$

$$X_{c2} = \frac{1}{2}X_c$$

Capacitive reactance is halved.

Quantum Mechanics – Explanations

1. D is correct.

The energy of each incident photon is transferred to an electron, which must then overcome the material's work function to be ejected.

Therefore:

hc / λ = Work function

$\lambda = (6.626 \times 10^{-34} \text{ J·s} \cdot 3.00 \times 10^{8} \text{ m/s}) / (1.90 \text{ eV} \cdot 1.60 \times 10^{-19} \text{ J/eV})$

$\lambda = 6.53 \times 10^{-7} \text{ m}$

$\lambda = 653 \text{ nm}$

2. B is correct.

The power varies with the number of photons per second and the energy of the photons; therefore, I is incorrect.

The energy of the photons varies with the frequency of the light; therefore, III is incorrect.

The intensity of a laser beam depends on the number of photons and the energy of each photon.

The energy of the photons varies linearly with the frequency. If the frequency doubles, the energy doubles.

Since the number of photons is unchanged, the intensity doubles.

3. C is correct.

The energy of each incident photon is transferred to an electron, which must then overcome the material's work function to be ejected.

Therefore, the maximum kinetic energy remaining in any electron is:

E = Energy in 240 nm photon − work function

$2.5 \text{ eV} = hc / \lambda$ − work function

Work function $= (6.626 \times 10^{-34} \text{ J·s} \cdot 3.00 \times 10^{8} \text{ m/s}) / (240 \times 10^{-9} \text{ m}) - 2.58 \text{ eV}$

Work function $= (8.28 \times 10^{-19} \text{ J}) / (1.60 \times 10^{-19} \text{ J/eV}) - 2.58 \text{ eV}$

Work function $= 2.6 \text{ eV}$

4. C is correct.

The minimum energy of the electron-positron pair is its rest mass ($E = 2m_{electron} c^2$).

The photon that creates the pair must have more than the minimum energy.

The energy of the photon ($h\nu$) must therefore be:

$$hv > 2m_{electron} c^2$$

$$v > 2m_{electron} c^2 / h$$

$$v > 2 \cdot (9.11 \times 10^{-31} \text{ kg}) \cdot (3.00 \times 10^8 \text{ m/s})^2 / (6.626 \times 10^{-34} \text{ J·s})$$

$$v > 2.47 \times 10^{20} \text{ Hz}$$

5. D is correct.

The energy of each incident photon is transferred to an electron, which must then overcome the material's work function to be ejected.

Therefore:

$$hc / \lambda > \text{Work function}$$

$$\lambda < (6.626 \times 10^{-34} \text{ J·s} \cdot 3.00 \times 10^8 \text{ m/s}) / (2.20 \text{ eV} \cdot 1.60 \times 10^{-19} \text{ J/eV})$$

$$\lambda < 564 \text{ nm}$$

6. C is correct. Anderson used a cloud chamber to observe the effects of cosmic rays. A cloud chamber is a device filled with saturated water or alcohol vapor and held in a magnetic field.

As the cosmic rays interact with the molecules in the vapor, they form high energy charged particles. These high energy charged particles then move out from their point of creation in curved paths because of the magnetic field. Their path is visualized as they condense droplets from the saturated vapor.

Anderson observed an event in which a pair of charged particles was created at the same point, moving out in opposite directions and with equal but opposite curvature. This corresponded to the earlier prediction by Dirac of a positively charged electron (a positron) based upon an extra solution to the equations of a relativistic invariant form of Schrodinger's Equation.

The electron and positron pair (pair production) was produced in a collision of a cosmic ray photon with a heavy nucleus in the vapor.

7. C is correct.

$$E = hv$$

$$E = (6.626 \times 10^{-34} \text{ J·s}) \cdot (6.43 \times 10^{14} \text{ Hz}) / (1.60 \times 10^{-19} \text{ J/eV})$$

$$E = 2.66 \text{ eV}$$

8. B is correct.

The kinetic energy of the emitted electrons (KE) is the energy of the incident photon minus, at least, the work function of the photocathode surface.

Therefore:

$KE = 3.4 \text{ eV} - 2.4 \text{ eV}$

$KE = (1.0 \text{ eV}) \cdot (1.60 \times 10^{-19} \text{ J} / \text{eV})$

$KE = 1.60 \times 10^{-19} \text{ J}$

9. D is correct.

The energy of each incident photon is transferred to an electron, which must then overcome the material's work function to be ejected.

Therefore, to eject an electron:

$h\nu = hc / \lambda >$ Work function

$\lambda < hc /$ (Work function)

$\lambda < (6.626 \times 10^{-34} \text{ J} \cdot \text{s}) \cdot (3.00 \times 10^8 \text{ m/s}) / (2.9 \text{ eV} \cdot 1.60 \times 10^{-19} \text{ J/eV})$

$\lambda < 428 \times 10^{-9} \text{ m}$

The illumination range of 400 nm–700 nm that does not satisfy this requirement is:

$\lambda > 428 \text{ nm}$

10. A is correct.

Photons move at the speed of light because they are light.

Since the momentum of photon A is twice as great as the momentum of photon B, its energy is twice as great, and therefore its wavelength is half as great.

11. A is correct.

The Balmer formula for Hydrogen is:

$1 / \lambda = (1 / 91.2 \text{ nm}) \cdot (1 / m^2 - 1 / n^2)$

The energy difference of the $n = 20$ and $n = 7$ state corresponds to a photon of wavelength:

$1 / \lambda = (1 / 91.2 \text{ nm}) \cdot (1 / 7^2 - 1 / 20^2)$

$\lambda = (91.2 \text{ nm}) / (1 / 7^2 - 1 / 20^2)$

$\lambda = 5092 \text{ nm}$

The energy of a photon with wavelength λ is:

$E = hc / \lambda$

$E = (6.626 \times 10^{-34} \text{ J} \cdot \text{s}) \cdot (3.00 \times 10^8 \text{ m/s}) / (5092 \times 10^{-9} \text{ m})$

$E = (3.93 \times 10^{-20} \text{ J}) / (1.60 \times 10^{-19} \text{ J/eV})$

$E = 0.244 \text{ eV}$

12. D is correct.

The de Broglie wavelength is given by:

$$\lambda = h / p$$

When the energy ($E = p^2 / 2m$ for a non-relativistic proton) is doubled, the momentum is increased by $\sqrt{2}$.

Therefore, its de Broglie wavelength decreases by $\sqrt{2}$.

13. D is correct.

(Trivially, it is known that the incoming photon must lose energy to the electron in the scattering and therefore its wavelength must increase.

There is only one answer with a longer wavelength.)

Using the Compton equation at 120°:

$$\Delta\lambda = \lambda_{Compton} (1 - \cos \theta), \text{ where } \lambda_{Compton} = 2.43 \times 10^{-12}\, m$$

$$\Delta\lambda = .00243\, nm\, (1.5)$$

$$\Delta\lambda = 0.00365\, nm$$

$$\lambda = 0.591\, nm + 0.00365\, nm$$

$$\lambda = 0.595\, nm$$

14. C is correct.

The brightness of a beam of light is linearly proportional to the energy of the photons in the beam and the number of photons in the beam.

If the color of the light beam, which is dependent on its frequency distribution or energy distribution, is unchanged, then the frequency and energy distribution of the light beam must be unchanged.

15. B is correct.

The Balmer formula for Hydrogen is:

$$1 / \lambda = (1 / 91.2\, nm)(1 / m^2 - 1 / n^2)$$

$$1 / \lambda = (1 / 91.2\, nm)(1 / 4^2 - 1 / 9^2)$$

$$1 / \lambda = (1 / 91.2\, nm)(1 / m^2 - 1 / n^2)$$

$$1 / \lambda = (1 / 1818\, nm)$$

The frequency of light is given by:

$$v = c / \lambda$$

$$v = (3.00 \times 10^8\, m/s) / (1818 \times 10^{-9}\, m)$$

$$v = 1.65 \times 10^{14} /s = 1.65 \times 10^{14}\, Hz$$

16. D is correct.

The Balmer formula for Hydrogen for the emission of radiation from the nth level down to the mth (i.e., $n > m$) is:

$$1 / \lambda = (1 / 91.2 \text{ nm}) \cdot (1 / m^2 - 1 / n^2)$$

Therefore:

$$(1 / m^2 - 1 / n^2) = 91.2 \text{ nm} / 377 \text{ nm}$$

$$(1 / m^2 - 1 / n^2) = 0.2419$$

$$1 / n^2 = 1 / m^2 - 0.2419$$

For n to be real, it must be either $m = 1$ or $m = 2$.

If $m = 1$:

$$1 / n^2 = 1 - 0.2419 = 0.7581$$

n is not an integer (i.e., the photon has less energy than the emission photon expected in a transition from $n = 2$ to $m = 1$).

Therefore, m must be 2 (i.e., the emission is from the n level down to the $m = 2$ level) and:

$$1 / n^2 = 1 / 4 - 0.2419 = 0.0081$$

$$n = 11$$

17. C is correct.

Wein's displacement law describes the wavelength of maximum emission of radiation of a black body at temperature T. It is:

$$\lambda_{max} \cdot T = \text{constant} = 0.00290 \text{ m} \cdot \text{K}$$

At $T = 5000$K:

$$\lambda_{max} = 0.00290 \text{ m} \cdot \text{K} / 5000 \text{ K}$$

$$\lambda_{max} = 580 \text{ nm}$$

18. D is correct.

Dirac factored the Schrödinger equation into a simpler equation that had two solutions; one solution described the electron, and the other solution described an identical particle with an opposite electric charge.

Four years later, such a "positively charged" electron was found in cloud chamber pictures of cosmic rays.

19. B is correct.

The electron absorbs the full energy of the photon and loses the work function energy as it escapes from the material.

Therefore, it has a maximum kinetic energy of:

Max KE = E – Work function

Max KE = 3.4 eV – 2.4 eV = 1.0 eV · (1.60 × 10^{-19} J/eV)

Max KE = 1.60 × 10^{-19} J

20. D is correct.

Consider the problem from the center of mass frame, a frame that is moving in the same direction as the incident photon. In this frame, the electron starts moving with the speed of the center of mass frame and in the opposite direction of the center of mass frame. In the center of mass frame, the electron is scattered with the same speed into one direction, and the photon is scattered in the opposite direction, the scattering angle.

Transforming back into the laboratory frame, the electron has a final velocity equal to the vector sum of its scattered velocity in the center of mass frame and the velocity of the center of mass.

This sum is greatest when the scattering angle of the electron is in the same direction as the velocity of the center of mass frame, the direction of the incident photon. The photon is then scattered in the opposite direction of the center of mass frame at a scattering angle of 180°.

If the velocity of the electron is maximal at that scattering angle, then the energy of the photon is minimal at that scattering angle.

Since wavelength is inversely proportional to energy, the maximal change in wavelength occurs when the photon is scattered at 180°.

21. C is correct.

This is a trick question that has nothing to do with the photocathode or the work function. If the radiation has energy 3.5 eV, then its wavelength is given by:

$E = h\nu = hc / \lambda = 3.5$ eV

$\lambda = hc / (3.5$ eV$)$

$\lambda = (6.626 \times 10^{-34}$ J·s$)\cdot(3.00 \times 10^8$ m/s$) / (3.5$ eV$)$

$\lambda = (6.626 \times 10^{-34}$ J·s$)\cdot(3.00 \times 10^8$ m/s$) / (3.5$ eV$)$

$\lambda = (5.679 \times 10^{-26}$ J·m /eV$) / (1.6 \times 10^{-19}$ J/eV$)$

$\lambda = 355$ nm

22. A is correct.

The energy of a photon is given by:

$E = h\nu = hc / \lambda$

Therefore, if the wavelength is doubled, the energy is halved.

23. D is correct.

The energy of each incident photon is transferred to an electron, which must then overcome the material's work function to be ejected. Therefore:

$hv >$ Work function

$v > (2.8 \text{ eV} \cdot 1.60 \times 10^{-19} \text{ J/eV}) / (6.626 \times 10^{-34} \text{ J·s})$

$v > 6.8 \times 10^{-14} /\text{s}$

24. B is correct.

The de Broglie wavelength of a matter wave is:

$\lambda = h / p = h / mv$

$v = h / (m\lambda)$

$v = (6.626 \times 10^{-34} \text{ J·s}) / [(9.11 \times 10^{-31} \text{ kg}) \cdot (380 \times 10^{-9} \text{ m})]$

$v = 1.91 \times 10^{3} \text{ m/s}$

25. B is correct.

Using the Compton Equation:

$\Delta\lambda = \lambda_{\text{Compton}} (1 - \cos\theta)$, where $\lambda_{\text{Compton}} = 2.43 \times 10^{-12} \text{ m}$

For $\theta = 90°$:

$\Delta\lambda = 2.43 \times 10^{-12} \text{ m}$

and

$\lambda_{\text{scattered}} = \lambda_{\text{incident}} + \Delta\lambda$

$\lambda_{\text{scattered}} = (1.50 \times 10^{-10} \text{ m}) + (2.43 \times 10^{-12} \text{ m})$

$\lambda_{\text{scattered}} = 1.5243 \times 10^{-10} \text{ m}$

26. B is correct.

As the intensity of light increases, the photon flux increases but not the energy of the photons. The kinetic energy of the ejected electrons depends solely on the energy of the incident photons and the work function of the metal. Since the energy of the incident photons is unchanged, the kinetic energy of the ejected electrons does not change.

However, the probability of an electron being ejected, and therefore the number of electrons ejected per second, depends on the flux of incident photons. It increases as the intensity of the light increases. The electron is ejected at the same instant as the light is absorbed, independent of the intensity of the light. Therefore, the time lag does not change.

Note: the time lag between the illumination of the surface (not the absorption of light) and the ejection of the first electron depends on the probability of ejection, which depends on the intensity of the incident light.

27. D is correct.

The de Broglie wavelength of a matter wave is:

$\lambda = h / p$

$\lambda = h / (mv)$

The energy of a photon with this wavelength is:

$E = hv = hc / \lambda$

Substituting in for λ:

$E = hc / [h / (mv)]$

$E = mcv$

$E = (1.67 \times 10^{-27} \text{ kg}) \cdot (3.00 \times 10^8 \text{ m/s}) \cdot (7.2 \times 10^4 \text{ m/s})$

$E = 36.1 \times 10^{-15} \text{ J}$

$E = (36.1 \times 10^{-15} \text{ J}) / (1.60 \times 10^{-19} \text{ J/eV})$

$E = 225 \times 10^3 \text{ eV}$

28. B is correct.

The Compton effect measures the change in energy as an x-ray scatters off of an electron. Both the total momentum and total energy of the x-ray and the electron, initially at rest, must be conserved.

As the scattering angle of the x-ray increases monotonically, its change in momentum increases and therefore the momentum imparted to the electron must increase.

If the momentum of the electron increases, then its energy must increase and the energy of the X-ray decreases.

If the energy of the X-ray decreases, then the frequency, which is proportional to its energy, must decrease.

29. A is correct.

The Rydberg formula for Hydrogen for the emission of radiation from the nth level down to the mth (i.e., n > m) is:

$1 / \lambda = (1 / 91.2 \text{ nm}) \cdot (1 / m^2 - 1 / n^2)$

If n = 16 (since the first spectral line is from n = 2) and m = 1, then:

$1 / \lambda = (1 / 91.2 \text{ nm}) \cdot (1 / 1^2 - 1 / 16^2)$

$\lambda = 91.2 \text{ nm} / (1 - 0.004)$

$\lambda = 91.6 \text{ nm}$

30. D is correct.

If the frequency of light in a laser beam is doubled, the energy of each photon in that laser beam doubles, since each photon has energy $E = h\nu$. The wavelength of each photon is divided by 2, since $\lambda = c / \nu$.

The intensity of the laser beam is the power per unit area.

The power is the energy delivered per unit time.

The energy delivered is proportional to the energy of each photon times the number of photons. If the energy of each photon is doubled and the number of photons remains unchanged (assuming the area of the laser beam is unchanged), then the intensity doubles.

Therefore, I and III are correct.

31. B is correct.

Order diffraction occurs when the incident and scattered beams hit the crystal at the same angle (i.e., in this case, the crystal planes are oriented at $58° / 2$ to the normal).

The neutron matter waves add coherently (i.e., constructive or destructive interference) if the extra distance that the neutrons must travel as they scatter off the next plane of the crystal is equal to an integer number of de Broglie wavelengths.

At $58°$, the extra distance is:

$$2 \cdot 159.0 \text{ pm} \cdot \cos(58° / 2) = 278 \text{ pm}$$

The de Broglie wavelength of a matter wave is:

$$\lambda = h / p$$

Therefore:

$$p = h / \lambda$$

and

$$E = p^2 / 2m = (6.626 \times 10^{-34} \text{ J·s} / 278 \times 10^{-12} \text{ m})^2 / (2 \cdot 1.67 \times 10^{-27} \text{ kg})$$

$$E = (1.70 \times 10^{-21} \text{ J}) / (1.6 \times 10^{-19} \text{ J/eV})$$

$$E = 0.0106 \text{ eV}$$

32. A is correct.

The energy of each incident photon is transferred to an electron. The electron's energy goes into overcoming the photocathode's 2.5 eV work function.

The remaining energy is then stopped by the stopping potential.

The greatest amount of energy an electron can have comes from a photon with a wavelength of 360 nm.

The remaining energy is then:

$$\text{remaining energy} = h\nu - 2.5 \text{ eV}$$

remaining energy = $hc / \lambda - 2.5$ eV

remaining energy = $(6.626 \times 10^{-34}$ J·s)·$(3.00 \times 10^8$ m/s) / $(360 \times 10^{-9}$ m) $- 2.5$eV

remaining energy = $[(5.52 \times 10^{-19}$ J) / $(1.6 \times 10^{-19}$ J/eV)] $- 2.5$ eV

remaining energy = 3.45 eV $- 2.5$ eV $= 0.95$ eV

The electron has a charge of e. Therefore, this energy can be stopped by a voltage of 0.95 V.

33. D is correct.

The de Broglie wavelength is given by:

$\lambda = h / p$

$\lambda = (6.626 \times 10^{-34}$ J·s) / $(1.95 \times 10^{-27}$ kg·m/s)

$\lambda = 340$ nm

34. C is correct.

The Balmer formula for Hydrogen for the emission of radiation from the nth level down to the mth (i.e., n > m) is:

$1 / \lambda = (1 / 91.2$ nm$)·(1 / m^2 - 1 / n^2)$

If n = 9 and m = 6, then:

$1 / \lambda = (1 / 91.2$ nm$)·(1 / 6^2 - 1 / 9^2)$

$1 / \lambda = (1 / 91.2$ nm$)·(0.01543)$

Thus:

$v = c / \lambda$

$v = (3.00 \times 10^8$ m/s$)·(1 / 91.2$ nm$)·(0.01543)$

$v = 5.08 \times 10^{13}$ /s

$v = 5.08 \times 10^{13}$ Hz

35. A is correct.

$E = hv$

$E = (6.626 \times 10^{-34}$ J·s$)·(110$ GHz$)$

$E = (6.626 \times 10^{-34}$ J·s$)·(110 \times 10^9$ / s$)$

$E = 7.29 \times 10^{-23}$ J

36. C is correct.

The visible spectrum ranges from 400 nm to 700 nm.

The Balmer formula for Hydrogen for the emission of radiation from the nth level down to the mth (i.e., n > m) is:

$1 / \lambda = (1 / 91.2 \text{ nm}) \cdot (1 / m^2 - 1 / n^2)$

Consider emission from any level down to the m = 1 level. The lowest energy is from the n = 2 level, and its wavelength is:

91.2 nm · (4 / 3) = 121 nm, which is not visible.

Therefore, no visible lines are radiating down to the m = 1 level.

Consider emission from any level down to the m = 3 level.

The highest energy comes from n = ∞ and its wavelength is:

91.2 nm · 9 = 820 nm, which is not visible.

Therefore, no visible lines are radiating down to the m = 3 level, nor are there any visible lines radiating down to any m level higher than 3.

Consider radiation from various levels down to the m = 2 level.

From n = 3, the wavelength is:

91.2 nm / (1 / 4 − 1 / 9) = 91.2 nm · 7.2 = 656.6 nm

From n = 4, the wavelength is:

91.2 nm / (1 / 4 − 1 / 16) = 91.2 nm · 5.333 = 486.4 nm

From n = 5, the wavelength is:

91.2 nm / (1 / 4 − 1 / 25) = 91.2 nm · 4.762 = 434.3 nm

From n = 6, the wavelength is:

91.2 nm / (1 / 4 − 1 / 36) = 91.2 nm · 4.5 = 410.4 nm

From n = 7, the wavelength is:

91.2 nm / (1 / 4 − 1 / 49) = 91.2 nm · 4.355 = 397.2 nm, which is not visible.

Therefore, there are 4 visible lines:

m = 2 to n = 3   656.6 nm

m = 2 to n = 4   486.4 nm

m = 2 to n = 5   434.3 nm

m = 2 to n = 6   410.4 nm

37. B is correct.

$E = h\nu = hc / \lambda$

$\lambda = hc / E$

$\lambda = (6.626 \times 10^{-34} \text{ J·s}) \cdot (3.00 \times 10^8 \text{ m/s}) / (4.20 \text{ eV})$

$\lambda = (4.73 \times 10^{-26} \text{ J·m/eV}) / (1.60 \times 10^{-19} \text{ J/eV})$

$\lambda = 2.96 \times 10^{-7} \text{ m}$

$\lambda = 296 \text{ nm}$

38. C is correct.

The energy of each incident photon is transferred to an electron, which must then overcome the material's work function to be ejected.

Therefore, if a wavelength of light is just able to eject an electron, then:

$hv = hc / \lambda$ = Work function

$(6.626 \times 10^{-34}$ J·s)·$(3.00 \times 10^8$ m/s) / $(500 \times 10^{-9}$ m) = Work function

$(3.98 \times 10^{-19}$ J) / $(1.6 \times 10^{-19}$ J/eV) = Work function

2.48 eV = Work function

39. C is correct.

In the Bohr theory, there is a fixed number of de Broglie wavelengths of the electron in orbit.

This number is the principal quantum number:

$n = 2\pi r / \lambda$

The de Broglie wavelength is given by:

$\lambda = h / p$

Therefore:

$n = (2\pi / h)rp$

or:

$n^2 = (2\pi / h)^2 r^2 p^2$

The attractive force of the proton keeps the electron in a circular orbit. The attractive force is proportional to $1 / r^2$, and if that force keeps the electron in orbit, $1 / r^2$ must be proportional to v^2 / r.

Therefore, v^2 (or p^2) is proportional to $1 / r$.

Since $r^2 p^2$ is proportional to n^2, and p^2 is proportional to $1 / r$, then r (i.e. $r^2·1 / r$) is proportional to n^2.

40. B is correct.

Heisenberg's Uncertainty Principle states that:

$\Delta p \Delta x \geq h / 2\pi$

Therefore:

$m\Delta v\Delta x \geq h / 2\pi$

$\Delta v \geq (6.626 \times 10^{-34}$ J·s) / $(2\pi \cdot 0.053$ nm $\times 1.67 \times 10^{-27}$ kg)

$\Delta v \geq 1.19 \times 10^3$ m/s

41. C is correct.

The Balmer formula for Hydrogen for the emission of radiation from the nth level down to the mth (i.e., $n > m$) is:

$$1 / \lambda = (1 / 91.2 \text{ nm}) \cdot (1 / m^2 - 1 / n^2)$$

$$1 / \lambda = (1 / 91.2 \text{ nm}) \cdot (1 / 9^2 - 1 / 11^2)$$

$$\lambda = (91.2 \text{ nm}) / (0.00408)$$

$$\lambda = 22,300 \text{ nm}$$

42. D is correct.

Heisenberg's Uncertainty Principle states that:

$$\Delta E \Delta t \geq h / 2\pi$$

Therefore:

$$\Delta t \geq (h / 2\pi) / \Delta E$$

$$\Delta t \geq (6.626 \times 10^{-34} \text{ J·s} / 2\pi) / (10^{-18} \text{ J})$$

$$\Delta t \geq 1.05 \times 10^{-16} \text{ s}$$

43. C is correct.

The energy of each incident photon is transferred to an electron, which must then overcome the material's work function to be ejected.

Therefore, if a wavelength of light is able to eject an electron with energy 2.58 eV, then:

$$h\nu = hc / \lambda = \text{Work function} + 2.58 \text{ eV}$$

$$(6.626 \times 10^{-34} \text{ J·s}) \cdot (3.00 \times 10^8 \text{ m/s}) / (240 \times 10^{-9} \text{ m}) = \text{Work function} + 2.58 \text{ eV}$$

$$\text{Work function} = [(8.28 \times 10^{-19} \text{ J}) / (1.6 \times 10^{-19} \text{ J/eV})] - 2.58\text{eV}$$

$$\text{Work function} = 2.60 \text{ eV}$$

44. C is correct.

The de Broglie wavelength of a matter wave is:

$$\lambda = h / p$$

$$\lambda = h / (mv)$$

$$\lambda = (6.626 \times 10^{-34} \text{ J·s}) / [(1.30 \text{ kg}) \cdot (28.10 \text{ m/s})]$$

$$\lambda = (6.626 \times 10^{-34} \text{ J·s}) / [(1.30 \text{ kg}) \cdot (28.10 \text{ m/s})]$$

$$\lambda = 1.81 \times 10^{-35} \text{ m}$$

45. D is correct.

By doubling the frequency of the light, the energy of each photon doubles, but not the number of photons (hence B is wrong).

Although doubling the energy of each photon would cause more electrons to be ejected, it does not, necessarily, double that number, since the number is not linearly proportional to the incident energy (hence A is not always true).

The kinetic energy of the ejected electrons would more than double since the initial kinetic energy is less than the energy of the incident photons - the work function of the surface reduced it (hence C is wrong).

The kinetic energy would increase by at least 2 but not necessarily by 4 (hence D is wrong).

46. D is correct.

The Balmer formula for Hydrogen is:

$$1 / \lambda = (1 / 91.2 \text{ nm})(1 / m^2 - 1 / n^2)$$

From the $n = 3$ level, the transition to the $n = 2$ level has the lowest energy and therefore the longest wavelength.

The Balmer formula for $n = 3$, $m = 2$ is:

$$1 / \lambda = (1 / 91.2 \text{ nm})(1 / 2^2 - 1 / 3^2)$$

$$1 / \lambda = (1 / 91.2 \text{ nm})(5 / 36)$$

$$\lambda = 656 \text{ nm}$$

47. C is correct.

Photons are light, and the speed of light is invariant. Therefore, I is wrong. The energy of the photons in a beam of light determines the color of the light. If the color is unchanged, then the average energy of the photons is unchanged, making II wrong.

Changing the brightness of a beam of light increases the number of photons in the beam of light.

48. B is correct.

Using the Compton Equation:

$$\Delta \lambda = \lambda_{Compton} (1 - \cos \theta), \text{ where } \lambda_{Compton} = 2.43 \times 10^{-12} \text{ m}$$

At $\theta = 180°$, it is required that $\Delta \lambda = \lambda$.

Thus:

$$\lambda = 2\lambda_{Compton}$$

$$\lambda = 4.86 \times 10^{-12} \text{ m}$$

49. D is correct.

The energy of the photons in the beam depends linearly on the frequency of the beam. Since the frequency of beam B is twice the frequency of beam A, the photons in beam B have twice the energy as the photons in beam A.

The intensity depends on the energy of the photons and the number of photons per second carried by the beam. Nothing is known about the intensity or the number of photons per second.

50. A is correct.

The Balmer formula for Hydrogen is:

$$1 / \lambda = (1 / 91.2 \text{ nm}) \cdot (1 / m^2 - 1 / n^2)$$

From the n = 3 level, the transition to the n = 1 level has the greatest energy and therefore the shortest wavelength.

The Balmer formula for n = 3, m = 1 is:

$$1 / \lambda = (1 / 91.2 \text{ nm}) \cdot (1 / 1^2 - 1 / 3^2)$$

$$1 / \lambda = (1 / 91.2 \text{ nm}) \cdot (8 / 9)$$

$$\lambda = 102.6 \text{ nm}$$

51. D is correct.

The uncertainty principle states that the uncertainty in position and momentum must be at least:

$$\Delta x \Delta p \approx h / 2\pi$$

$$\Delta p \approx h / (2\pi \Delta x)$$

If:

$$\Delta x = 5.0 \times 10^{-15} \text{ m}$$

Then:

$$\Delta p \approx 6.626 \times 10^{-34} \text{ J·s} / (2\pi \cdot 5.0 \times 10^{-15} \text{ m})$$

$$\Delta p \approx 2.11 \times 10^{-20} \text{ kg·m/s}$$

The uncertainty in the (non-relativistic) kinetic energy of the proton is then:

$$\Delta KE \approx (\Delta p)^2 / (2m)$$

$$\Delta KE \approx [h / (2\pi \Delta x)]^{\,2} / (2m)$$

$$\Delta KE \approx [(6.626 \times 10^{-34} \text{ J·s}) / (2\pi \cdot 5.0 \times 10^{-15} \text{ m})]^2 / (2 \cdot 1.67 \times 10^{-27} \text{ kg})$$

$$\Delta KE \approx (1.33 \times 10^{-13} \text{ J})$$

Converting to MeV:

$$\Delta KE \approx (1.33 \times 10^{-13} \text{ J}) / (1.6 \times 10^{-13} \text{ J/MeV})$$

$$\Delta KE \approx (0.83 \text{ MeV})$$

52. B is correct.

The electron absorbs the full energy of the photon, losing 2.4 eV as it escapes from the photocathode and an additional 1.1 eV of kinetic energy after it escapes from the photocathode. This allows it to be stopped only with a potential exceeding 1.1 volts. It therefore absorbs 2.4 eV + 1.1 eV = 3.5 eV from the incident photon.

A photon with energy 3.5 eV has a wavelength given by:

$hv = hc / \lambda = E$

$\lambda = hc / E = (6.626 \times 10^{-34}$ J·s$)·(3.00 \times 10^{8}$ m/s$) / (3.5$ eV $· 1.60 \times 10^{-19}$ J /eV$)$

$\lambda = 355$ nm

53. B is correct.

The Compton effect is a measure of the reduction in wavelength of an x-ray beam as it scatters off a sample.

The reduction in wavelength can be explained if the incident x-ray beam is considered as being made up of individual particles each with momentum and energy, and electrons scatter those particles in the sample.

Hence, the Compton effect demonstrates the particle nature of electromagnetic radiation.

While the energy content and momenta of the individual x-rays are included in the scattering calculation, they are not directly demonstrated in the Compton effect.

54. B is correct.

The de Broglie wavelength of a matter wave is:

$\lambda = h / p$

$\lambda = h / (m\gamma v)$

(Since $v / c < 0.1$, this will equal about 1.005 and can be ignored)

$\lambda = (6.626 \times 10^{-34}$ J·s$) / [(9.11 \times 10^{-31}$ kg$)·(2.5 \times 10^{7}$ m/s$)]$

$\lambda = 29 \times 10^{-12}$ m

$\lambda = 29$ pm

55. D is correct.

The energy uncertainty is given by the uncertainty principle:

$\Delta E \Delta t \geq h / 2\pi$

$\Delta E \geq (6.626 \times 10^{-34}$ J·s $/ 2\pi) / (30 \times 10^{-12}$ s$)$

$\Delta E \geq (3.5 \times 10^{-24}$ J$)$

Converting to eV (1.6×10^{-19} J /eV):

$\Delta E \geq 2.2 \times 10^{-5}$ eV

AP prep books by Sterling Test Prep

- AP Chemistry Practice Questions
- AP Chemistry Review
- AP Biology Practice Questions
- AP Biology Review
- AP Physics 2 Practice Questions
- AP Physics 2 Review
- AP Environmental Science

- AP Psychology
- AP U.S. History
- AP World History
- AP European History
- AP U.S. Government and Politics
- AP Comparative Government and Politics
- AP Human Geography

Your purchase helps support global environmental causes

Sterling Test Prep is committed to protecting our planet by supporting environmental organizations for conservation, ecological research, and preservation of vital natural resources. A portion of our profits is donated to help these organizations continue their critical missions.

  The Ocean Conservancy advocates for a healthy ocean with sustainable solutions based on science and cleanup efforts.

 The Rainforest Trust saves critical lands for conservation through land purchases and protected area designations in over 16 countries.

Pacific Whale Foundation saves whales from extinction and protects our oceans through science and advocacy.

We want to hear from you

Your feedback is important to us because we strive to provide the highest quality prep materials. Email us any comments or suggestions.

info@sterling–prep.com

Customer Satisfaction Guarantee
Contact us to resolve any issues to your satisfaction.

*We reply to all emails – **check your spam folder***

Thank you for choosing our products to achieve your educational goals!

SAT Subject Test prep books by Sterling Test Prep

- SAT Chemistry Practice Questions

- SAT Chemistry Review

- SAT Biology Practice Questions

- SAT Biology Review

- SAT Physics Practice Questions

- SAT Physics Review

- SAT U.S. History

- SAT World History

To access the online AP tests at a special pricing visit:
http://AP.Sterling-Prep.com/bookowner.htm